Enlightenment Phantasies

Enlightenment Phantasies

Cultural Identity in France and Germany, 1750–1914

HAROLD MAH

Cornell University Press

ITHACA AND LONDON

First published 2003 by Cornell University Press
First printing, Cornell Paperbacks, 2004

Printed in the United States of America

Library of Congresss Cataloging-in-Publication Data

Mah, Harold.
   Enlightenment phantasies : cultural identity in France and Germany, 1750–1914 / Harold Mah.
       p. cm.
Includes bibliographical references and index.
   ISBN 0-8014-4144-7 (cloth : alk. paper)
   1. Enlightenment—France—Influence.   2. France—Intellectual life.
3. France—Civilization.   4. Enlightenment—Germany—Influence.
5. Germany—Intellectual life.   6. Germany—Civilization.   I. Title.
   B1925.E5M34   2003
   940.2—dc21

                                                          2003009504

ISBN 0-8014-8895-8 (pbk. : alk. paper)

Cornell University Press strives to use environmentally responsible suppliers and materials to the fullest extent possible in the publishing of its books. Such materials include vegetable-based, low-VOC inks and acid-free papers that are recycled, totally chlorine-free, or partly composed of nonwood fibers. For further information, visit our website at www.cornellpress.cornell.edu.

Cloth printing   10 9 8 7 6 5 4 3 2 1
Paperback printing   10 9 8 7 6 5 4 3 2 1

To my mother

馬周蕙蘭

unmatched in her ability to endure historical change

Contents

Acknowledgments

The support of friends, colleagues, and certain institutions has made this book possible. Research fellowships to the School for Historical Studies at the Institute for Advanced Study at Princeton and to Cornell University's Society for the Humanities provided opportunities to read, think, and write in fields beyond my then customary ones. The broad and intense intellectual activity of these institutions encouraged me to attempt something more ambitious than the usual historical monograph. I am indebted to Peter Paret, Joan Scott, Carla Hesse, and Shaun Marmon for the many wonderful conversations at Princeton. Carla Hesse has served as an ongoing interlocutor, whose critical and innovative thinking about the Enlightenment has offered me a standard of what cultural and intellectual history might aspire to. At Cornell, Dominick LaCapra and other members of the Society for the Humanities and the Department of History, in particular Rachel Weil and Michael Steinberg, provided the best possible experience of a university, of a community of intellectually engaged and engaging scholars, supporting and rigorously challenging one another's work.

My work has benefited from colleagues' responses to earlier versions of chapters, which I gave as lectures and papers at Cornell, Rice University, and UCLA. Martin Jay's scrupulous, critical reading of some preliminary chapters—and his amazing breadth of knowledge—corrected my mistakes and helped to focus my arguments. Cathy Conaghan provided support at critical junctures, and Fritz Ringer's and David Sabean's readings of some sections improved them. Milen Jissov has been an indispensable research assistant, and John Ackerman has shown himself an exemplary editor, who has saved me at times from my own worst instincts. Ann Hawthorne was a scrupulous, demanding copyeditor.

x   *Acknowledgments*

When this book was only a dim intuition, Felix Gilbert offered, as he had in previous work, unfailing advice and support. When I was writing one of the book's key chapters, George Mosse also offered generous encouragement, notwithstanding my disagreement with his views on German classicism and gender. The death of these men has felt to me like the final passing of a great generation of European scholars, whose intellectual and cultural breadth is now rarely found in historians. (Notable exceptions to the rule are mentioned above.) I lament the passing of that generation, and its astounding erudition, and I hope that in its own minor way—and possibly in a way they would have criticized—this book honors their example and spirit.

Parts of chapters 2 and 5 first appeared in different forms in *Representations* 47 (summer 1994), 64–84, and in *New German Critique* 50 (spring/summer 1990), 3–20, respectively.

Enlightenment Phantasies

Introduction

Identity as Phantasy in Enlightenment
France and Germany

In various significant writings of the mid-eighteenth century, the French *philosophe* Voltaire proclaimed that France since Louis XIV had achieved a new level of refined society, a civilization of elegant manners, language, and sensibility. Evident in the great cultural accomplishments of the previous century and now sustained by the accomplishments of the French Enlightenment, such a civilization, Voltaire concluded, had surpassed even ancient Athens and Rome in the gracious "art of living." Voltaire asserted that eighteenth-century French civilization and its Enlightenment offered the rest of Europe a universal standard of culture—of language, conduct, and thought.[1] And Europeans agreed. On the continent, courts, aristocracies, and hautes bourgeoisies of the period adopted French tastes, manners, and language. Frederick II of Prussia spoke and wrote better French than German. Philosophes of the French Enlightenment traveled to foreign capitals on the invitation of their monarchs, and French officials and intellectuals assumed leading positions in foreign bureaucracies and academies.

An image of elegant France provided the dominant standard of civilization for other continental European countries throughout the eighteenth century. But in the last part of the century intellectuals and writers in those countries began to rebel against conceptions of universal culture and of a generalized French and Enlightenment standard in particular. In Germany especially, young writers and philosophers considered French cultural dominance an alien imposition that displaced what was most authentic and meaningful in German culture. In a variety of ways Germans advocated, against French and Enlightenment universalism, the value of specific, concrete aspects of German culture. They wrote appreciative stud-

1

ies of the German language; collected folk songs; cultivated a new, intense poetic sensibility; rejected sweeping conceptions of history for histories focused on specific cultures; sought alternative cultural inspiration in other national models—such as ancient Greece—and made arguments for not just the distinctiveness but also the superiority of German cultural and intellectual life. In the late eighteenth century these affirmations of a unique and valuable German character circulated in an expanding public realm of publishing and reading, producing what the historian Friedrich Meinecke describes as a "cultural nationalism"—a sense of belonging to a distinct and significant cultural whole.[2]

These Germans decisively altered the dominant conceptual framework of the period, so that cultures came to be thought of as valid not just in universal terms but also in terms of their own unique characteristics. To grasp German cultural identity in its concrete specificity; to conceive of each culture as a singular whole, each developing on the basis of its own conditions and principles—these were the innovative ideas that German writers and thinkers of the late eighteenth century articulated and disseminated. And this German notion of identity—that it is properly and naturally an outgrowth of particular circumstance, character, and history—has proved immensely influential in how we have since come to conceive of cultural identity in both popular and academic terms. From the rebellion against the idea of universal standards of culture contained in the idea of a dominant French and Enlightenment civilization, we have come to embrace the specifically national, regional, and local as the source of a culture's deepest values and identity.

Germans provided the first influential models of cultural particularism opposed to the imposition of a general, overarching standard of universal civilization. This characterization of the nature and outcome of a clash between eighteenth-century French and German thought and of the diverging tendencies of French and German intellectual and cultural development has long influenced how much of the cultural and intellectual history of Germany has been and continues to be written. But though still largely accepted, and in certain senses still accurate, that characterization has been enormously complicated by tendencies in the historiography of the European Enlightenment since the 1960s and in theoretical work on culture and cultural identity. These developments have together suggested a far more complex and uncertain history of French and German cultural identity and of the relationship between universal and particularist models of identity.

Both the original French and German formulations of identity and current histories of those formulations share the conventional assumption that identities are singular, discrete entities. These identities are coherent

and well-functioning on their own terms because those terms directly reflect a set of specific social and political conditions. Eighteenth-century
German identity flows naturally out of distinctive eighteenth-century German conditions and French identity out of French ones. The historiography of the Enlightenment, however, suggests that the terms of eighteenth-
century identities seldom operated according to these assumptions. Asserted as a singular and self-consistent entity, an identity often turned out
to be multiple and self-conflicted. Presumably fixed and discrete, identities showed themselves to be porous, inconsistent, and changeable. Identities frequently did not register or reflect factual conditions but ignored
or exceeded them. Identities always involved to some extent an idealization of character, which meant that they were always to some extent phantasies. And when those phantasies, with their multiple, conflicting, and
self-contradictory terms, were enacted, they often malfunctioned, setting
in motion wayward urges and desires and producing paradoxical consequences. Problematic at their inception, phantasies of identity became increasingly more so through the nineteenth century. Under the influence
of events—notably, the French Revolution—or because of a gradual internal unraveling of the terms of identity, the problems and paradoxes of
phantasmatic identities became acutely evident to French and German
writers, artists, and thinkers who in different ways came to find their cultural identities at an impasse.

This book rethinks some of the key terms of French and German identity. It rewrites some of the most significant histories of French and German cultural identities that arose in the Enlightenment and continued
through the nineteenth century. Challenging conventional assumptions
about the naturalness, coherence, and factual rootedness of identities, the
following chapters reconstruct different trajectories of identity emphasizing their convolutions and paradoxes. This approach casts a very different
light upon both the terms of French universalism and German attempts to
produce specific forms of German culture. The foundational figure of German cultural nationalism, Johann Gottfried Herder, turns out to be a critic
of German nationalism and a believer in French cultural superiority.
French claims to the natural superiority of the French language and civilization yield the conclusion in France that its language and civilization are
based on deception and decadence. The resulting German counterclaims
to the superior authenticity and profundity of German language and culture inspire a German cultural resurgence from the late eighteenth century to the late nineteenth, until those claims are ironically undercut by
the devastating anti-German criticisms of Friedrich Nietzsche. The eighteenth-century use of classical revival to construct German identity as a rational, autonomous self reveals a compulsive desire to surrender that self,

to give up personal autonomy in a strange condition of aesthetic submission. This reversal of classicist intentions becomes increasingly apparent from the founder of modern art history, Johann Winckelmann, to the writer Thomas Mann. At the end of the eighteenth century, France's most celebrated artist, Jacques-Louis David, draws on classical revival to effect a cultural renovation based on the transformation of genders. This project becomes policy in the Jacobin French Revolution, but in the hands of Goethe and Germaine de Staël, David's and the Jacobins' reworking of gender is shown to be not a cultural renewal but an affliction, a suicidal destruction of society. In the late eighteenth century, German identity is redefined as authentic spiritual depth and German progress, but in the nineteenth century that same identity comes to seem retrograde and fraudulent in relation to the new criteria of "modernity" set by the French Revolution. This new sense of German culture's dislocation from the flow of history leads the young Karl Marx to repudiate German cultural identity and to invent a new agent in history defined precisely by its lack of culture: the proletariat.

Throughout all these complex and paradoxical projections of identity, the oppositions of universal and particular and of France and Germany continue to be asserted in different forms, and for different historical reasons these simple formulas of opposition have often veiled the many contradictions and convolutions of identity. Recognizing how multiple and conflicting terms of identity were at work in French and German culture and how they both functioned and malfunctioned requires a brief overview of the historiography of the European Enlightenment and its crucial influence on historians' narratives of cultural and intellectual development in the nineteenth century.

"There are many philosophers in the eighteenth century, but there was only one Enlightenment"—so begins Peter Gay's monumental study of the Enlightenment published in 1966 and 1969. As he tells us in the preface to the first volume, Gay's purpose in writing this enormous study is to rescue the Enlightenment from those "who held [it] responsible for the evils of the modern age." Since the French Revolution, critics of the Enlightenment have accused it of suffering from "superficial rationalism, foolish optimism, and irresponsible Utopianism." Against these criticisms, Gay offers an encouraging, affirmative view: "The men of the Enlightenment united on a vastly ambitious program, a program of secularism, humanity, cosmopolitanism, and freedom, above all, freedom in its many forms— freedom from arbitrary power, freedom of speech, freedom of trade, freedom to realize one's talents, freedom of aesthetic response, freedom, in a word, of moral man to make his way in the world." Eighteenth-century writers collectively worked to realize these aims by using "pagan" or ancient texts to liberate themselves from the dominance of a retrograde Christianity and of arbitrary political authority. This use of the ancients was not backward looking or nostalgic in intention but, on the contrary, provided the necessary means to engineer a breakthrough to the future: Enlightenment "paganism," Gay notes, was thoroughly "modern," ultimately emancipating the Enlightenment "from classical thought as much as from Christian dogma." A unified project of multiform individual emancipation, the Enlightenment marked the crucial passage from "tradition" to "modernity."[3]

Gay seeks to reaffirm the Enlightenment as a liberal phenomenon, indeed, to establish it as the proper foundation of a heroic modern liberalism. And while he directs his project against a long tradition of nineteenth- and twentieth-century critics of the Enlightenment's putative liberalism, he also more directly addresses the situation of Western liberalism in the middle decades of the twentieth century. In those years, Western inheritors of the liberal tradition had fallen into self-doubt. World war and the emergence of fascism and communism had disillusioned some American liberals and led them to a critique of the Enlightenment as a genuinely liberal movement. In the 1950s Gay sought to counter the influential attack on the Enlightenment by the disenchanted American liberal Carl Becker in *The Heavenly City of the Eighteenth-Century Philosophers* (1932).[4] Gay's subsequent massive study, *The Enlightenment,* constitutes his overwhelming positive rejoinder, a clarion call to a renewed liberal self-confidence in the unity, efficacy, and relevance of Enlightenment principles as the proper source of liberal values. Gay describes the Enlightenment as a "recovery of nerve," a recovery of the ancients' affirmation of the autonomy and force of human reasoning; but the book also announces another "recovery of nerve"—that of post–World War II progressive liberalism, which, in having defeated fascism and contained communism, was able to reassert the supremacy of Enlightenment values.[5]

The popular and academic success of Gay's interpretation of the Enlightenment was emblematic of the dominance in 1960s academe of a progressive liberalism, and in its message and importance it can be grouped with other texts of the period that affirmed the historical victory of liberal modernity and modernization.[6] In historical studies, this liberal view of the Enlightenment and modernity often served as the touchstone for subsequent interpretations of nineteenth-century European cultural and intellectual history. The conventional view of the divergence of the French and German cultural trajectories relies, in fact, on the idea of a normative liberal Enlightenment. On this view, where the French Enlightenment and the French Revolution manifested modern liberal ideas, Germany's choice of an anti-Enlightenment cultural particularism rendered the Germans fatefully vulnerable to political authoritarianism in the nineteenth and twentieth centuries.[7]

In the decades since Gay's study, the liberal view of European intellectual and cultural history—and its presupposition of a unified liberal Enlightenment disseminated through the next century—has come to be challenged in a number of significant ways. Notwithstanding its desire to annunciate a new era of liberal thought, Gay's book can be seen to set a highwater mark of a postwar progressive liberal consensus in the universities in general and of the liberal interpretation of the Enlightenment in particular. As the Vietnam War produced countercultural movements and a political radicalism that challenged liberalism in universities and society, corresponding intellectual developments in Enlightenment historiography unsettled liberal interpretation. The push and pull of those historiographical developments have rendered European cultural and intellectual history contentious, often contradictory, and highly complex.

In part, the historiographical developments of the late 1960s and 1970s derived from a desire for greater empirical and historical specificity than was found in Gay's liberal history of ideas. Criticizing what he believed was Gay's abstraction of ideas from their institutions and social conditions, Robert Darnton advocated a more concrete "social history of ideas" that would approach the philosophes of the eighteenth century on their own specific social and institutional terms. Other historians also argued for greater attentiveness to the national differences between Enlightenment thinkers and to their multiple, often conflicting intellectual traditions.

All these developments challenged Gay's synthesizing liberal narrative of the Enlightenment. Darnton's studies of publishing, patronage, and the poor, would-be philosophes of "grub street" pointed to a kind of hypocrisy in the French Enlightenment. As Darnton argues in "The High Enlightenment and the Low-Life of Literature in Pre-Revolutionary France" (1971), French philosophes ascended after midcentury into the privileged institutions of the French old regime and, once there, closed ranks against newcomers. By the late eighteenth century, the French Enlightenment had become a pillar of the old regime. The French Revolution, on Darnton's account, drew its strength not from Enlightenment ideas but from its opposition to the Enlightenment's social exclusiveness.[8]

Studies that considered national differences in the European Enlightenment also tended to challenge Gay's image of a harmonious and cosmopolitan unity of purpose. Although some intellectual and cultural figures in Germany—such as Immanuel Kant—seemed to fit neatly into Gay's image of a European Enlightenment philosophe, others, such as Kant's student Herder, both subscribed to a cosmopolitan Enlightenment culture and strongly resented its universalist or cosmopolitan claims. National cultural differences, as historians noted, inflected national and regional Enlightenments and produced reactions against the idea of a single, general intellectual and cultural order.[9]

These studies suggested further that one crucial aspect of Gay's *Enlightenment* synthesis, its absorption of the classical revival of the eighteenth century into a cosmopolitan Enlightenment liberalism, was particularly misconceived. Although that revival reinforced certain aspects of that Enlightenment, in other respects it proved to be the liberal Enlightenment's most potent adversary. J. G. A. Pocock's influential *The Machiavellian Moment: Florentine Political Thought and the Atlantic Republican Tradition* (1975) traces a vital strain of ancient "civic republican" thought that gained a powerful hold in Renaissance Florence and was then transmitted throughout Europe, landing in the eighteenth century at the center of Anglo-American political thought. Following Pocock, other historians have argued that civic-republican ideas also exerted a powerful influence in eighteenth-century France, whose spokesmen included Montesquieu and Rousseau of the *Discourses* and *The Social Contract*. In Germany, ancient civic republicanism appeared in the thought of Herder, the young Hegel, and early German liberals. Identifying moral rigor, political obligation, patriotism, and self-sacrifice as the constituent characteristics of ancient "virtue," eighteenth-century civic republicans served as some of that century's most compelling critics. They opposed, unsurprisingly, centralizing princely courts, which they believed had usurped the power of the citizenry and corrupted its morals.[10] But the same principles that led them to criticize monarchies and aristocracies also led them to criticize the strongest eighteenth-century representatives of Gay's cosmopolitan liberal Enlightenment, the advocates of liberal commerce.

Civic republicanism attacked the luxury and deferential sensibility—the politeness or civility—of courtly and aristocratic culture. That culture's dissemination of soft living, easy morals, and luxury, it believed, taught citizens to forget their civic obligations, to seek instead their own narrow enjoyments and selfish interests. Civic republicans sought to restore to their cultures and polities the same austere, virtuous political community that they believed had characterized ancient republics. Their fear of the corrupting power of luxury and selfishness was directed not just at the court and aristocracy, but at another activity that seemed also to be based on a narrow egoism and the production of material excess—namely, unrestrained commerce.

In objecting to unfettered commerce, civic republicans placed themselves in direct opposition to a current of Enlightenment thought that has been central to its putative liberalism, as Gay acknowledges by including "freedom of trade" in his list of defining Enlightenment liberties. Theorists of a new political economy, such as Adam Smith and other Scottish writers, advocated the beneficial, civilizing effects of commerce. Commerce, for them, increased the wealth and prosperity of a nation; it eased the hardships of life and brought people together to engage in sociable exchange. When trade extended to other countries, it made militarily combative nations engage in peaceful interrelations, as they then learned a pacifying, cosmopolitan language of commercial exchange.[11]

Civic republicans interpreted in a less benevolent way the liberal notion that commerce was the great engine of economic development and material prosperity. For them, wealth always bred self-interest, extreme material inequality, and extravagance—all things that introduced the corruption of virtue that they found in the courts and aristocratic venues of Europe.[12] The fear of moral contamination from an expanding commerce indicates the streak of xenophobia that sometimes ran through civic republicanism's so-called political communitarianism. Notwithstanding the fact that it was an international political ethos, in certain local, regional, and national manifestations it tended to imagine an ideal republic that preserved the austere virtue of its citizenry by sealing itself off from the rest of the world.[13] Contrary to Gay's view of an easy assimilation of ancient ideas into the Enlightenment as part of a harmonious "modern" consciousness, this eighteenth-century republican ethos conflicted with Enlightenment notions of progressive cosmopolitan commerce. Against an international liberal order of self-interested individuals, civic republicanism pointed toward the revival of a putatively ancient political community.[14]

The impetus of Darnton's populist critique and social history of an elitist Enlightenment and the civic-republican critique of Enlightenment commerce and individualism reflected the political and countercultural concerns of the 1960s.[15] Reinforcing the social-historical and civic-republican challenges to Gay's image of a unified liberal Enlightenment were other historiographical developments in the 1980s. The popularity of bringing interpretive ethnography to historical analysis, combined with the importation of semiotic cultural analysis, further deflected attention from the ideas of the elite Enlightenment and toward cultural institutions and practices. The influence of Michel Foucault's studies of eighteenth-century institutions additionally undercut a liberal understanding of the Enlightenment, as he inverted the liberal view of the Enlightenment as an era of progressive, humanitarian reform. According to Foucault, the Enlightenment reshaping of institutions—the madhouse and the prison—brought about more oppressive systems of surveillance and order that were designed not to ease but to rigidify exclusion and control. The Enlightenment's claims of pursuing liberty only masked a more sinister domination.[16]

The cultural agitations of the 1960s and 1970s produced a strong feminist movement in the universities that by the 1980s significantly influenced Enlightenment studies. In some respects the concern with gender fitted well with the tendency of historians since Gay to challenge the liberal understanding of the Enlightenment. Joan Landes's influential *Women and the Public Sphere in the Age of the French Revolution* attacks the Enlightenment's negative representations of women, which she argues issued in a rigidified gender differentiation in the liberal and modern era. Sara Maza's *Private Lives and Public Affairs: The Causes Célèbres of Prerevolutionary France* brings the issue of the invidious representation of women to Darnton's grub street, as she considers how the would-be philosophes Darnton identified as resentful political agitators were motivated by an intense misogyny.[17]

But while strengthening one of the currents of historiography that was at odds with Gay's synthetic view of liberalism and the Enlightenment, the focus on gender in the Enlightenment also in another sense returned to Gay's view. In part, this was accomplished by the criticism that feminist historians brought against civic republicanism. Where historians of the 1960s and 1970s, who were interested in civic republicanism, focused on its explicit and implicit conflicts with liberal notions of commerce and progress, historians of the 1980s and 1990s, interested in gender, examined civic republicanism's treatment of its other great nemesis, the putatively decadent court and aristocracy. In looking at civic republicanism's representations of gender, recent feminist historians have arrived at a much less flattering view of the recourse to antiquity and a much more favorable view of the cultural institutions of the old regime. Civic virtue, from a feminist (and Foucauldian) perspective, did not express so much a longing for a revived sense of human community as a desire for a new regulative order based on an oppressive system of rigid gender differentiation. Formulated by Rousseau, disseminated by his followers, and implemented by the Jacobins, the misogyny of civic republicanism, according to these historians, exerted a strong influence into the modern era.[18]

In criticizing the gender politics of civic republicanism, feminist historians have rehabilitated what civic republicanism attacked—namely, the court and that institution of aristocratic society, the salon. In those forms of the old regime, these historians have argued, women exerted considerable and benevolent social influence and cultural power, which were then lost with the French Revolution. This rehabilitation of the refined institutions and sociability of the old regime, from the point of view of the role of women, has challenged the populist social historian's critique of the Enlightenment pioneered by Darnton. In Dena Goodman's analysis of the salon in the Enlightenment, the *salonnière* emerges as the great impresario of the Enlightenment. The salonnière, according to Goodman, mediated between combative men to produce a domain of free, candid conversation and intellectual exchange. Without the mediation of that female figure, the French Enlightenment might never have unfolded as productively as it did.[19] The feminist rehabilitation of the institutions of the old regime has thus also ended up rehabilitating the philosophes who attended them, those whom Darnton regarded as having been co-opted into the exclusivist practices of the old regime.

In her emphasis on how an institution of the old regime produced free, open, and critical discussion, Goodman joins other recent historians who have helped to revive a work of Jürgen Habermas, *The Structural Transformation of the Public Sphere* (1962). According to Habermas, eighteenth-century Europe witnessed the birth of institutions of critical rational discussion. In British coffeehouses, German reading societies and masonic lodges, and French salons, ideas circulated unimpeded by concerns of social hierarchy and religious and political censorship, creating a new "public sphere" of rational debate and criticism. Goodman has interpreted the institutions and cultural practices of late eighteenth-century France according to Habermas's criteria of a public sphere, factoring in as well an argument about gender. According to Goodman, this golden era of the public sphere recognized the role of women as crucial participants in intellectual exchange.[20]

Habermas's theory of the public sphere is bound up with particular liberal notions of modernity and modernization. Writing in the era of a triumphant liberalism and of Gay's *Enlightenment,* Habermas considers the eighteenth-century public sphere the manifestation of a "bourgeoisie" emancipating itself from the constraints of a traditional society dominated by aristocratic privilege and absolute monarchy. A person's entry into the public sphere was an assertion of rational autonomy, for within the public sphere one was to act strictly as a critical, rational interlocutor, as a free individual, relying only on his or her own reason. The public sphere, in short, was the accomplishment of liberal modernity. In using Habermas's theory of the public sphere to underwrite their characterizations of the Enlightenment, recent historians such as Goodman have, intentionally or unintentionally, returned to Gay's image of a liberal Enlightenment, of a unified intellectual movement that gave birth to the individual liberties associated with an ideal modernity, even if, for some, this ideal modernity existed no longer than the Enlightenment itself.[21]

Gay's attempt to write a synthetic liberal interpretation of the Enlightenment has thus been followed by a series of challenges and modifications in interpretation that have, in turn, produced their own interacting challenges and modifications, including, ultimately, a rehabilitation of a liberal understanding of the Enlightenment in the notion of the public sphere. These many challenges and counterchallenges have produced considerable intense debate about the meaning of the Enlightenment and the intellectual and cultural identity that issued from it.[22] Was the Enlightenment intellectual a modern liberal advocate of commerce and material progress or a backward-looking civic republican, a political reformer or a compromised would-be aristocrat, a cosmopolitan universalist or a figure defined by national character, a misogynist or a supporter of women?

Different commentators have argued for each of these possibilities as they have sought to make sense of the Enlightenment, to affirm a distinct, characteristic, consistent Enlightenment identity in the face of the multiple, conflicting terms of eighteenth-century identity. This procedure—to seek a single, definitive characterization of Enlightenment identity—registers the remarkable transformations of Enlightenment historiography, but it has not, I believe, drawn the fullest conclusions from those transformations. Rather than offering a single Enlightenment identity, either as an alternative to or as an affirmation of Gay's liberal philosophe, historiographical developments suggest a different implication for the intellectual and cultural history of the eighteenth and nineteenth centuries. Where Gay considered the philosophes of the eighteenth century to have a single, uniform identity—the modern liberal—the various challenges to Gay's interpretation have produced an eighteenth century that appears to be crisscrossed by conflicting terms and discourses of identity. The projection of a modern liberal Enlightenment has been undercut by its elitism, altered by national differences, challenged by ancient republicanism, undone by its skewed notions of gender, or perhaps reaffirmed by its elite embrace of women during the old regime. And in contradistinction to those historians since Gay who have argued that one of these currents constitutes a general cultural or intellectual identity that defines the Enlightenment, no such definitive general conclusion seems possible. Writers or texts taken to be exemplary of a particular identity often show signs of multiple, conflicting, or jumbled terms of identity.[23] The study of the eighteenth century now shows that era to be neither the coming together of intellectuals into a single, unified liberal movement nor fully definable by any single, fixed character. The eighteenth century can be looked on as a field of intellectual and cultural movement and conflict between contradictory terms of identity. The constant fusion and friction of ideas produced identities that were in crucial senses uncertain or unstable.[24] Those instabilities in Enlightenment terms of identity formed the basis of the multiple and paradoxical projections of identities in France and Germany and determined how they further developed, especially under the pressure of external events such as the French Revolution.

This study of French and German cultural identities takes as its point of departure the complex history of challenges to and restorations of the liberal view of the Enlightenment. In applying this historiography, I also seek to refine and, where appropriate, amend it. One general amendment helps to explain how I earlier characterized French and German cultural identities. As with conventional characterizations of national cultural identities, historians who seek to define (and often endorse) a characteristic Enlightenment identity—say, the Enlightenment advocate of progressive commerce, or the benevolent, intellectual salonnière—have assumed or sought to establish that identity's full reality, its entire basis in empirical fact. But although cultural and intellectual identities did sometimes have a basis in social and political reality—commerce did sometimes generate civilizing wealth; aristocratic women did facilitate intellectual discussion in salons—they, like characterizations of national identity, were also constituted on another basis. Taking over the most affirmative self-descriptions of the figures they study, historians often do not recognize that terms of identity are in some ways idealized phantasies; and, as I indicated above, these are constructions of self that showed themselves to be intensely problematic.[25] The multiple, contradictory, and phantasmatic nature of the terms and discourses of Enlightenment identities, how they interacted in France and Germany, and how they affected nineteenth-century projections of identity are the concerns of this book. In different French and German cultural trajectories that flowed out of the Enlightenment, we can see phantasies of identity weaving together and tearing apart, projected forth by desires and aspirations only to be undone by their own contradictions, conflicting notions of selfhood, and intense cultural and political conflict.

This book offers a "synthetic" study in the sense that it brings together many of the major topics and themes of Enlightenment historiography and their connections, and it extends its analysis to cover developments into the nineteenth century. But the study is not synthetic in the conventional historiographical sense of offering a single comprehensive narrative. The multifarious and contradictory character of Enlightenment terms of identity in France and Germany necessarily precludes writing one master narrative into which all major cultural and intellectual developments can be assimilated. The diversity and conflicted character of terms of identity and their effects require reconstructions of cultural identity to differ according to the kind of instability of identity one is dealing with, its context, and its historical duration.[26]

The organization of the chapters that follow is based on this conclusion. Their narratives vary according to the nature of the identities in question and the angle from which they are seen. Chapter 1 focuses on a few key formative years when Herder emerged as an important writer in the German public sphere, a perspective that, while referring to much broader developments, allows us to see all of Herder's identity troubles at work during a convergent moment. Later those problems would be distributed over a broad range of his writings and concerns and many more events. Chapters 4 and 5 consider how specific historical events critically affected cultural identities, intensifying their instabilities and contradictions during the era of the French Revolution. In chapters 2 and 3, historical events play a more general and diffuse role, while the most significant factors at work in these trajectories of identity are the internal conceptual impasses and inconsistencies in long-standing discourses of civility and aesthetics. Chapter 3 extends its analysis over a long nineteenth century to bring out the most far-reaching effects of the instabilities of an important Enlightenment identity of neoclassical revival in its German form.

A central concern in one trajectory of identity points in another trajectory of identity to a deeper and broader set of issues. The focus in chapter 2 on what I call the French discourse of civility thus directs us in chapter 3 to larger and even longer-persisting anxieties in aesthetics and classicism. What is of secondary importance in one set of debates turns out to be at the center of controversy in another set, as the issue of the trustworthiness of language and civility in chapter 2 passes into the high-stakes politics of gender in chapter 4. The figures, texts, and works of culture that I deal with are chosen according to their prominence and the exemplary roles they play in the development of certain identities. There is no attempt to cover exhaustively all the figures, texts, and works exemplifying a particular identity.

This book rewrites our understanding of important figures, texts, and developments over shorter and longer durations of historical time, determined by the changing terms and implications of unstable cultural identities. While some chapters focus on a shorter, more discrete historical period to offer a "close-up" view, in these chapters, as well as in those with a longer-term perspective, I have tried to indicate some important consequences of each development in order to make clear that the self-descriptions of a historical period should not be taken as impervious to further change or contradiction. Each chapter is thus in a sense self-contained, not just incorporating the development of a topic up to and within a particular period, but also indicating a particular future. Other futures of a particular subject might be possible, and these would coexist and possibly interact with the increasingly ironic views of identity I describe in this book.

The following chapters draw on relevant contemporary, often post-structuralist theories of culture that, rightly or wrongly, are associated with "postmodernism." But while contemporary theory informs my analysis, I have not attempted to derive the latter from the former. Rather, as I have argued here, the ambiguous and conflicted nature of identity can be derived from historiography and from an empirical, close reading of texts and documentary evidence. In emphasizing how conventional historical practices can lead us to conclusions in principle similar to those of contemporary cultural theorizing, I hope to counteract what I believe are the wrongheaded notions that historians using theory are necessarily proceeding unempirically and incomprehensibly. On the contrary, the acute concern of contemporary literary and cultural theory with the slippages and contradictions of culture can make the historian more clearheaded, more attentive to the empirical record, taking seriously the evidence of the inconsistencies and ambiguities of identities that are often elided in order to produce a phantasy of a fully coherent and uniform self.

CHAPTER ONE

The Man with Too Many Qualities

The Young Herder between France and Germany

The eighteenth-century writer Johann Gottfried Herder is conventionally thought of as a consistent thinker. In a variety of pursuits, he seemingly advanced a single program of German cultural nationalism that opposed Enlightenment cosmopolitanism and rationalism and the European dominance of French culture and language. All his activities as a literary critic and linguist, collector of German folk songs, and philosopher of history emphasized the primacy of national cultural differences, particularist—as opposed to universalizing—history and thought, and the advantages of German language and culture.

This general view of a consistent, singleminded Herder has been proffered even as studies have long noted that he thought and acted in ways that seem to contradict this conventional view. Biographers and commentators have observed, for example, several ways in which he did not challenge but followed the Enlightenment, both European and German.[1] And they have noted that his other behavior and thought often failed to fit the conception of Herder as a rigorous proponent of German cultural nationalism. On this aspect of Herder, Friedrich Meinecke is particularly eloquent, as he writes in his classic work, *Historism:* "Herder, considered as a man in the development of his powers, strikes us as an inharmonious and puzzling personality. He never struck firm roots in any profession or in any particular place. As he himself says in a mood of self-reflection, he was 'driven by a vague unrest that sought another world, but never found it.'"[2]

Meinecke's observation and Herder's self-characterization are at odds with what we expect from a founder of German cultural nationalism and its notion of Germany as a privileged homeland, or *Heimat*. The image of Herder as a single-minded German nationalist, cultural particularist, and historicist, particularly appreciative of the uniqueness of historical periods, does not do justice to the complexity and strangeness of his thought and personality. His thinking and behavior were not just attracted to those ideas but were also driven from them. The oscillation and uncertainties in his views and actions, in his sense of where he belonged, are particularly visible in the first years of his career as a writer, when he was employed as a pastor and teacher by the German community in the Baltic city of Riga in the mid-1760s.

The manner in which commentators have treated Herder's time in Riga follows the conventional interpretive approach. Herder's stay in Riga is considered a crucial period in his development. Within a few years of leaving university, he had established himself as a notable figure in the German community in Riga; at the same time, he made his mark in German letters, obtaining a national reputation for his essays on German language and literature. These essays appeared at a particularly opportune time, when German literature and criticism were experiencing a revival in an expanded literary public sphere. Herder's essays, which are concerned with the nature of German language and literature, thus identified him as an emerging public spokesman for German cultural nationalism. So much of his activity and of German literary history in this period thus supports the conventional image of Herder as an emerging champion of German cultural revival, and, consequently, the confusion, oddness, and vacillation that he also displayed in his thought and behavior at this time have been downplayed, generally assimilated without further comment into the conventional image of the writer. This standard procedure in analyzing Herder is here especially understandable, since he himself explicitly endorsed it, as he later remarked how his life and career in Riga had perfectly suited him and his intellectual work.

But notwithstanding the many ways in which his development at this time and his later self-description fit the conventional image of Herder, his life and thought in this period were also characterized by such intense uncertainty and vacillation that they cannot be easily absorbed into the conventional view. Herder had serious, destabilizing doubts about the conventional persona that he was cultivating, about his successful career in Germany and his successful entry into the German public sphere. And these doubts ultimately drove him from the city and from Germany. What happened to Herder when he left Riga emphasizes the importance of the often-overlooked oscillations and doubts of Herder's formative Riga period. For over and against his unsettled identity in Riga, he now imagined an alternative person, one that he had earlier stylized as the direct opposite of the figure of the German cultural nationalist. Herder left Riga to make a coastal voyage that ended in France. That trip constituted a kind of imaginative holiday, an ellipsis in the usual trajectory of cultural nationalism that is attributed to Herder. On this voyage, he allowed himself to indulge in a phantasy of becoming precisely what he denounced in his published writings: a French philosophe in a culture of refined French sociability.

Herder's formative period in Riga provides a particularly good example of the multiplicity of terms and discourses of identity in the eighteenth century, of how they might simply be joined together, but also of how they could come apart, in this case in a figure who was acutely conscious of their conflicts and problems. Herder manifests the unsettled nature of eighteenth-century subjectivity. Despite efforts to impose a harmonizing narrative on his persona and writings in Riga, Herder's texts and the oddities of his behavior break apart into conflicting terms and discourses of identity. No matter how much he sought to ignore their contradictions and problematic implications, he could not fuse the clashing terms and discourses of enlightened commercial society and civic republicanism, of German cultural nationalism and commitment to a national public sphere. As he traversed the various discourses, in what seemed like an involuntary displacement from one to the next, the prospect of a harmonious identity in Riga became increasingly untenable. What he then sought as an alternative to the conflict of identities in Riga was an image drawn from yet another eighteenth-century identity, one of French refinement and Enlightenment worldliness. He phantasized about this identity, and as he did so, he encountered not just its considerable advantages but also its defects. The young Herder's particular phantasy of French civility shows with particular clarity that he was not a unified subject, in possession of a fixed identity, but a persona in flux, driven by clashing terms and problematic discourses of the self.

THE GOOD CITIZEN AND THE GOOD GERMAN

After graduating from the University of Königsberg, where he had studied with Immanuel Kant and Friedrich Hamann, twenty-one-year-old Johann Gottfried Herder arrived in the Baltic city of Riga in 1764 to assume the duties of a teacher at the Lutheran Cathedral school, one of the major social and cultural institutions of Riga's dominant German trading class.[3] This German commercial patriciate had long dominated the former Hansa city. The ruling council of Riga consisted of fourteen of its wealthier members. The corporations and guilds alone elected members to the council and chose the *Bürgermeister.* Its well-established institutions of self-government nourished the belief that the city was part of a tradition of proud, autonomous European republics. Thus the city adopted the title

"Respublica Rigensis." In 1710 Riga was incorporated into the Russian empire, and an upper class of Russian aristocracy and bureaucracy was implanted in the region. The city, however, under the political guarantee of Peter the Great retained its traditional rights of self-government, and those privileges, along with the protection of the Lutheran church, ensured the continued dominance of a German commercial class.[4]

Herder proved an immediate success, both in his work and in patrician German society. His reputation as a teacher spread to St. Petersburg, whose Lutheran community in 1767 offered him a position in its new secondary school. The city of Riga responded by making him a pastor of two suburban churches and admitted him into full membership in the clergy. His sermons, according to his English biographer, were admired for their "graceful and appealing manner."[5]

Herder also easily made his way through patrician social circles, where he found favor as a "charming conversationalist."[6] His social successes led to an invitation to join the local lodge of freemasons, a society of some of the city's most important and enlightened citizens. And once there, he became so amiable and impressive a member that he was apparently chosen as its secretary even before he had attained the usual rank for such a position.[7]

All this activity did not prevent him from embarking on an additional literary career. After writing small pieces for regional publications, he received national attention by producing a series of essays, the *Fragments on Recent German Literature (Über die neuere deutsche Literatur: Fragmente)* (1766–1767), which analyzed the contributions to *Literary Correspondence concerning Recent Literature (Literaturbriefe, betreffend die neuste Literatur)*, published in Berlin by Friedrich Nicolai, the prominent advocate of a German Enlightenment. In the *Fragments*—commentaries on language, literature, poetry, and aesthetics—Herder significantly intervened in some of the controversies concerning the revival of German literature and outlined some of the concerns that would preoccupy him for the rest of his life.[8] The author of these commentaries on Nicolai's *Literary Correspondence* was immediately identified as an important new voice in a reforming German literature, and although Herder published those commentaries anonymously, before long his identity was well known in literary circles. Nicolai in fact saw in Herder a kindred spirit in a movement to reinvigorate German culture against what both men regarded as its domination by derivative pedantry. Nicolai consequently recruited Herder as a contributor to his next literary venture, the *General German Library (Allgemeine deutsche Bibliothek).*[9]

Identified as an important critical contribution to a national debate about the character of German language and literature, Herder's *Frag-*

ments injected him into the emerging public sphere in Germany. According to Jürgen Habermas, the modern public sphere is a domain of unrestricted discussion and criticism focused initially on literature and then on politics. Unlike traditional intellectual and cultural institutions of the European old regime, the modern public sphere is open to all regardless of social status, location, or origin.[10] Through his work as a publisher of new literary journals and newspapers directed at reforming German literature, Nicolai had made himself an impresario of an emerging modern public sphere in Germany, and Herder's contributions from Riga are a good example of the public sphere functioning as Habermas described it. From far-off Riga, an unknown writer, on the basis of his criticism alone, came to play a formative role in the shaping of the concerns of a new literary public. At the same time that his writings testified to the formation of a new literary public sphere and gave Herder an important place in it, they also allowed him to advance an agenda that was still forming in his mind—namely, the attempt to define and celebrate the unique qualities of German language and literature. His entry into the public sphere was thus also a first step on his path to cultural nationalism.

Herder's reputation as an emerging writer of national importance was recognized by his employers and the Riga community, and that recognition made him only more valuable to both. When he first contemplated resigning his position to make a coastal voyage, a member of the city's senate called on that body to do whatever it could to keep its "famous" author. And when he could not be dissuaded from leaving, the city promised to promote him, if he returned, to a rectorship of a prestigious imperial school and to a pastorate at the important Church of St. Joseph.[11]

The German patrician class thus embraced Herder, and he apparently responded in kind. His very first writings in Riga, before he published the *Fragments,* consisted of short essays and addresses for regional publications and public occasions. These endorsed the world of his patrons. The mainstream European Enlightenment, and the Scottish Enlightenment in particular, supported commerce, not just because it produced wealth and prosperity, but also because it taught human beings to be restrained and sociable. Through trade, according to many eighteenth-century writers, commerce fostered understanding between cultures and development within them. Commerce, in short, was often incorporated into the eighteenth century's discourse of an enlightened civilizing process according to which European society had evolved from a ferocious, xenophobic egoism, a condition of barbarism, to refinement, cosmopolitan understanding, and culture. "Commerce," as Montesquieu wrote, "polishes and softens barbarian ways as we see every day."[12]

This eighteenth-century view of *doux commerce* appeared as a defense and a rehabilitation of commerce against earlier suspicions that it undercut social ties rather than strengthened them. Christian and civic-republican thought stressed the moral dangers of unconstrained economical egoism. To get around the civic-republican critique, eighteenth-century apologists for commerce who were also republicans developed what J. G. A. Pocock has called "commercial republicanism," which claimed to harmonize republican and commercial values. This hybrid ideology was particularly influential in British commercial circles, was supported by some French writers such as Montesquieu, and had widespread adherence in the American colonies and later republic.[13] A similar idea of a commercial ethos superimposed onto a republican constitution was evident in eighteenth-century Riga, and in his first short essays aimed at local consumption and in his public addresses, Herder functioned as the spokesman—the "organic intellectual," to use Antonio Gramsci's term—of the "commercial republicanism" of his German patrons.

In an essay that appeared in the *Riga Gazette (Rigische Anzeige)* in 1769, "On Diligence in the Study of Several Languages," Herder seeks to justify the value of learning languages in terms of enlightened commercial activity. Training in foreign languages, he writes, is necessary for ever-expanding commerce, not just because it expedites trade but also because it helps to realize the moral mission of commerce. Trade and commerce produce prosperity for all, and they enlarge human understanding. They allow people to learn about one another more fully and accurately. As a spokesman of enlightened commerce, Herder embraces its cosmopolitanism; the idea of studying other languages issues in a joyous embrace of other nations: "I seek to join through English temperament, the wit of the French and the resplendence of Italy with German diligence. I encompass the spirit of each people in my soul!—Rewards sufficient, I think to raise our diligence in the study of many languages."[14]

On the occasion of Catherine II's visit to Riga in October 1765, and at her dedication of the new courthouse, Herder delivered an address whose success led the city council to encourage its publication. In this address, entitled "Do We Still Have the Public and Fatherland of Yore?," Herder not only displays the eighteenth-century view of civilizing commerce but also explicitly indicates its distance from and superiority to a civic republicanism based on ancient models. Comparing the public life of eighteenth-century Riga with that of ancient Athens and Rome, he points out that both the ancient public and the orators who addressed it have long vanished. And what has disappeared as well, he tells us, is the intense, overheated patriotism of ancient polities, which necessarily led to conflict and war. Trade and commerce have made the modern age more tolerant, so that the freedom enjoyed today is no longer "the *brazen audacity* of the ancients" but "a finer, more modest *freedom,* the freedom of *conscience,* to be an honest man and a Christian, the *freedom* to enjoy in the shadow of the throne one's dwelling . . . in peace and quiet, and to possess the fruits of one's labors; the freedom to be the shaper of one's happiness and comfort." This paean to a commercial and *bürgerlich* republicanism precisely summarizes for Herder the meaning of Riga and its relationship to the benevolent rule of Catherine: "it is the *jewel* that *Riga* has received so splendidly from the hands of its just *Empress* and enjoys most gratefully."[15] In this Baltic city, an enlightened commercial community has become harmoniously wedded to an enlightened monarch, and the result is not an ancient but a modern, self-governing republic of commerce, culture, and calm sociability; or, as Herder put it in an earlier address, Riga was "a city where one unites industry and utility with refinement, friendship and comfort with obedience, thought with piety." Indeed, "Riga under the shadow of Russia is nearly Geneva."[16]

From his arrival in Riga, the young Herder thus successfully negotiated a complex and potentially conflicting set of offices, loyalties, and identities. He was at once a dutiful Lutheran pastor and teacher, a sociable member of society, a spokesman for Riga's commercial and republican patriciate, a loyal subject of an enlightened Russian monarch, a celebrated writer of national reputation in Germany's developing public sphere, and an emerging German cultural nationalist.[17] This array of social, political, and cultural claims in Herder is on the surface a particularly striking example of how terms and discourses of identity could be various yet blended together. And the happy result of that blending was Herder's success in Riga society and in German letters. As he wrote to his future wife in 1770, the particular mix of social and political forces was never constraining but afforded him a unique opportunity for expression. In Riga, he said, "I lived, taught, acted so freely, so without restriction—I will perhaps never be in a position to live, teach, and act so freely again."[18]

In Riga, Herder was, in the words of his English biographer, a "cosmopolitan, Enlightened lion of patrician society," who from this base was well on the way to becoming a major participant in Germany's newly expanding literary sphere.[19] But instead of setting forth on this path marked out for him, Herder abruptly decided in 1769 to resign his position and to leave Riga for a coastal voyage that ended in France. Notwithstanding his own testimonies of satisfaction with these years in Riga, something bothered him about his life in the city, and it bothered him sufficiently to make him feel the need to leave what appeared to be an extremely favorable situation.

COMMERCE WITHOUT VIRTUE

The harmonizing narrative of Herder's thought and experience in Riga offered above agrees both with older biographies and interpretations of his evolving cultural nationalism and with more recent investigations of such things as Herder's politics and his notion of the public sphere. All these studies allow the different aspects to merge together to form a single personality assumed to be coherent and well functioning.[20] But these interpretations have exaggerated the consistency of Herder's remarks and the enthusiasm with which he asserts each of the positions attributed to him. They have tended to ignore the various and intense contradictions, frictions, and slippages that also appear between and within the terms and discourses of identity that flow through Herder's writings, actions, and phantasies.

In his address "Do We Still Have the Public and Fatherland of Yore?" Herder carefully distinguishes between an "ancient" and a "modern" republic. The former fosters a tumultuous overheated politics; the latter produces a calm, cultivated, more rational commercial governance. An ancient republic is based on a polity that is democratic but also demagogic and unstable, while a modern commercial and bourgeois republic pursues policies that encourage order and prosperity. This distinction between republics supports Herder's even more explicit defense of commerce in his essay "On Diligence in the Study of Several Languages," a defense that relies on conventional eighteenth-century arguments: commerce and trade produce prosperity, encourage understanding between nations, and thus advance civilization.

But although these writings strongly endorse Riga's commercial republic, they also contain remarks that call it into question. In these criticisms, Herder does not draw on the reasoning of an eighteenth-century commercial republican but reiterates the views of classic civic republicanism, which are strongly hostile to a commercial ethos.[21] One of the objections of ancient and Renaissance civic republicanism to commerce is that while it yields economic growth and prosperity, it does so unevenly, and thus inevitably produces dependency. In contrast to a polity of relatively equal, self-reliant citizens, people in commercial societies necessarily fall into more differentiated economic hierarchies, in which some citizens become economically dependent on the will of others. Commerce, in other words, always lends itself to exploitation and domination. As Rousseau writes: "The word 'finance' is slave language; it has no place in the city's lexicon."[22]

This is how Herder also characterizes trade and commerce in "On Diligence in the Study of Several Languages," as he slips in, between the conventional praises of those activities, strong statements that reiterate ancient republican complaints. Alongside the view of commerce as fostering prosperity and understanding, Herder tells us bluntly that "trade is the pillage of distant lands." Learning another language does not so much facilitate mutual understanding as serve the cause of exploitation: "Treasures that the sweat of a foreign nation dug from the veins of the depths are shared as booty among other peoples through that nation's language." At one point Herder asserts that the benevolent rationales of commerce are no more than cynical pretexts: "The *raison d'état* of commerce thus masters languages so that other nations may at least be deceived in words of their own tongue."[23]

In keeping with the classical republican critique, Herder worries not just about what commerce does to other cultures, but also about what it does to one's own. In producing wealth and social and economic complexity, commerce and trade, according to ancient civic republicanism, threaten to undercut the polity's most important values. With commerce come more material goods, luxury, and social affectation. As some people then no longer need to work, physical softness and self-indulgence follow. Citizens hire others to perform their civic duties, particularly military service. And thus this society, becoming decadent, eventually collapses or gives way to its enemies.

In his article on language, Herder criticizes commerce and trade in this disparaging rhetoric of civic republicanism. These activities, he writes, yield new "glittering needs," "the gold of royal diadems, the delicacies of our tables, all the appurtenances of splendid display and luxury." If nations were satisfied with their own goods, there would be no "need to trade the citizen's birthright of his fatherland to ape the gallantries and ambiguous courtesies of others."[24] On his coastal voyage to France in 1769, as Herder passes the Netherlands, he thinks about how that country, though now energetic, will inevitably decline. Its commercial spirit, he writes, will ultimately kill the "spirit of valor" (*J,* 320/417).

Commerce and trade are dangerous to the well-being of the republic and to the independence of the republican self. As Herder pursues this train of thought in his article, his belief in a beneficial commercial cosmopolitanism, signified in the learning of foreign languages, comes to be displaced by the opposite urge: a turning inward, moralistic isolationism, and the cultivation solely of one's own language and culture. Herder writes: "If each nation were to enjoy, within the confines of its frontiers and attached to its soil, nature's gifts from the womb of the earth without asking illicitly for tribute from other people's riches, perhaps no one would need to trade the citizen's birthright of his fatherland for foreign advantages." In this state of contented self-reliance, "no city would become a hodgepodge of ten languages of commerce."[25]

International commerce and trade thus undercut a republic in this further sense: they erode natural, local, or regional identity. As republics accept foreign goods and ideas, they risk dependency on other cultures; they begin to forget what was distinctive about their own traditions and customs. When Herder thinks about how a state is best off relying on itself, it occurs to him that this is in fact how nature intended cultures to exist: alone, self-reliant, focused on developing their own cultural resources. "All these objections [that he has just given against learning foreign languages] appear to have nature on their side," since "we may ape haltingly the sounds of foreign nations, without, however, penetrating to the core of their uniqueness. I may perhaps, with much effort, learn dead languages word by word, from their monuments, but their spirit has vanished for me." Herder's culturally narrowing republicanism merges here with his cultural nationalism, both together leading him to a radically relativist position: that one can genuinely or fully know only one's own culture and never the culture of another people. Herder concludes: "If thus each language has its distinct national character, it seems that nature imposes upon us the obligation only to our mother tongue, for it is perhaps better attuned to our character and coextensive with our thinking."[26]

Herder's mitigating "perhaps" in the preceding sentence signals his own recognition that he is saying something at odds with what he should be saying in defense of the commercial republicanism of his employers. Herder's problem now is that he senses that his own reasoning is heading toward an impasse, as his strenuous criticisms of commerce threaten to undercut completely his justification of commercial Riga and its basis in international trade. In "On Diligence in the Study of Several Languages," his strongest reservations about commerce are on the verge of undoing the article's intention. Herder must find a way back to the article's purpose of justification; so, after pointing out that the mandate of nature is cultural separation and self-reliance, Herder adds that the mandate no longer holds: "The contemporary condition of culture is quite remote from nature."[27]

On this not-altogether-convincing disclaimer that he is speaking of contemporary societies and not of the ancient republics,[28] Herder returns to the view that one is authorized in trading with other cultures, learning their languages, and acquiring, however imperfectly, some greater knowledge of the world. But though returning to his article's original purpose, after having rehearsed the republican criticisms of commercial society, he cannot bring himself to endorse wholeheartedly that original purpose. His acceptance of commercial society is at best grudging. Given the modern, unnatural condition of culture, learning foreign languages, Herder tells us, is an "indispensable evil and thus almost a genuine good."[29] In that equivocating "almost" Herder indicates that he has not forgotten the republican ideal of a self-contained national culture and language, one whose naturally impermeable borders ensure the virtue of its citizens and the vigor of its culture.

The logic of Herder's republican and particularist criticisms of commerce drives toward cultural relativism and isolationism according to which one is naturally and necessarily limited by one's own culture and nation. While this conclusion was radically at odds with the commercial cosmopolitanism of the German patrician class in Riga, it must seem fully consistent with Herder's contributions to the emerging German literary public sphere, where he proclaimed the unique natural advantages of the German language and its literature. But as we shall see, just as the ethos of commercial Riga and that of civic republican belief showed the strains of being forced together, so too were there tensions between, on the one hand, republican belief and Herder's specific life in Riga, and, on the other, the implications of success in a modern public sphere.

DISPOSSESSION IN THE PUBLIC SPHERE

On first view, Herder's republicanism seems to go hand in hand with his developing cultural nationalism, since both Herder's Riga republic and the emerging national literary public sphere were German in language and culture. But beyond this general correspondence, conflicts arose between the kind of selves that each discourse of identity entailed. Republicanism has always centered on small, self-reliant, and self-governing cities, in which citizens recognize and know one another in direct, face-to-face relationships. Herder's interest in German culture and language refers to cultural phenomena he found in Riga, but the space of discussion on these matters extends far beyond the city itself to address a putative German nation and a putative German public sphere.

Recent studies of the eighteenth century have emphasized the role of the public sphere in constituting new types of identity. As Jürgen Habermas describes it, the institution of the public sphere refers to a growing circulation in the late eighteenth century of opinion and argument in a variety of institutions, including French salons, British coffeehouses, German masonic lodges and literary societies, and journals and newspapers throughout Europe. This increased intellectual production and circulation of reporting, reviewing, and debating constituted what appeared to be a domain of impersonal rational criticism and hence a seemingly objective realm of judgment, which, as Habermas argues, was eventually extended from literature to politics.[30]

The quick and widespread success in Germany of Herder's *Fragments,* its stimulation of debate, and its recognition by important figures such as Nicolai injected Herder into the developing literary public sphere in Germany. Herder's *Fragments* specifically addressed issues of the formation of a public sphere in Germany as it sought to determine the characteristics appropriate to the cultivation of a national German culture and language. Herder's writing gained widespread attention because of the expanding circulation of opinion in Germany, and his new fame as a writer meant that he could have moved to a more important cultural center. His friends and his former mentor Hamann offered in fact to find him a new position, but Herder demurred. He gladly accepted Nicolai's offer to contribute to the *General German Library,* but he turned down the publisher's offer to bring him to Berlin.[31] Riga suited Herder, as he told his friends and later his fiancée, and from there he was able to launch himself successfully into the larger German literary world.

Herder plainly benefited from and supported the formation of a modern literary public sphere. But as some recent writers have noted, he did not fully endorse it in the form described by Habermas. According to Anthony LaVopa, Herder had qualms about the public sphere's reliance on print, as opposed to oral, culture, a concern that is reflected in his later work as a collector of folk songs. In a similar vein, Benjamin Redekop points out that Herder wanted an "organic" public sphere, one that met the specific conditions of German folk culture and language.[32] These qualifications about Herder's embrace of the forming public sphere are valid, but they do not fully explain what he felt or experienced as the general problematic aspect of the public sphere, one that eventually led him to hope for an "organic" public sphere and that placed him directly at odds with his specific sense of self in Riga. This conflict can be seen in one of the most bizarre episodes in Herder's literary career, an episode that ultimately drove him temporarily from both Riga and Germany.

In keeping with a still-strong convention, Herder published his *Fragments* anonymously;[33] but his identity was immediately revealed in Königsberg and then made known in the rest of Germany and in Riga. Yet Herder continued to insist strenuously on anonymity. He asked his friends to deny his authorship. He told those who approached him for an autograph to keep his identity a secret, and he even asked his major literary adversary, the Halle formalist, neoclassical aestheticist Adolf Klotz, not to refer to him by name when writing about him. Herder continued to insist on an impossible anonymity even as he looked increasingly ridiculous for doing so.[34]

In his next work, on the writings of the deceased author Thomas Abbt, again published anonymously, Herder took yet more elaborate precautions to protect his identity:[35] he altered his writing style; criticized his own mentor, Hamann; and even referred to the author of the *Fragments*—that is, himself—as if he were another person. But all this maneuvering was to no avail. In journals from Riga to Königsberg to Berlin and Halle, Herder was immediately identified as the author and discussed by name. That his pleas for anonymity went unheeded provoked him to further extraordinary gestures of self-concealment: he placed false announcements in prominent newspapers asserting that his writings had been misattributed to him, he threatened to stop writing altogether, and he criticized his own writings as if they were the writings of another person.[36]

Herder's exaggerated sensitivity to public identification provided an ideal target for his literary enemies. In early 1769, Klotz, whose classicist formalism Herder had criticized, published in his journal a review of Herder's revised edition of the *Fragments,* which was still in press. The critic of this presumably stolen preliminary copy of Herder's book condemned him by name for proffering shoddy scholarship, accused him of aspiring to become a cultural dictator, and ridiculed his teacher Hamann. Herder was infuriated by this provocative violation of his desired anonymity, and although Hamann and Nicolai advised him to accept the *fait accompli* of his notoriety, he futilely continued his attempts to mislead the reading public. This behavior, Hamann told Herder, irritated all his Königsberg friends.[37] The more he had tried to conceal his identity, the more it was ridiculed and demeaned. The more Herder refused a literary and public persona, the more subject he was to personal attack and isolation. Yet he still could not tolerate the public identification of his authorship.

Herder's difficulty in accepting his national fame was a difficulty in accepting the modern conception of the public sphere. On Habermas's theory a modern public sphere is constituted when people set aside their social differences to engage in discourse and debate using only their reason. On the basis of this circulation of rational and impartial discussion and debate, persons in the public sphere come to a judgment that is deemed to be the judgment of a rational and critical public. As I have argued elsewhere, this process of arriving at a judgment in the public sphere involves an extraordinary transformation. Many persons from disparate backgrounds and with conflicting opinions enter the public sphere, but the strange dynamic of the public sphere fuses these heterogeneous opinions into a single judgment, a unified voice. People enter the public sphere as if they were entering a "space," but once inside that space, they are transformed into a collective subject, a single authoritative persona.

Throughout the late eighteenth into the twentieth centuries, many observers were dumbfounded at this transformation and particularly at what this remarkable conceptual and rhetorical slippage implied. The public sphere yielded an image of a unified and authoritative collective opinion, but given the diversity of conflicting persons and groups in the public

sphere, there was always a struggle between individuals and groups to assume the voice of a unified group. Situated in strategic social and cultural
positions, a small number of important critics in particular could seize the
mantle of a rational everyone.[38] In his early writings, Herder shared the
views of those who were amazed by this development. In "Do We Still Have
the Public and Fatherland?" he shows a characteristic puzzlement when he
writes that "the term the *public* often remains an enigma." Herder finds
completely unintelligible the idea that a single unified voice can emerge
from multiple opinion and debate: "Is this the voice, the judgment of the
public? Of the public? I expect ten, twenty, a hundred who represent almost all their citizens: these think, judge for themselves, and perhaps remain silent. But the large head of this many-headed creature, where does
it have its seat and voice? Where must one stand to be judged by this public? In the marketplace or in private homes?"[39]

   In the ancient republics of city-states, the "public" consisted of fellow citizens one personally knew, who met in a real physical site; but the modern
public is a ghost, without a real location, an "everyone," in Mona Ozouf's
nice turn of phrase, who is actually "no one."[40] The modern public defined
itself as a collective being that could be known concretely only in the opinions of the few people who claimed—always spuriously—to speak for it.
The national success of Herder's *Fragments* benefited from the emergence
of the new modern public, and he was well on the way to becoming one of
the real voices who could claim to represent it, as Klotz's accusation of
Herder's aspiring to cultural "tyranny" indicates. But notwithstanding his
success in the new public sphere, Herder could not bring himself to accept
the modern notion of a public; although he made use of its mysterious
power in which collective authority could be commandeered by a few
voices, he also feared it, particularly once he was made the object and not
the subject of judgment in the public sphere.

   Resisting full absorption into the abstract and phantasmatic space of the
modern public sphere, Herder clung to an ancient republican idea of public life—of concrete, face-to-face relations that, in republican theory, ensured transparency, mutual recognition, and individual dignity. In his reply
to Nicolai's offer to find him a position in Berlin, Herder made clear his
republican view of daily life: "My local situation is not brilliant, but it is independent, peaceful, and at least accompanied by personal regard for
me."[41] The real public space of republican Riga was a site of existential security, a place where one obtained not only a quiet autonomy but also a socially sustained self-coherence; the direct personal "regard" of others
confirmed his stability of self.[42] A literary career in a cultural center might
bring a "brilliant" reputation, but by implied opposition to genuine republican sociability and transparency, it was also associated with depen-

dency, disquiet, and a disregard of one's actual self. To be a figure in the public sphere is to leave oneself open to definition by people one might never directly know. This danger was precisely what he felt realized in Klotz's attacks: that a critic, who did not really know him, could formulate and disseminate an opinion of him that might then, mysteriously, be taken as the opinion of an overawing public.

Like the widening relations of Enlightenment commerce and trade, the circulation of opinion in the modern public sphere offered an aggrandizement of the self (by wealth and celebrity), but it also paradoxically engendered the opposite: a loss of the self, the dispossession of the self by a phantom authority. Eminent membership in the public sphere offered fame but also distortion and dependency, an unsettling vulnerability to the opinion of distant and invisible others. Herder's intense sensitivity to maintaining his anonymity in the public sphere was an attempt to ward off this dispossession of the concrete self. But being able to choose how one is known in the public sphere was (and is) of course impossible. Its lack of real location, its unbounded circulation of opinion, and its strange transformation into the form of a single, authoritative judgment—all these conditions foreclosed the possibility of controlling how one's self was to be defined.[43]

Michael Warner has pointed out how the modern public sphere subjects writing to a process of abstraction, stripping it of the particularities of production and ownership. This abstraction allows it to be apprehended by everyone in society with the appropriate technical skills (such as literacy and access to venues). The process of abstract circulation gave to Herder's work an influence on distant others, but the same process of abstraction allowed distant others who did not know the author to criticize his writing. The abstract reciprocity of the public sphere was what Herder found intolerable: writing remained for him intimately personal, an expression not just of an "author" but also of a "person." For the same reason, Herder preferred folk oral expression, as LaVopa notes, over modern writing; the former seemed an authentic expression of the personality of a culture, a quality lost in the abstract media of writing.[44] Herder's ambivalent entry into the public sphere resulted in his sense of suffering loss of control over how he defined himself. As he wrote in his *Journal,* all these experiences had so "debased" him that he was "scarcely" able to recognize himself (*J,* 237/374).

As Herder experienced the different terms and discourses of eighteenth-century identity-making—of enlightened commercialism, of the new literary public sphere, of German cultural nationalism, and of civic republicanism—he encountered their conflicts and internal problems. The expanding prosperity of enlightened commercialism suggested to Herder, the civic republican, an inevitable moral corruption and a loss of linguistic and cultural identity. The expanding literary public sphere offered intellectual exchange and national celebrity but also a loss of republican self-possession and self-transparency. Traversing the conflicts between the terms of different discourses of identity and their contradictions, Herder appeared to be opting, above all, for a stable self and for the communal transparency of an idealized republican Riga. He seemed to be writing his life as a narrative of refusal and return, a rejection of the faulty experience of other cultures and of a broadened national public, in favor of a secure, transparent, and settled life in a small self-governing city. Herder's thinking tended toward this republican ideal, but as with all his other discourses of identity, this particular narrative of identity was also subject to defects, aborted its projected trajectory, and led Herder to opt in the most surprising way for a completely different model of self.

THE FRENCH PHILOSOPHE

In the play of the conflicting terms and discourses that constituted eighteenth-century identities, the ones that for Herder seemed to trump all others were those of his republicanism. At odds with enlightened cosmopolitan commercialism and with the new public sphere of German literature, Herder's republicanism appeared to emerge as the dominant claim on his identity, the aspect that criticized commercialism and made him especially sensitive to the abstracting processes of the modern public sphere. Herder expressed, both publicly and privately, his satisfaction about living in republican Riga. Yet in the late spring of 1769 he resigned his position and set out on a coastal voyage that ultimately took him to France. He never returned to Riga.

As a means of shedding light on what was at work behind this surprising departure, Herder's *Journal of My Voyage in the Year 1769* is an important if sometimes puzzling document. The *Journal* is not a coherent travelogue structured around the physical voyage but an amalgam of scattered cultural and political observations, introspective inquiry, and outlines of writing and pedagogical projects—all written after the voyage and during Herder's first months in Nantes.[45] In a letter to his teacher Hamann, Herder described his voyage as a dream,[46] and his *Journal* faithfully conveys that image in its rambling organization and internal momentum. It advances by a process of association that discharges into multiple narratives, bursts of self-doubt, and self-exaggeration—the last particularly embodied in Herder's expressed desire to launch enormous political and pedagogical undertakings.

This loose, rambling text is most often read for confirmation of some of the themes we have discussed—Herder's republicanism, his notion of the public sphere, and his concern with German cultural nationalism—that led him, among other things, to criticize French cultural dominance in Europe.[47] This approach to the *Journal* interprets it as a harmonizing narrative of Herder's life and thought. But in Herder's *Journal* the assertions of his usual concerns coexist with a problematization of those concerns. Here, for the first time, he calls into question the social life of the Riga republic. And although he criticizes France and French sociability in the *Journal,* he also praises the advantages of French language, literature, and society.

Given both the movement of terms of identity that we have seen so far and Herder's new critique of republican life, the positive remarks about France point to something else that emerges systematically in Herder's stream of associations. The loose, rambling introspective character of the *Journal* allows some of Herder's deepest desires to emerge. Summoned up in his associations is a cultural wish-fulfillment—a surprising dream of being a French philosophe in a refined French society. This dream does not persist long, but the fact of its intense allure to Herder points to the importance, even for a would-be German nationalist, of the claims of what I call the French discourse of civility. At an impasse in Riga, Herder turns to an idealized image of a refined French identity, even though its limitations will ultimately disillusion him and send him back to Germany. Herder's rehearsal of the attractions and repulsions of a French ideal of gracious sociability is especially significant because it brings out with particular clarity the dynamic and structure of Herder's identity problems.

Herder's departure from Riga must have puzzled his friends and patrons. He had had a bad experience in the German public sphere, but he remained nonetheless an important influence in it, as well as a social success in republican Riga. What emerged only when he had left Riga, as he confesses in his *Journal,* was that the entire time, beneath or coexisting with all his successes, growing influence, and republican and German allegiances, he felt a deep sense of discontentment. Herder's republicanism showed a marked tendency toward isolationism and the cultivation of one's own culture and polity. This turning inward was a means of protecting republican virtue against the corruption and dependency that, on republican theory, necessarily followed from enlightened cosmopolitan commerce and intercultural contact. But this advantage of isolationism, as Herder also clearly recognized, came at a cost. When he thought as a republican, he embraced this isolationism, regardless of its costs. But when he assumed the alternative persona of the enlightened cosmopolitan, he suffered from the turning inward of a culture, which brought with it, he recognized, parochialism and intellectual narrowness. As a republican, he ignored those consequences of virtue; but in the *Journal* his enlightened cosmopolitanism reasserts itself. He acknowledges the small-mindedness of his republican life, and this acknowledgment brings him back to an Enlightenment cosmopolitan position, if now no longer of a commercial sort.

As a teacher and minister, his world, he writes, consisted of no more than a "student's chair in a musty study, a place at a monotonous boardinghouse table, a pulpit, a lecture desk" (*J*, 211/360). The narrowly circumscribed life of an author in the small city made him feel like a "pedantic scribbler" (*J*, 209/359). His success in the wider German public sphere did not mitigate his sense of dissatisfaction. His recent experiences with Klotz had spoiled whatever sense of expansiveness it offered, so that even his activities there now seemed only to reinforce the feelings of intellectual constraint and waste: his "dead research" had produced only "useless criticisms," pointless "disputation," and the vain pursuit of a minor "literary fame" (*J*, 236/373). "All this," Herder writes, "was repugnant to me" (*J*, 209/359). In his official and public writings and addresses, he has linked small-town republican life with nature and the study of German language and literature with organic, national expression. But in his *Journal* Herder describes this same life in Riga in precisely the opposite terms, in figures of deformity—"How narrow and cramped, finally, the whole spirit" (*J*, 211/360)—all of which coalesce into an overpoweringly forlorn feeling of having become old without ever having been young (*J*, 210/359–360, 386/451–452).

These bitter and self-pitying ruminations present a strange antithesis to Herder's earlier and later writings and to conventional interpretations of those writings and the man himself. Even more surprising is the alternative that he sees to a constricted life in republican Riga and the German public sphere. In the form of a lament for a lost opportunity Herder repeatedly invokes the French language. Thinking of his time in Riga, it occurs to him that he should have made better use of its library. He should have read systematically in areas he neglected—in the political history of empires, in mathematics, and in physics and natural history. To these he adds, as a rhetorical question: "And the French language combined with all this and made the chief object of study?" (*J*, 208/358). His implicit answer is that he should have read much more French literature; but he also wishes that he had emphasized "practice in speaking French and what is associated with that activity": "social intercourse and aptitude for lively discussion" (*J*, 208/358).

And as he dwells on this combination—practical knowledge; facility in French, particularly in sociable conversation—he projects himself beyond Riga, into a more generalized social space: "had I made French, history, natural science, mathematics, drawing, social intercourse and aptitude for lively discussion my principal objects, into what society could they not have brought me?" (*J,* 209/358). When Herder first invokes the use of French in his *Journal,* he speculates that it would have made him satisfied with his situation in Riga (*J,* 208/508). But as his chain of associations continues, they clearly reveal another purpose—not to reconnect him to Riga and his literary work, but to sever him from them, to allow him to enter "any society." Finally, Herder writes that if he had been endowed with practical knowledge and the ability to read and speak French, he would have never become a small-city minister and parochial author (*J,* 209/359). Herder is projecting himself into the world at large and in this sense seems to be reasserting a belief in Enlightenment cosmopolitanism, but on this occasion cosmopolitanism is defined not by enlightened commerce but by facility in the French language.

A self, constituted by facility in French and by a pragmatic set of studies, gives rise to a figure who is the converse of the narrow republican or German pedant. As the French-reading and -speaking man of letters and practical knowledge, Herder writes, "I would have been spared from losing myself." Natural biological evolution would have superseded premature aging: he imagines himself "sensitive, rich, full of real knowledge and not book-learning, vigorous, living like a youth, to enjoy at some future time a happy maturity and a happy old age!" (*J,* 210–210/359). And as he dwells on the joys of the kind of life made available by speaking and reading French, one last set of associations surfaces: pleasure and the company of women. One of his most intense dissatisfactions with "virtue" in Riga was that it brought with it a sensuous and sensual austerity, a "weakness," he now says, in that it led to sexual distortion and frustration.[48] When he dreams of France, he projects himself from this repressed and desiccated society into a world regarded as natural, healthy, worldly, pragmatic, and now also feminine and sensually gratifying. Where up to now in Riga he has had only "a false *intensive* knowledge of human nature," he imagines his French spirit "should rather have learned to know the world, men, societies, women and pleasure *extensively*—with the noble, fiery curiosity of youth, who enters the world and runs quickly from one experience to another" (*J,* 209/359). Herder's invocation of the French language thus summons up associations that frame a striking dichotomy: opposed to a stunted life of narrow pedanticism, sexual distortion, and premature aging in republican Riga is a dream of regaining a self in its natural, youthful form as it confidently enters a broader, more worldly and sensual domain. In Herder's phantasizing of another identity, the French language is the ennabling mode of expanded and more direct sensuous experience and, with it, of a renewed self-possession.

*

Herder's phantasies of a richer world of practical knowledge, worldly sociability, and greater sensation, all defined by reading and speaking French, derive from an idealized set of French conceptions about identity and social behavior summed up by the terms *civilité, politesse,* and the *honnête homme.* Emerging in the French court and Parisian salons of the seventeenth century, these terms referred to a code of gracious appearance, behavior, and refined sociability. In the salon in particular the proper mode of social interaction was intelligent and charming conversation. The salon was metaphorically charged with feminine characteristics—conversation and conduct were soft, pleasing, and gracious—and literally organized by a woman, the refined salonnière.[49]

When Herder links facility in French and engaging in "lively discussion," he is playing on a conventional notion of the previous two centuries that French was the perfected language of conversation.[50] And when he then links French speech and lively discussion with the possibility of "entering any society," which he later associates with the company of women, he is likely projecting himself into a French salon. Moreover, the kind of knowledge that was to serve as the basis of salon discussion—worldly, free-thinking, open-ended, "natural"—was stylized as the opposite of a dry, bookish, claustrophobic academicism[51]—in short, the kind of knowledge Herder imagines himself escaping. Herder thus appears to be fleeing republican Riga for a classical French salon.

By the time of his voyage to France, the salon had also acquired additional associations, which Herder's phantasy also draws upon. Although the French Enlightenment was sometimes critical of civility and politeness, its social tendency was to reoccupy the same spaces, especially the salon. And the result was for many philosophes a fusion—at times problematical—of the figure of the philosophe with the characteristics of civility. In seventeenth-century France the philosopher, according to Hans Ulrich Gumbrecht and Rolf Reichardt, was often thought of as someone removed from society, figured as the outsider, be it the unworldly truth-seeker or the bookish misanthrope.[52] In the course of the eighteenth century and because of the Enlightenment, the philosophe took on the features of an engaged critic of society doing battle in particular with religious superstition.[53] The movement from without to within was completed after mid-century, when, despite their continued claims to beleaguered outsider status, Enlightenment philosophes had become fully integrated into society—as seen in their entry into the academies, government offices, the company of princes, and in their public reception.[54] In the second half of the eighteenth century, educated opinion had in fact so warmly embraced the philosophes that their image, as Gumbrecht and Reichardt put it, had become "immune" from attack.[55] In the French public sphere—as in the courts and academies of north German princes—there formed what Robert Darnton has called the "cult of the philosophe."[56]

The integration of the philosophe into French society was expedited by his association and fusion with civility and politeness.[57] In the anonymously written article "Philosophe" in Diderot's *Encyclopedia,* the author ascribes to the philosophe the usual characteristic of critical rationality opposing ignorance and superstition, but he also marks him with a set of social attributes. He explicitly differentiates his philosopher from earlier ones: "Our philosophe does not believe in exile for this world." Like that of the figure of seventeenth-century civility, the philosophe's knowledge is not bookish and unworldly but useful and sociable. And to be useful and sociable, his critical reason must be made appealing, presented with wit and charm.[58] The absorption of earlier notions of sociability into the image of the philosophe is made explicit as the author identifies him repeatedly as the "*honnête homme* who wants to please to render himself useful." "The philosophe is, then, *un honnête homme* who acts in all according to reason, and who joins a spirit of reflection and of soundness [*justesse*] with manners and sociable qualities."[59]

In his *Journal* Herder imagines himself entering the French salon. What would have crucially enabled this entry, he acknowledges, was more reading in the masters of a refined French style—"Crébillon, Sévigné, Molière, Ninon, Voltaire, Beaumelle, etc." But much of the rest of his list consists of figures of the French Enlightenment, such as Montesquieu, again Voltaire, d'Alembert, and Maupertuis (*J,* 208/358). Herder's reading list would educate him not just in the general style of French civility but also in the substance of the French Enlightenment. The implication of his phantasy of becoming adept in French language and culture is that he is imagining himself a French philosophe endowed with the characteristics of French civility and able to enter Parisian salons. Yet to enter the "republic of letters"—that is, the Enlightenment salon in Paris—is also to authorize entry to "any society." Going to France, in fact, paradoxically would prepare him to return to Germany. In an era of French cultural dominance, it was a conceit of the French philosophe that his combination of critical rationality, practical knowledge, and the charms of urbane civility uniquely equipped him to present himself anywhere in the world and, implicitly, to intervene wherever he went. Diderot, in his *Supplement to the Voyage of Bougainville* (1772), gives this notion of Enlightenment cosmopolitanism hyperbolic expression as he folds the figure of the philosophe as *honnête homme* into the image of the explorer-adventurer: "Bougainville has a taste for the amusements of society. He likes women, the theater, delicate foods. He gives himself to the whirl of the world with as much good grace as to the inconstancy of the elements on which he has been tossed. He is amiable and lighthearted: it is a true Frenchman, ballasted on the one side by a treatise on differential and integral calculus and on the other by a voyage around the globe."[60]

The assumption of the identity of a French philosophe offers Herder a powerful self-possession, an ease in any social sphere because he carries with him, internalized, the gracious manners of refined French sociability and the good sense and practical knowledge of the Enlightenment. When he arrives in Nantes, Herder's thoughts of a happier, alternative identity give way to daydreaming about returning to Riga as a social reformer. And although this may be a sign of his loyalty to his former home, it nonetheless follows as part of an imagined French-centered intellectual subjectivity.[61] The assumption of enlightened French civility would restore him to Riga because it would make him an active citizen of the world. He would return not as a German intellectual but as a French-speaking philosophe.

THE PROBLEM OF DISPLACEMENT

All the terms and discourses that Herder drew on to fashion an identity in Riga proved much less viable than they initially appeared. Terms and discourses conflict or contain internal problems. Enlightened commercial republicanism attempted to elide civic republicanism's objections to commerce, but those objections, as we saw in Herder's early writings, could not be so easily denied, resurfacing as they did in the same writings that praised commerce. The public sphere offered Herder fame, but only because it created an abstract self at the expense of concrete personal recognition. Herder's little republic in Riga brought virtue and self-certainty, but also parochialism, constrained experience, and frustration. French sociability and the persona of the French philosophe offered a remedy to that limited life in a republic; they promised practical knowledge, a pleasing and feminine social interaction, expanded experience, and ease in the world. Herder phantasized all these aspects of an idealized French culture and self, but like the other terms and discourses of identity that he drew on, this one, too, had its uncertainties.

In the next chapter, we shall see how both Herder's attractions to and criticism of refined French civility fit into a long-standing discourse of French civility. For now, we will focus on how his first, general misgivings about French culture spoil his phantasy of being a French philosophe. In this sense, his ambivalence about the persona of the cosmopolitan French philosophe continues the uncertain, equivocating adherence he had shown to other eighteenth-century models of identity.

Herder's rejection of the persona of a French philosophe is carried out in a series of associations that on the surface engage familiar themes in his thought, but that, on inspection, show a deeper, recurring concern. When

Herder's ship passes Courland, he thinks of Prussia's Frederick II, whose belief in the supremacy of French language and culture had led him to attempt to gallicize Prussian culture. Frederick brought to Prussia prominent philosophes (notably and disastrously Voltaire) and restored the Prussian Academy of Sciences in French form, modeling it after the French Academy, placing it under the directorship of the French philosophe Maupertuis, and making French its official language.[62] Herder is plainly skeptical of all these actions, and he seems to show some of his earlier German cultural nationalism.

On Herder's view, Frederick's application to Prussia of French cultural standards not only has failed to bring about a cultural revival but in fact has produced a further German decline. The Prussian Academy has published only uninspired tracts and misapprehensions of German philosophy. With works accomplished in form but lacking in substance, the Academy's members have failed to live up to the standards of their predecessors: "What are the philosophers themselves, with all their fine style, in comparison to men like Locke and Leibniz?" The Academy's tracts on language are at best mediocre, lacking even the practicality of earlier German writings (*J*, 313/413). At first sight, Herder's criticism of Frederick's cultural policies seems to stem from cultural nationalism and to anticipate the notion customarily identified with Herder—the idea that cultures are unique and therefore incommensurable.[63] What is French does not suit Germany. But although the notion of cultural incommensurability is evident in the *Journal*, it is not, as some have suggested, the controlling preoccupation.

What mainly bothers Herder about Frederick's cultural reforms is the fact that they are copies of phenomena and not the originating phenomena. This theme of derivativeness, of the insubstantial copy, regardless of its connection to Herder's cultural nationalism, has a certain independent force, the guiding force of a more fundamental preoccupation. That theme returns again in his next set of travel observations, this time attached not to his cultural nationalism but to his republicanism. As he passes the Netherlands, he thinks, in good republican fashion, about how that country's commercial spirit will undercut its republican spirit, and with that decline, its "spirit of valor" will disappear (*J*, 320/417). Here Herder seems about to pursue one of the main concerns of his period in Riga—the antithesis between commerce and republican virtue. But the invocation of the idea of decline deflects his thoughts from commerce and republicanism to the theme of French derivativeness (*J*, 326/419).

The invocation of decline in the Netherlands sets Herder to thinking about how the French Enlightenment is now also in decline: the great philosophes—Voltaire and Montesquieu, for example—are passing, and the new ones have failed to live up to the Enlightenment's original spirit.

The epigonic phase of the Enlightenment is evident, according to Herder, in its apotheosizing of the *Encyclopedia,* which for him is merely a mechanical labor of compilation: "this very book which the French regard as their triumph is . . . the principal sign of their decline" (*J,* 327/419–420). That reflection about the derivative and degraded nature of the *Encyclopedia* then breaks loose into a jeremiad on the general derivativeness of the current genres of the Enlightenment: "they [the philosophes] have nothing to write and so make *abrégés, dictionnaires, histoires, vocabulaires, esprits,* encyclopedias, etc. Original works have fallen away" (*J,* 327–328/420).

Herder is here reiterating the same criticism he has made of Frederick's French reforms. The idea of decline suggests to him the same problem of derivativeness, of the deficient copy replacing the original substance. As Herder continues, the theme of derivativeness becomes more and more emphatic. After briefly pondering the situation of England, he again turns his thoughts to France, and the subject of France immediately issues in another emphatic restatement of the country's present derivativeness: "Its age in literature is finished—the century of Louis XIV is past; men like Montesquieu, d'Alembert, Voltaire and Rousseau are past also; the nation is living on the ruins" (*J,* 328/420).

The French Enlightenment assumes a degraded, derivative form in Prussia; the work of the younger philosophes is derivative from that of the older; the Enlightenment in general is derivative from the great age of classicism under Louis XIV. French derivativeness thus projects itself from one standard of measure to another, displacing the ultimate value of authentic originality from one term to the next. At the beginning of this section of his *Journal,* Herder measures derivativeness against seventeenth-century French classicism, but unsurprisingly, given the displacements so far, only a page later he calls into question the originality of French classicism: "What was really original in the century of Louis XIV?"[64]

In Herder's series of associations every French claim to substantive cultural originality is immediately excavated, so that taken together these French claims form a regression of derivativeness that recedes into cultural nothingness. French culture is always already derivative; its cultural and philosophic achievements are always empty of an actual French content. French culture, sociability, and the persona of the philosophe are to provide, Herder phantasizes, an expanded realm of direct experience of the world and with it a new self-possession, a self at home in the world. But as he contemplates further the nature of French accomplishments, he compulsively returns to a sense that those accomplishments are in fact hollow, and he explains this odd shuffling between his expectation of cultural value and his expectation of being disappointed with what he finds by attributing it to the derivativeness of the product at hand. The problem with this explanation is that derivativeness is displaced from one cultural product to the next, until original substance seems barely to have existed. Like "the spirit of monarchic manners . . . the French Nation," Herder concludes, "has little real virtue, little inner strength. . . . National strength . . . originality—these it does not have in large measure" (*J,* 349/431).

What Herder is finally driven to recognize is that the defect of French culture is one that affects all its cultural products. The allure of French culture that Herder has felt is precisely what also ruins it. The imperative to communicate in exquisite sensuous media overwhelms and displaces the substance and intentions of the communication. Herder notes this process at work even in the writings of the philosophes. Voltaire, he tells us, writes history—but only so that it is a "supplement to and occasion for his wit, his mockery, his sardonic observation" (*J,* 335/424). Montesquieu's weakness for the "faux-brillant" leaves his *Persian Letters* in a representational impasse: he "finds himself in a dilemma when he at once has his Persian use French turns of phrase and at another wants to have him speak as an Oriental and so must deny him these devices!" (*J,* 337/425, 355/435).

As we shall see in subsequent chapters, writers of civic-republican persuasion such as Rousseau questioned the social function and consequences of French refinement. But according to Herder, their substantive critique is couched in the same representational modes of French refinement, so that the critique proves to be self-defeating. The imperative of French writers to produce elegant, refined, and striking presentation of material ensures that all the cogent criticisms by philosophes end up distorted. One cannot, as Herder shows in his discussion of Rousseau, hope to abolish French refinement while still using that refinement: "However strongly Rousseau may combat the philosophes, one can see that he too is not concerned with the correctness, the intrinsic worth, the reasonableness, the usefulness of these thoughts but with greatness, their extraordinariness, their novelty, their striking quality. Where he can find these qualities he is a sophist and an apologist" (*J,* 350/431–432). Notwithstanding his criticism of refined French society, Rousseau's ultimate allegiance to its underlying cultural principle—its desire for extravagant self-presentation—subverts the intentions of his writings: "everything," for Rousseau, "must have a paradoxical turn"; and this, Herder writes, "spoils him, seduces him, leads him to make commonplace things new, small things great, true things untrue, and untrue things true. Nothing is simply stated in his writings: everything is new, *frappant,* wonderful" (*J,* 335/423).

The signifier contaminates and confuses the signified; the refined forms of French culture obscure and undercut the moral and critical intentions of the Enlightenment. And for Herder the desire of the French to excel in producing refined forms implies that they were never really interested in the content in the first place. Herder writes in his discussion of a scene from Pierre-Claude Nivelle de la Chausée's *Préjugé à la mode* (1735): "The

Frenchman cannot conceive that a deeply moved husband can return and fall at his wife's feet, and that the whole scene can develop naturally; he must have the feelings dissimulated, the language tortured into epigrammatic verse, and a *bout rime*. . . . Everything is byplay, sobbing, wringing of hands, declaration of scenes, the [formal] connection of scenes, etc." (*J,* 362–363/438). What Herder thinks should be the presentation of a natural scene of direct feeling and immediate sensation is unimaginable to the French; immediacy is unthinkable, always already altered into artifice by the canons of French classicism. All the world, to the French, is a "coup de théâtre" (*J,* 362/438).

Contrary to the conventional harmonizing image of the young Herder, which blends his various concerns into a unified figure, his identity was remarkably unstable. Drawing on conflicting and problematic terms and discourses of identity, he traversed them as a series of displacements from one to the other, driven by the conflicts between them or the problems within them. To escape this anxious shuffle of identities, Herder leaves Riga and phantasizes an alternative persona and a prospect of a more rewarding fullness of experience in the figure of the French philosophe at home in a milieu of refined sociability that equips him for the world at large. But here, too, Herder does not escape the cycles and epicycles of displaced and unstable identity that he experienced in Riga. On the contrary, as he ponders his feelings about French culture, he is brought to the recognition that it in fact seems to incarnate in its ever-present sense of derivativeness and extravagant presentation a pure principle of displacement and the deceptions, disappointments, and uncertainties that displacement entails. Herder's analysis of the attractions and problems of refined French culture constitutes in this sense the *reductio ad absurdum* of his shuffle of identities; it brings home with particular clarity his experience that identity is not the presence and fullness of pleasing sensuous refinement, or the realization of austere civic virtue, or the happiness and prosperity of enlightened commerce, or the fulfillment of national character, but one's removal from those or from any other putative essence. Herder's desire to experience the actualization, the presence, of a particular eighteenth-century identity always gives way to a troubling sense of its absence, of something defective or lacking. The French philosophe and French sociability have made, for Herder, an art out of this deficiency and lack.

GERMAN AGAIN

As we shall see in the next chapter, the concerns Herder expressed in his journal about French culture were widespread not just in Germany but also in France, and not just in the late eighteenth century but over a *longue durée* of cultural discourse. This recurring anxiety about French culture became a problem for many French intellectuals and artists in the late eighteenth century up to and through the French Revolution. But the anxiety about the dislocating, deceiving attractions of French civility also provided an opportunity for Germans in the late eighteenth century and beyond to make their own claims for the superiority of a German identity over and against French culture.

In the next chapter, we will see Herder acting as one of these Germans in his best-known public persona as a German cultural nationalist. But here, in his private journal, we can see that his concerns about French culture operate in a different fashion, not to empower him but to worry him, as they undo his phantasy of being a French *philosophe*. Here Herder wants to imagine himself a figure schooled in French refinement and adept in French sociability and language, a persona that would make him at home both with himself and anywhere in the world. But this dream of broad and intense experience, of pleasure and youth, is ruined, as it also unavoidably summons up associations of decline, deception, and absence. Unsurprisingly, Herder's subsequent stay in France—four months in Nantes, then two months in Paris—were characterized by halfhearted attempts to learn more about French culture. He made little effort to meet the philosophes he had once hoped to emulate. In Paris, he visited d'Alembert and possibly Diderot, the French Academy, the Louvre, and various picture galleries, but on the whole he found these experiences uninspiring. After contemplating a return to Riga, he accepted a position as a tutor of the prince of Holstein, and he returned to Germany at the beginning of 1770.

Passing from enthusiastic phantasy to general indifference at the possibilities of French culture, Herder, once back in Germany, resumed his earlier thinking about German literature and language. He adopted once again the persona of the German cultural nationalist, and in a series of publications he reestablished himself as an innovative and influential voice in Germany's literary public sphere. Later in 1770, accompanying the prince on a trip to Italy, the destination of the prince's coming-of-age "grand tour," the party stopped in Strasbourg. For various reasons, Herder decided to resign his position and to stay in the city—a decision, as many commentators have noted, of momentous significance for German literary history. In Strasbourg Herder met the young Goethe, who had recently arrived in the city to study law. Animated by their discovery of shared views on the state of literature, the two published one of the major texts of the so-called German *Sturm und Drang,* a movement of young writers who emphasized the intensity and immediacy of natural expression over and against French refinement, rationalism, and classicism. In their manifesto

On German Nature and Art, Herder and Goethe argued for the supremacy of *Sturm und Drang* impulses as the basis of culture and to which they linked the poet Ossian, Shakespeare, the Gothic Strasbourg cathedral, and the German people in general.[65] In the same *Sturm und Drang* spirit, Herder began to collect and publish German folk songs. Calling them voices of the "Volk," Herder considered these songs the direct expressions of a simple common people, constituting a poetry of natural immediacy.[66]

In 1771 Herder accepted a post as superintendent of schools in Bücke-burg, but before moving there he wrote his famous *Essay on the Origin of Language,* which argued against rationalist conceptions of language and won the Berlin Academy's essay competition in 1772. In Bückeburg Herder continued to collect and publish German folk songs, and he composed one of the most significant texts in the philosophy of history. Herder's polemical essay *Also a Philosophy of History* (1774) challenged the dominant Enlightenment and French conception of history, which asserted that progress was inevitable given the dissemination of knowledge and the refinement of civilization. Against this universalist history—and again seeking to distance Germany from Enlightenment France—Herder's essay offered a foundational statement of what is now often called "historicism," the view that cultures, because of their unique characteristics, cannot be judged according to universal standards. There is not one general history but many different incommensurable national histories, each operating according to its own particular principles. Germany, as Herder noted, thus properly evolved from its own unique feudal past, which, in his polemic against Enlightenment and French notions, he construed in a highly idealized form.[67] Like the writings of the Strasbourg period, Herder's *Also a Philosophy of History* thus reinforced his image as the consummate German cultural nationalist.

In 1775 Herder left Bückeburg to become the general superintendent of the clergy in Weimar, a position arranged by Goethe, and there, in the 1780s, Herder extended his thinking about history in another well-known study, the multivolume *Ideas for a Philosophy of History.* Some of the material intended for that study ended up in one of his last important works, *The Letters for the Advancement of Humanity* (1793–1797). While promoting and predicting the further cultural development of humanity, this work contained some of Herder's most scornful attacks on the idea of the supremacy of French refinement and culture.[68]

In all these works, for which Herder is best known, he continued the trajectory of the German cultural nationalist he had begun in Riga and had set aside to make his coastal voyage to France. One might conclude that his disappointment with French culture and sociability renewed his faith in his earlier endeavors, particularly when we consider the fierce animosity with which he now portrayed France and opposed Enlightenment universalism and the highly idealized manner in which he presented German culture. His encounter with what to him was a chain of empty forms of French culture sent him back on his life's course of pursuing things more substantial and more immediate, things identified as particularly German.

Such a conclusion may be warranted to some extent, but it does not take fully into account the lessons of his phantasy of French culture. Although Herder now turned against refined and universalist French culture with a consistent ferocity and seemed to phantasize a superior, German particularity, the problem of displacement that he experienced in his Riga identity troubles and that he saw operating in French refinement continued to motivate and (dis)organize his thought. He was indeed again concerned with establishing the uniqueness, authenticity, and immediacy—the undeniable substance—of German culture in different ways, and all these efforts reinforce the image of Herder as a thoroughly anti-Enlightenment, anti-French, and proto-Romantic writer. But what is often overlooked or underestimated is how each of these positions also broke down, deformed or distorted by the persistent influence of other conflicting terms of identity.

Herder's publication of folk songs in the 1770s was strongly criticized by Nicolai and others because of their lack of polish and refinement. Herder attempted to justify his work, but he also accepted the criticism. The result was considerable conceptual contortion as Herder attempted to save his faith in popular expression from the demands of a refined sensibility. In one instance, he thus separated the "Volk" from the actual people itself, managing at once to elevate popular culture and to despise it: "The 'Volk' is not the rabble in the streets; the rabble never sings and composes; it shouts and mutilates."[69] Who actually composed this idealized "Volk" Herder never made clear, and in the 1770s he stopped collecting and publishing folk songs. The *Sturm und Drang* notion of the immediate organic expression of the untutored common people collapsed before the dominance of a more refined, civilized taste.

Herder's rigorously relativist polemic, *Also a Philosophy of History*, denies the possibility of writing Enlightenment universal histories that align and compare many different cultures according to universal standards. But in the 1780s, in *Ideas for a Philosophy of History*, he attempts his own universal history, affirming a progression for all of humanity, and he sets up this progression by using precisely the tropes of universal development that he explicitly repudiated in *Also a Philosophy of History*. The German particularist here succumbs to the cosmopolitan Enlightenment philosophe.[70]

When other adherents of relativist German historicism gravitated toward a conservative German nationalism in response to the French Revolution, Herder's republicanism again showed itself. He welcomed the

Revolution and supported it long after other initial German enthusiasts had abandoned it. Well into the Terror and after the French invasion of the Rhineland, he affirmed the Revolution's principles as universal, cosmopolitan ideals of right. Herder finally suppressed his support because of pressure from the Weimar court, whose aristocratic Francophile tastes harked back to the refined world of aristocratic French sociability.[71] In this case the collision of shifting terms of identity was worsened by Goethe's own shift from his *Sturm und Drang* enthusiasm of his time in Strasbourg to his embrace of classicism at Weimar, which made him more sympathetic to French principles of sociability even though he continued to denounce France itself. The shifts in Goethe's ideas resulted in various tense periods in his relations with Herder, whose own views continued to be upset by their instabilities.

After his voyage to France, Herder sought to perform a more consistent cultural identity, but the complexity of events and the constant diversity of cultural discourses continued in key respects to frustrate that attempt at consistency. Notwithstanding the myth of Herder the proto-Romantic, cultural nationalist, and champion of the German Volk,[72] his thought and life continued to be unsettled by the continuous displacement of terms and discourses of identity, and by the problem that he saw with particular clarity concerning France: that immediacy and essential substance might never assume a coherent form. In a still largely "premodern" world, Herder showed many of the signs of a "postmodern" instability and multiplicity of selves, characteristics that call into question his own pursuit of fixed essences.

CHAPTER TWO

The Language of Cultural Identity

Diderot to Nietzsche

THE LANGUAGE OF REASON

In his *Letter on the Deaf and Mute for the Use of Those Who Hear and Speak* (1751), Diderot reiterates a seventeenth-century view. He provocatively remarks that the Roman Cicero must have thought in French before he wrote in Latin. Diderot's point is that the "direct order" of the French sentence, its linear syntax standardized in the seventeenth century, is equivalent to the linearity of reasoning itself. Cicero may have deployed syntactical inversions—such as placing the object of a sentence before its subject—but such grammatical twists are, for Diderot, second-order embellishments, stylistic construals of an original linear path of thinking. And that primary path, because it is linear, corresponds to the grammatical directness of French syntax. At some point, Cicero must have thought the inverted sentence in an uninverted form—that is, in the arrangement of the standard French sentence. Because French syntax corresponds to the linear structure of reasoning itself, French, according to Diderot, is "the language of truth," while languages that allow second-order inversions are the languages of "dream."[1]

Diderot's interest in the direct order of the French sentence occurs at the intersection of several debates in the eighteenth century over language and culture. His reference to Cicero is an allusion to the so-called Quarrel of the Ancients and the Moderns, and with his elevation of the French language, he signals the triumph of the modern.[2] But while positioned on the winning side of one debate, his point about the French sentence is also entangled in other disputes that render his view of the French language problematic and ultimately untenable. In the first instance, those further arguments concern the epistemological status of the French language, which had been complicated by sensationalist psychology in the eighteenth

45

century. But those technical philosophical issues lead further into the larger cultural concerns about refined French culture. Arguments about the epistemological advantages—and defects—of the French language take us to the decentering center of the French discourse of civility, to its aporias of representation that both enabled and disabled the ideals of a refined French persona and sociability.

The debates in sensationalist epistemology and on the conflicted nature of the discourse of civility eroded the foundations of the claim that French was the language of rational transparency. Germans seized that loss of cultural self-legitimation to make their own claims for a special cultural identity. Noteworthy in that movement were the linguistic criticism of the young Herder, in his familiar persona as a German cultural nationalist, and Johann Gottlieb Fichte's *Addresses to the German Nation,* the latter given at a time when the issue of establishing a German identity over and against French domination was at its most pressing. After Herder and Fichte, the terms of eighteenth-century debates continued to inform the articulation of German identity, culminating in the young Friedrich Nietzsche's universalization of those terms into fundamental conditions of human nature, and then, remarkably, his ironic repudiation of both the original terms of French and German identity and his own extension of them. This last shift marks, with particular clarity, a crucial turn both in Nietzsche's thought in particular and in thinking in general about the link between language and culture: from a Romantic elevation of German language and culture to a poststructuralist problematization of that relationship.

Proceeding from linguistic speculation that went back to antiquity, seventeenth-century theorists of language and propagandists for the standardization of French argued that the order of the ideal sentence follows the hierarchy of logical categories given by natural reason. The subject has a natural logical priority in the sentence, coming necessarily before its action and the object of its action. One cannot, the argument goes, conceive of an action without presupposing an agent of the action. This ideal sentence structure, actualized in the standardized grammar of reformed French, presents ideas with a simplicity and directness not found in the syntax of other languages. The French sentence alone necessarily allows for an immediate and full comprehension of intended meaning.[3]

Writings in the eighteenth century reiterated this view of the supreme transparency of the French sentence. We have already seen it in Diderot's *Letter on the Deaf and Mute.* In his entry in the *Encyclopedia* on the French language, Voltaire attributes the "genius" of the language to its "order" and "clarity," traits, he says, given by a grammar that requires "words to arrange themselves into the natural order of ideas."[4] The grammarian Nicolas

Beauzée, in his *Encyclopedia* entry "Inversion," asserts that if the principal object of language is to communicate ideas, then the language best suited to that end is one whose sentences are always direct or linear in structure. He reaffirms that judgment in his *General Grammar*, where the superiority of the direct order of the French sentence appears as a self-evident grammatical truth, irresistible in its influence on other languages and no less than the mark of a properly human utterance: "It is the unique construction that has had a necessary influence on the syntax of all languages, the only one that the failure to observe would make the human language a vain and simple noise, similar to the inarticulate cries of animals."[5]

Beauzée's assertion of the universal validity of the French sentence obtained some legitimacy from the fact that others outside France shared his view. In 1679 Leibniz noted that recent reforms of the French language had transformed it into "pure, polished glass" that gave "the understanding a penetrating clarity." He counseled Germans to refine their own language before it was displaced by a superior French.[6] In the eighteenth century, Frederick II sought to fulfill Leibniz's prediction. In his 1780 essay on German literature, Frederick criticizes Germany's apparent linguistic disorder, which he attributes in part to what he considers a German weakness for obscure syntactical constructions. As the standard that Germans should emulate, he points to the writings of the French, who follow, he says, the primary obligation of ensuring clarity of expression by never straying from the fixed rules of their linear syntax.[7] Frederick had already institutionalized his linguistic preferences in his renovation of the Prussian Academy in the 1740s; although papers could be presented in German or Latin, the academy's official language was French. Conferring on French the mantle of the language of learning was justified by appealing to its unique clarity.[8]

The academy endorsed Frederick's views and its own institutional practices in its 1784 essay competition. Asking the question why French had become and would continue to be the universal language of Europe, it awarded the prize to two essays that praised the language for its superior clarity, a quality that was given, they argued, by the direct order of the French sentence. Or as one of these writers, the Frenchman Antoine Rivarol, proclaimed: "French syntax is incorruptible. It is from there that results that admirable clarity, the eternal foundation of our language. . . . What is not French is not clear."[9] We have seen how Herder, on his coastal voyage to France in 1769, imagined himself a French philosophe. What set that phantasy in motion was his reflection on all that the French language could accomplish. There, phantasizing about that language, he calls it "the most general and indispensable in Europe," in large part because it was already "philosophical, rational," ideally suited for "exploration and reasoning."[10]

Both within and outside France, eighteenth-century writers reaffirmed the seventeenth-century belief in the supreme transparency of the French sentence. But while this view of the language was triumphantly reiterated, it was also apparent that it could no longer be legitimated in the traditional manner. Eighteenth-century philosophy had called into question the rationalist assumptions of the previous century, so that for many writers of the Enlightenment the notion of a rational language given by nature was unacceptable. In his 1746 *Essay on the Origin of Human Knowledge,* Condillac tells his fellow French that although they "flatter" themselves that their language is superior to the languages of the ancients, this belief, founded on the supposed natural rationality of the linear sentence, is mere prejudice. For to be "natural" in the terms of sensationalist psychology, the French sentence would have to mirror a fundamental order of sense perception. And that, Condillac says, is not the case. Projecting a hypothetical primordial scene of original sense perception, he argues that the most likely first language would have been a language of gesture, whose "sentence" would have placed objects (e.g., by pointing) before verbs and subjects. In other words, the first language, the language of initial sense experience, was probably one of inversion.[11]

Diderot in his *Letter on the Deaf and Mute* makes a critical move that would seem to render moot the issue of establishing a primordial sentence structure. Also postulating a condition of original sense perception, he concludes that such perception must be a simultaneous recognition of many different sensory events. The communication of that initial totality of empirical experience requires its decomposition into a succession of grammatical parts. What one perceives all at once and therefore in no particular order is disassembled and rearranged into the structure of a sentence. All sentences, whether direct or inverted, are in some way removed from the simultaneity of multifaceted initial perception.[12]

But after concluding that no sentence occupies the site of initial perception, Diderot allows some sentences to be more removed from primordial knowledge than others. In a later appendix to the *Letter,* in which he responds to his critics, he clarifies his view of sentence structure and its relation to a language of gesture, asserting that the gestural language of the deaf and mute, which is predicated on inversions, is "the order according to which ideas are placed in the language of animals." Syntactical inversion, in short, is characteristic "of the primitive order of words and of the ancient sentence."[13] By the time Rivarol writes in the 1780s, the sensationalist view of first languages is well established. He simply assumes that knowledge of the external world derives solely from sense perception and that what he calls the "straight line" of the French sentence must have emerged after an earlier language of inversion.[14]

Eighteenth-century sensationalist epistemology thus repudiated any direct connection between the French sentence and immediate sense perception, and it in fact concluded the opposite—that the French sentence is a second-order arrangement of ideas, a work of reflection and artifice rather than of sensuous immediacy. For sensationalists who were also partisans of the French language, this repudiation was apparently untroubling. We have already seen that Diderot and Rivarol confidently went on arguing that French could still lay claim to being the clearest, most direct, and therefore most rational of languages. Condillac explicitly reassures his readers that the loss of an older epistemological grounding does not affect the traditional virtues of the language. For although he grants that as a language of artifice French lacks the "natural liveliness" of other languages, it "makes amends," he says, by "choosing such constructions as are always agreeable to the greatest connexion of ideas . . . and gradually invests the mind with that character of clearness and simplicity by which this language is so superior in many respects."[15]

Sensationalist psychology uncoupled the French language from immediate sense perception, and that uncoupling seemed to have left intact the conventional endorsements of French as the universal language of reason. But notwithstanding that apparent undiminished faith in the rational transparency of the language, its displacement from a situation of primary knowledge posed some unsettling problems for the traditional view of the language. For one thing, this dissociation of language from sensation turns into a puzzle Diderot's assertion that Cicero must have thought in French before he wrote in Latin. Sensationalist argument could now counter Diderot's assertion by saying not only that Cicero might have perceived first in Latin before he had any thoughts, but also that Diderot might have perceived in Latin before he thought in French. Both the inverted sentence of sense perception and the necessary linear sentence of reasoning make contradictory claims to epistemological priority in Diderot's essay.

The issue of priority is important, especially if we grant it to the sensationalist sentence of inversion. For that would suggest a further problem for the French sentence. It may still order our ideas in a clear and direct fashion, but that order, on sensationalist theory, would probably be a reordering of the sense impressions that gave rise to those ideas. The question then is whether that reordering alters significantly, even distorts, what is conveyed by the primary sense impressions. Something is plainly lost, as Condillac indicates when he says that French lacks the "natural liveliness" of languages of inversion.[16]

The issue, to put this in contemporary terms, is whether the French sentence provides a reliable representation of empirical experience. Condillac begs the question when he says that French "makes amends" for a loss of "natural liveliness" by making us reason more rigorously. That response derives some of its force from an implied notion of historical development, whose beginning and end points are a natural confusion and a rational reordering. Others make a similar gesture. To vindicate the conventional claims of French, Beauzée positions it as the fully developed, human opposite of the "inarticulate cries of animals." And Diderot relies on the same implied evolution in the *Letter on the Deaf and Mute* when he asserts that the sentence of inversion is the syntactical order of the language of animals, and even more plainly when he says that French has fewer than other languages of those defects that derive from "the stammer of the first ages."[17]

In order to substantiate the claim of the language to a superior transparency that is epistemologically reliable, these writings situate it as something fully human over and against what is still primitive or animal-like. They have recourse, that is, to a traditional opposition between civilization and barbarism. The emergence of a rational language is a sign of humanity's development away from a disorderly, sensuous barbarism.[18]

This reliance on the telos of a civilizing process to legitimate the superiority of French is especially striking in the second winning essay of the 1784 competition of the Prussian Academy, Johann Christoph Schwab's *On the Origins of the Universality of the French Language*. French arose, according to Schwab, because "northern barbarians" overran the western parts of the disintegrating Roman Empire. Though more powerful than the people they conquered, they readily exchanged their "raw, defective, and indeterminate" language for one that was "milder, more accomplished, and firm." That linguistic substitution occurred smoothly and inevitably, Schwab says, because people are always drawn to a form of expression that promises nuanced feeling, sophisticated social pleasures, and the intellectual rewards of the arts and sciences. Even in the savage there is an inherent proclivity for civilization.[19]

Eighteenth-century sensationalist psychology undermined the epistemological grounding of the conventional claims of the French language to transparency. Yet partisans of the language who were also sensationalists continued to reiterate those claims and could justify doing so by comprehending the formation of the language as a good work of civilization. But that appeal to a civilizing process, invoked to shore up the legitimacy of the claims of the language, carried with it the danger of undercutting in an even more obvious fashion the view that the language provided transparent representation. For that appeal enmeshed the language in another cultural debate, in the conflicted discourse of French civility.[20]

THE DISCOURSE ON CIVILITY

We might approach this consideration by examining an ambiguity in eighteenth-century descriptions of the "elegance" of the language. Sometimes that description of the language referred to the clarity and precision of the French sentence—to its linear form. But the attribution of elegance could also refer to other qualities—to the softness of the language, for example, or to its nobility.[21] Elegance, in other words, was a product not just of rational structure but also of pleasing figures and tropes. Now sometimes the elegance of agreeable metaphor could be fused with the rational clarity and precision of the French sentence, as Voltaire suggests when he says in an *Encyclopedia* article that the refinement of language emerges from the "delicacy of expressions" carefully aligned in a linear order. Frederick II, in his polemic against German literature, locates the precision of French in both the direct order of its sentence and the appropriateness of its metaphors.[22]

But at the same time that writers tried to subsume metaphor and syntactical clarity into a single principle of elegance, they also recognized that such a formula was unstable. The figurative nature of the language could also deviate from its direct communicative function, because French was not just a vehicle of reason; it was also the language of French civility or politeness. The ideas of civility—and its linked terms *politesse* and the *honnête homme*—constituted a new social and cultural code in France first at the court and then in the salons of the seventeenth century. The aim of that code was to produce a pleasing effect in every appearance, gesture, and word, all in the service of fashioning a refined and agreeable sensibility and sociability. The eighteenth-century Enlightenment philosophes assimilated the ethos of civility into their ideas of practical knowledge and cosmopolitan worldliness, and they participated in the old regime's institutions of refined sociability, such as the salon. But while endorsing the ideals and institutions of civility, they also criticized them. We have already seen some of these criticisms at work in Herder's phantasy of French refinement and they were shared as well by many other eighteenth-century writers, most vehemently by Rousseau and his followers. What is important to recognize—and what is currently often overlooked—is that these eighteenth-century criticisms of civility were of long standing. They were not inventions of the late eighteenth century but had been around since the inception of the discourse of civility.[23]

All French codes of civility, whether of the court, the salon, or the philosophe, ultimately relied on the same rationale to legitimate the adoption of a code of civility: namely, the connection, established by earlier humanist writing and prescriptive literature on courtly behavior, between virtue and manners. The theory of civility assumed a direct circuit of signification between inner states and external appearances. A virtuous sensibility—to be such—had to show itself, and an attentive virtue made itself known in carefully controlled self-presentation. Moral character and intelligence were thus directly manifested in stylized sensuous form—as graceful movement and dress, agreeable behavior, and charming conversation.

Because of this direct circuit of signification, sensuous surface appearances were always available for moral readings. The shape of a gesture, the softness of one's voice, or the elegance of an expression—all these gave direct access to moral character.[24] "Clothing," Erasmus wrote in *De civilitate morum puerilium* (1530), "is in some ways the body of the body and gives an idea of the disposition of the spirit."[25] Seventeenth-century theorists of civility, such as the Chevalier de Faret, liked to invoke the ancient adage that the eyes are the windows of the soul.[26] The Chevalier de Jaucourt, in his *Encyclopedia* article "Honnêteté," reiterated Erasmus's conventional formula of civility, first affirming its legitimating principle—*honnêteté* "is above all founded on the interior sentiments of the soul"—and then supporting that principle by invoking a well-established trope of civility: "The draperies ought always to conform to the character of the subject that they want to imitate."[27]

The theory of civility assumed the transparency of inner conviction and moral character, of direct access to virtue in sensuous figures of appearance, behavior, and speech. This was the often-invoked first principle of civility. But this assumption of a direct circuit of signification was deeply flawed in its conceptualization, and the problematical nature of that conceptualization guaranteed that the discourse on civility would be characterized by alternating attacks of self-criticism and evasion. The weakness of civility's centering assumption is particularly evident if we consider the position of the external recipient of the sensuous figurations of civility. On the logic of civility, the reactions of the perceiver of civility should be immediate and automatic. "The ideal of *honnêteté*," notes Jean Starobinski, "is perfect reciprocity: the individual who submits to judgement displays his merit, and in return the clairvoyant 'judicial faculty' of the chosen witness is presumed capable of giving that merit its due."[28] The logic of civility requires a closed and direct circuit of signification, but circuits of signification are in fact never direct, and particularly when they rely on sensuous signifiers, they are never closed.[29] Sensuous figures always summon up multiple associations—be they personal, social, cultural, political, gendered, aesthetic, sexual, or something else. And those associations may conflict with one another. In the practice of civility, this tendency of sensuous figures to hold multiple and even contradictory meanings is particularly pronounced. For civility's figurations tend toward aesthetic stylization, and as aesthetic phenomena they become especially susceptible to the free play of the imagination.[30]

The plural meaning of sensuous figures is a concern for the logic of civility because it suggests, not that the signified of moral character fails to gain some kind of signification, but that the signification it does obtain is always threatened with confusion, contamination, or negation by other, extramoral or antimoral intentions. The inability of signifiers of civility to hold a single, consistent meaning implies that there is no necessary or logical primary relation between those signifiers and what they are supposed to signify. And if there is no ultimate necessary connection between the signifier and its putative signified, there can be no secure readings of the sensuous figure. One can never be certain that virtue lies behind the sensuous surface.

The problematical nature of sensuous figuration thus produced moral perplexity where there was supposed to be clarity and confidence. At the heart of civility lay a destabilizing aporia: its inability to differentiate in representation between an affirmation and a denial of its putative moral signified. Because civility could not guarantee that its signifying forms signified properly, it could easily be accused of serving not morality but a moral perversity. Considered the conventional sign of moral character and intelligence, yet capable of enacting other kinds of intentions, civility offered a vehicle by which those of no or ill virtue could present themselves as virtuous. Its claim to moral transparency paradoxically made it a particularly effective mode of dissemblance.

The problematical nature of civility's closed circuit of signification was immediately evident to its theorists. Starobinski notes, "No sooner was the word civilization [that is, the historical stage of refined living, contrasted with barbarism] written down . . . than it was found to contain a possible source of misunderstanding."[31] From its inception, the discourse on civility displayed a conflicted, ambivalent character, alternating between self-affirmation and self-doubt.[32] As Chartier points out, in the seventeenth century Corneille negotiated both sides of civility—showing, on the one hand, that it was the correct form of noble social interaction and, on the other, that its refined manners and elegant dress were used to conceal one's true identity.[33] Molière, of course, repeatedly ridiculed civility's easy slide into the service of *amour-propre,* yet he also sought out ways to reestablish the integrity of civility.[34] The seventeenth-century theorist of civility the Chevalier de Méré anxiously circled again and again the issue of how to discern a genuine, that is, moral civility. After elaborating various unsatisfactory criteria—consistency of behavior, ability to please, a long period of training—Méré, according to Domna Stanton, was ultimately forced to reassert civility's premise of a direct circuit of signification as if it were self-evident: "To appear *honnête* one must in fact be *honnête*, for external appearances are only images of internal acts."[35]

The aporia of civility—its inability to differentiate in representation between an affirmation and a denial of its signified—thus resulted in skeptical questioning of the trustworthiness of civility. And by the end of the seventeenth century there was a desire to prevent that questioning from going too far. Recuperative efforts were made to rechristianize civility and to infuse it with additional ethical substance.[36] From the late seventeenth through the eighteenth centuries distinctions proliferated between civility and its onetime synonym, politeness. Here the strategy was to preserve the notion of the moral transparency of surface appearance by separating out the possibility of rhetorical dissemblance and conferring it on a single term. If one term could be made the receptacle of dissemblance, the other could be preserved as a signifier of a moral civility. That this was an arbitrary, evasive maneuver, rather than a logical or substantive development, is evident in the ultimate semantic indeterminacy of the two terms: each could function as a morally positive or negative term of refinement. In *The Spirit of the Laws* (1748), Montesquieu reaffirms (in an awkward rhetorical question) the direct connection between civility and virtue: "is not freeing oneself from the rules of civility the way one seeks to put oneself more at ease with one's faults?" And to protect this circuit of signification, he immediately differentiates it from its linked term, embedding in the latter the power of corruption. "Civility is preferred, in this regard, to politeness. Politeness flatters the vices of others, and civility keeps us from displaying our own; it is a barrier that men put between themselves in order to keep from being corrupted."[37]

But while some valued civility over politeness, the valences could easily be reversed. Civility could be criticized in the same way as politeness, as it was by Charles de Saint-Evremond: "Civility is nothing other than continual commerce in ingenious lies to deceive one another."[38] And while civility could be criticized, politeness could be rehabilitated, as it was in France in the second part of the eighteenth century. François Guizot in his *Universal Dictionary of the Synonyms of the French Language (Dictionnaire universel des synonymes de la langue française)* cites the view of the grammarian Beauzée: "Overly ceremonious civility is both tiring and pointless. Affectation causes suspicion of falseness, and enlightened people have banished it entirely. Politeness is exempt from this excess. The more polite one is, the more amiable."[39]

To protect civility, its negative, dissembling potential was distilled and displaced onto a related term.[40] The strategy here was to partition off its characteristics. The opposite strategy was also tried. To strengthen the ideas of civility—to forestall the slippage between its signifier and signified—the idea was joined to new signifiers of virtue. We have already noted that by the mid-eighteenth century some philosophes, by way of self-legitimation, assimilated the language of civility into the self-characterizations of the philosophe. Given the unstable nature of the language of civility, we can now see that this assimilation was reciprocally beneficial: to counter its own representational instabilities, civility's adherents sought support from the language of the philosophe.[41]

Reasserting civility's transparency, partitioning its meanings, assimilating it to other terms—all these were attempts to contain the discourse's tendency toward collapse. Yet all these strategies did not resolve but only deferred the consequences of the discourse's instabilities. For in the face of every attempt to reaffirm the first principle of civility's moral signification, one could always reinvoke the potential swerve of civility to mere dissembling appearance. Although the author of the article "Philosophe" in the *Encyclopedia* fuses the philosophe and the *honnête homme*, another article contains the familiar, delegitimizing criticism of refinement. Jaucourt writes in "Civilité, politesse, affabilité": "Without necessarily emanating from the heart, they give appearances of doing so, and they make one appear on the outside as he ought to be internally."[42] Mirabeau in 1760 reiterates this skepticism of the closed circuit of civility's signification:

> I am astonished, when it comes to civilization, at how distorted our thinking is. Ask most people what their idea of civilization is and they would answer that it is perfection of manners, urbanity, and politeness and diffusion of knowledge such that the proprieties are observed in the absence of detailed regulations—all of which to me is but the mask of virtue and not its true face, and civilization does nothing for society if it does not establish the foundations and form of virtue. It is in societies made soft by the aforementioned factors that the corruption of humanity begins.[43]

Originally projected as the signification of a moral content, civility slides toward another meaning. The discourse on civility repeatedly issues in self-referential preoccupations with the forms of civility, particularly with how those forms undermine what they are supposed to signify. And these preoccupations yield the same conclusion: that the sensuous forms of civility displace its moral content. But though displaced that content is not entirely eliminated, for the swerve from proper signification to the narcissistic self-presentation of the form is recognized as such. Indeed, the swerve is possible only because sensuous figuration continues to be measured against a standard of moral content. Or put another way, the conceptual instabilities of civility tend to collapse that notion into an unrealized ideal of virtue that underwrites yet might never be present in actual practice. The enactment of civility is always unsettled by an anxiety over the absence of its signified.

For those who recognized civility's potential for referential aberration, the result could be an extreme epistemological uncertainty that took the shape of both social criticism and introspective doubt. As Rousseau notes in *A Discourse on the Moral Effects of the Arts and Sciences* (1750), civility made direct knowledge of others impossible, for it rendered undecidable the question whether or not one was acting sincerely. And that undecidability, Rousseau asserted, permeated all social intercourse, at once constituting and undermining it. In a civilized society, he writes: "we never know with whom we have to deal. . . . What train of vices must attend this uncertainty. Sincere friendship, real esteem, and perfect confidence are banished from among men. Jealousy, suspicion, fear, coldness, reserve, hate, and fraud lie constantly concealed under that uniform and deceitful veil of politeness: that boasted candour and urbanity, for which we are indebted to the enlightened spirit of this age."[44]

In addition to destabilizing and distorting all social relations, the cognitive doubt engendered by a recognition of civility's contradictions also imperiled one's sense of self. Once civility became an internalized trait—a reflex of one's character—epistemological uncertainty could be planted in the heart of one's identity. Rousseau's notorious problems of self-transparency, in this respect, might be seen not as the product of an idiosyncratic psychology but as a fulfillment of the disintegrative rhetoric of civility.[45] If one's whole character automatically acted according to the dictates of civility, then one could also doubt the sincerity or authenticity of one's own actions and feelings; one could call into question the genuineness of one's self.

In his phantasy of enjoying the pleasures of French sociability and of becoming a French philosophe, the young Herder found himself rehearsing both the justifications of civility and its conventional criticisms, ones that Rousseau so strenuously elaborated. Herder's experience of the aporia of civility resulted in the sense of an always-existing absence or lack of genuineness in the forms of French culture and French selves, even in the writings of the French critics of civility, including Rousseau himself. In late eighteenth-century France, the conventional criticisms of civility obtained a particularly intense power as they were put in the service of the polarizing politics and the gender relations of the time. But the pervasiveness of these criticisms allowed them to be used in other debates and by other parties as well. As the case of Herder suggests, they played an important role in how Germans defined themselves over and against the French, and a key aspect of that differentiation was the way in which the problems of civility spilled over into views of national language.

Herder's phantasy of French refinement and sociability was set in motion by his thinking about French language. That association is unsurprising in that the qualities of the language were conventionally treated as emblematic of the entire sensibility and sociability of French civility. The reform of the French language in the seventeenth century proceeded at the same time as the emergence of a code of civility in the French court and salons. The new clarity of the French language lent itself to more elegant communication, which, combined with pleasing and appropriate images and tropes, rendered the language ideally suited to the requirements of civility. Besides its other usual characterization as the language of reason, French was thus also often described as the ideal medium of refined conversation, which, according to some, was constitutive of the language. In a letter to Madame d'Epinay, the abbé Galiani, for example, calls French the "language of dialogue" because it is the "language of the most social people in the world, of a nation which must talk in order to think and which thinks only in order to be able to talk."[46] Voltaire offers French as the model language for a universal sociability based on civility: "Of all the languages, French must be the most universal, because it is the most conducive to conversation."[47] As the manifestation and instrument of civility, French was also understood as the outer form of an inner character. Rivarol, for example, tells us that the changing nature of seventeenth-century France, the prosperity, good order, and happiness of its people in the era of Louis XIV, was registered directly in an increasing delicacy of language: the metaphors became "more exact, "comparisons nobler," and "pleasantries finer." And to seal the equivalency of outer and inner, Rivarol has recourse to the same conventional trope of civility that we find in Jaucourt: "Language being the clothing of thought, one wants the most elegant forms."[48]

The French language embodied all the virtues and benevolent social functions of civility, but, like other forms of civility, it could be suspected of subverting those same qualities. While expected to communicate sensibility and virtue, an elegant refined French might merely simulate those characteristics and put that simulation to other uses. Language, like other signifying forms, was subject to the instabilities of representing civility; French was thus both praised as the proper signification of moral character and intelligence and denounced as the instrument of pretense and manipulation. Writings on the French language acknowledge the aporia of civility. Beside the conventional affirmations of French, there appears the melancholy conclusion that all languages, even French, will inevitably decline, a decline that follows from having placed the language in the service of civility.

In his prize-winning essay on why French should become the universal language, Rivarol praises the elegance of the language. That elegance, he tells us, has its source not just in its clarity but also in its grace and politeness, which render it "sociable, charming, and flirtatious." In such a form, the language constantly gives pleasure. But to give pleasure constantly, the language must always be changing, and inevitably that continuous change issues in metaphorical innovation. This unleashing of metaphor pushes the language onto a slippery slope, a slide from transparent communication to dissemblance: "It is that perpetual lie of the language, it is the metaphorical style which carries a germ of corruption. . . . [For] errors in figures or in metaphors announce a falseness of the spirit and a love of exaggeration that can scarcely correct itself." The inevitable result, according to Rivarol, is a "fall into affectation."[49] Diderot and Condillac display the same worry—that the pursuit of refinement produces a figurative displacement and therefore a distortion of original meaning. What ultimately undermines the clarity of the French sentence, Diderot writes, is "that harmony of style to which we have become so conscious that we often sacrifice to it everything else." All too often, in order to refine our language we impoverish it, for, "having often only one proper term to render an idea, we prefer to enfeeble the idea rather than not employ a noble term."[50] In his *Essay on the Origin of Human Knowledge,* Condillac asserts that in current literary society no writer will settle for mere equality with predecessors who wrote in a clear, precise manner. In the search for constant refinement, the modern writer will inevitably try "a new road." And that, he concludes, is the beginning of linguistic corruption: "But as every style analogous to the character of the language, and to his own, has already been used by preceding writers, he has nothing left but to deviate from analogy. Thus in order to be original, he is obliged to contribute to the ruin of a language."[51]

In the eighteenth century the French language was thought to operate in two registers: it is the clear, direct language of rational exposition, and it is the pleasing figurative language of civility. Now sometimes those two registers may merge into one, but as various writers noted, what is more likely, what they tell us is in fact inevitable, is that the French language, to fulfill the requirements of civility, will sacrifice its logical exactitude to figurative excess. The language loses its logical rigor as it seeks to become a pleasing rhetoric. Emblem of French civility, the French language was susceptible to the same perceived uncertainties of representation that followed other forms of civility. And like those other forms of civility, the fate of the language of civility was the displacement of content or substance by an excess of form. The rational rigor of the language succumbed to its rhetoric.[52] And as writers concluded, the inevitable ascension of rhetoric has a devastating consequence: a loss of direct reference, a loss of the language's ability to say what it means and to mean what it says.

THE LINGUISTIC CONSTRUCTION
OF GERMAN IDENTITY

As we have seen, Frederick II and others in late eighteenth-century Germany accepted the French claim that French was the universal language of Europe. Those Germans who were already engaged in a literary revival rejected Francophile arguments and asserted the autonomy and even the supremacy of their own language. What made their work easier was that the French had themselves already provided the means of turning back French claims and of making German ones.

Germans drew on the epistemological criticism of the French language both as dissembling rhetorical excess and as dislocating abstract reason. On the epistemological locations where the legitimations of the French language collapsed Germans made their own assertions of identity. A striking literary example of this procedure is found in Goethe's *Wilhelm Meister's Apprenticeship,* when Aurelie surprises Wilhelm with her fierce antipathy to French: "I hate the French language," she says, "with my entire soul." When he asks her why she despises that "beautiful, cultivated" language, she tells him that her former male friend, a German, could be trusted when he wrote to her in his own "strong, honest, heartfelt" language. But when he wanted to mislead her, he wrote in French. Aurelie, seduced and abandoned with a child, thus scoffs at the conventional image of the French language: "French is rightly the language of the world, worthy of being the universal language with which people can lie and deceive one another!"[53]

We have seen that in the *Journal* of his voyage to France, Herder is both drawn to and repelled by an image of French sociability and the French *philosophe.* He rehearses both the positive enticements of the discourse of civility—its offer of pleasing sensuous appearances in various forms, especially linguistic—and its negative aspects, his sense that there is no content behind the refined appearances. Herder's phantasy of refined French sociability is initiated by his thinking about the French language, and he is particularly sensitive to how the problems of French civility affect the language. Observing that like "the spirit of monarchic manners . . . the French nation has little real virtue and little inner strength," he then notes that instead of virtue, another characteristic defines the language: "A certain nobility in thought, a certain freedom of expression, a *politesse* in the manner of using words and in turning phrases—these are the stamp of the French language as of French manners."[54] Herder is an especially discerning critic of the mechanisms of French civility. While feeling that French culture and language have no genuine substance or moral content, he also recognizes that they have come to obtain general acceptance; they set the standard for European culture. This cultural mastery paradoxically owes its success precisely to civility's lack of a guiding content. For in its detachment from its referent, civility asserts itself as pure rhetoric—as overpowering sensuous figuration. It gestures toward the rationale of representing a particular moral or cultural content only to put that aside in the further development of its pleasing forms; the power of French civility comes from a tacit recognition of its own rhetorical excess, its own surpassing of any signified. And once that recognition becomes explicit, it can be thought to signify nothing more than its own signifying power. What French language and culture unleash—and what they represent in the end—is simply their own rhetorical power of self-presentation.

Herder turns this analysis into a withering criticism of how the French language's performative mechanisms disable direct communication. The French, he says, under the pretext of communication, speak their language to construct a self-referential social situation that becomes the point of speaking:

> Whoever knows French in this way [i.e., as the "aesthetic, refined, gallant, graceful, polite" language of civility] knows it in the depths of its nature, knows it as the art of shining and of pleasing in our present-day world, knows it as the logic of a whole way of life. Its turns of phrase, in particular, must be taken into account here. They are always twisted around: they never express what they say, but always form a relationship between the speaker and the one spoken to, and thus relegate the main issue to a subordinate position. The relationship itself becomes the principal concern—and is not this the etiquette of social intercourse?[55]

In a society constituted by the requirements of civility, every linguistic act is a social performance, and every performance displaces the intellectual content of the linguistic act. The point of one's performance of the French language and its implied civility is not to communicate a moral principle or an edifying idea but to make the listener accept the rules and terms of such performances. This performative, rhetorical aggression originates from an absence of content, and it undercuts all attempts to reestablish content. It creates a narcissistic, self-referential world.[56] Herder finds the displacement of content by self-regarding form to be ubiquitous in French culture, at work even in the writings of philosophes who are critical of this very process. The desire for virtuoso linguistic performance ruins the ideas that they seek to communicate, covertly teaching the opposite of what they seek to communicate.

Herder's repudiation of French as the language of civility comes on the heels of his criticism of French as the language of rational transparency. In the work that first earned him national attention and entangled him in the literary disputes of the day, his 1766 *Fragments concerning Recent Literature,* he examines the controversies surrounding the technical epistemologies of national languages. Having by this time read Diderot and Condillac, he adopts their critique of the older rationalist conception of the French sentence. He points out how that view of the French sentence—as corresponding "to the metaphysical order itself"—is incompatible with sensationalist analysis. According to that analysis, Herder says, primary sense perception must result in syntactical inversions; thus the first languages had to have been characterized by a certain disorder. "If inversion therefore arises from sensuous attentiveness," he writes, "then the language of an entirely sensuous nation must be irregular and full of changes."[57]

Herder goes on to conclude that this must be true not just of ancient languages but of modern ones as well. Contemporary languages that allow for inversions have by implication maintained a continuous direct connection to primary sense experience, while a modern language that prohibits inversions must at some time have disconnected itself from that sensuous immediacy, making it into a second-order abstraction. In an early use of a terminology that will become common in German idealism, Herder calls the consciousness that thinks without inversions, that thinks in French, mere "Verstand," or abstract reasoning, which "has nothing to do with the eye and ear." The Germans, on the other hand, thinking and speaking inversions, maintaining an unbroken relationship to direct experience, have earned for their language the title of higher reason, of "Vernunft."[58]

Herder's distinction between two kinds of consciousness is based on an ideal of complete and closed referentiality. The French language suspends the mind above sense experience and therefore refers to nothing but itself; German goes all the way down to brute sense perception and, through it, goes all the way up to higher reason. The epistemological circuit is elaborate but continuous. Herder says that this unbroken epistemology, derived by opposing the German to the French sentence, belongs to "German freedom."[59] It distinguishes German from and raises it above a dominant French culture.

Germans thus made use of both the problems of French as a language of untrustworthy civility and its separation from immediate sense experience. Germans proceeded to reoccupy with their own language the epistemological spaces vacated by the French. German, not French, signified ideas and sensations in a reliable manner. Unlike the deceptive and abstractly detached French language, German offered a true and moral knowledge of the world. This particular strategy of grounding claims to cultural identity in the putative differential epistemologies of national languages plays a central role in another key text of German cultural nationalism, one that is always mentioned in discussions of the subject. In December 1807, following the collapse of Prussia and while Berlin was still occupied by French troops, the German philosopher Fichte began a series of lectures at the Prussian Academy. In these *Addresses to the German Nation,* he seeks to rouse defeated Germans, exhorting them to display stoicism in the face of the collapse of their country and to find in the current situation the opportunity for cultural and national renewal. He proposes a program of educational reform, derived from Johann Heinrich Pestalozzi but essentially Kantian in purpose. Now, Fichte argues, Germans have been given the opportunity to educate themselves into practical reason. The aim of educational reform is to produce a purely moral will, one that he calls "supersensuous" because it suppresses self-interest corrupted by sensuous necessity and desire. It is the special destiny of Germans, he argues, to become morally autonomous.[60]

Fichte realizes that to accomplish his aims of national rebuilding and philosophical actualization, he must first establish a source of German and philosophical distinctiveness not found in the French. Unlike other nationalists, he explicitly rules out place—that is, homeland, or *Heimat*—as the defining aspect of national identity. And he also discounts race, or racial purity; indeed, given the "intermingling" of peoples "it would not be easy," he writes, "for any one of the peoples descended from Teutons to demonstrate a greater priority of descent than the others."[61] Germans are for Fichte distinctively German in one sense: they have never abandoned their language.[62] And that continuity of language is significant for a reason that we might now expect: it indicates a history of uninterrupted contact with immediate sense experience. Fichte accepts the eighteenth-century notion that the structure of a language mirrors the structure of a people's sensuous experience of the world; the continuity of a people's language therefore indicates the continuity of their direct sense experience.[63] What he adds to this earlier view is the notion that the continuity of sense experience, embodied in a language, determines a people's access to the supersensuous realm of the ethical will.

Fichte's argument is this: to educate a person to recognize the supersensuous realm of morality one must first describe that realm in a language that the uninitiated person can understand—that is, in the language of that person's sensuous experience. The supersensuous initially can be made intelligible only in the conventional language of sense perception. One's ability to comprehend the ethical or philosophical concept depends on the clarity and immediacy of the signifying sensuous language.[64]

A problem therefore arises when people give up their own language to adopt a foreign one. For the loss of one's original language disables the apprehension of the supersensuous. One cannot intuitively or immediately comprehend the signification of an ethical or philosophical concept in a foreign language, because the linguistic signifier of that concept is based on a past sense experience that one or one's culture has never had. At best, one must have the significance of the term explained, and even then one will always feel that the connection between the sensuous signifying language and the ethical and philosophical signified is purely arbitrary. This sense of arbitrariness ensures that the supersensuous realm will never be taken seriously but will be treated as inessential, unimportant, as a means rather than an end. The consequence, Fichte says, is an easy "perversion and misuse" of moral language, "glossing over every kind of human corruption." Without a correlation in immediate sensuous experience, linguistic signifiers of the supersensuous realm constitute a language without compelling force, a language easily distorted and placed in the service of bad intentions.[65] Fichte summarizes his argument:

> The purpose and result of all admixture [of languages] has ever been this: first of all to remove the hearer from the immediate comprehensibility and definiteness which are the inherent qualities of every primitive language; then, when he has been prepared to accept such words in blind faith, to supply him with the explanation he needs; and finally in this explanation to mix vice and virtue together in such a way that it is no easy matter to separate them again.[66]

By maintaining the continuity of their language, Germans have ensured its moral and philosophical transparency. But for those Teutons who have abandoned their language, who have come to speak French instead, "incomprehensibility" is "the very nature and origin" of their moral language. French is a language without clear referentiality, and, detached from reference, it slides into "arbitrariness and artificiality," gives way to frivolous pleasure seeking. A culture based on this language, Fichte writes, "seeks nothing more than to pass the time away in a manner that is pleasant and in keeping with the sense of the beautiful and it has attained its object completely when it has done this."[67]

The French language, epistemically cut off from direct sense experience, thus takes on the features of the corrupted language of civility. In

Fichte's lectures the two forms of the language's referential instability—its dislocation from sense experience and its untrustworthy forms of sensuous self-presentation—merge into a single process, as cause to effect. In the era of military occupation those epistemological problems of the French language take on a fateful significance. Like Herder, Fichte identifies the performative displacement of content as the crucial operative mechanism of the language, but what once resulted in self-absorption and social theater now becomes epochally dangerous. French narcissism gives way to nihilism; the absence of direct referentiality is the generative principle of conquest: "Unable to apprehend anything in its actual state of existence," Fichte writes, the French "only want to destroy everything that exists and to create everywhere . . . a void, in which they can reproduce their own image and never anything else."[68]

Fichte's analysis of language brings together long traditions of French criticism in the service of remaking the defeated German nation. In doing so, it reinforces a new rhetoric of cultural identity and difference. Germans capitalized on the problems of establishing the stable referentiality of the French language both as a language of civility and in terms of sensationalist epistemology. They exploited those problems to legitimate a new identity, a new trope of Germanness. Wherever they criticized the dissembling, if pleasing, character of linear French surfaces, that criticism suggested an opposing and superior standard of German depth, complexity, and profundity. That distinction between cultures—the deeply moral and spiritual against the frivolous, superficial, and untrustworthy—could be underwritten by the putative differential abilities of French and German to mirror immediate sensuous experience. By use of linguistic contrast, Fichte carefully nurtures a trope of superior Germanness at a time when it was difficult to believe that the Germans could win any battle, cultural or otherwise.

IDENTITY IN QUESTION

In *The Order of Things: An Archaeology of the Human Sciences* (1970), Michel Foucault identifies a momentous shift in the structures of knowledge that occurred at the beginning of the nineteenth century. This shift, according to Foucault, entailed, among other things, a radical change in views of language. In the seventeenth and eighteenth centuries, language was thought of in terms of a "general grammar" whose main concern was the representational functions of words and grammar, with how well they mirrored sensation and thought. At the beginning of the nineteenth century, there appeared a very different view of language, one not focused on issues of representation but on lineage and derivation, in a word, philology. In many respects, Foucault's account of changing views of language explains why most notable nineteenth-century German philologists, such as Wilhelm von Humboldt, showed little interest in eighteenth-century debates regarding the representational character of different languages. These philologists never participated in the arguments outlined above concerning the link between a language's representational competence and national culture. But while Foucault is right about the lack of interest of most philologists in eighteenth-century issues of representation—of how well a language reflects direct experience—he is wrong to say that those debates and concerns ceased in the nineteenth century.[69]

In one of Hegel's lecture series on the "philosophy of spirit," given before an audience of students and civil servants at the University of Berlin in the 1820s, he points out that the French achievement of "the highest delicacy of social cultivation" carries with it a familiar danger: the French preoccupation with pleasing others easily degenerates into the "striving to please at any price—even at the cost of truth." And when he describes the nature of French *Verstand* as one of clarity and definiteness, he projects against that form of consciousness a superior German *Vernunft:* "Our spirit is generally, more than that that of any other European nation, turned inward. We live preeminently in the inwardness of the soul and thought." To mark the epistemological character of French consciousness, Hegel also makes the now-familiar gesture toward linguistic difference; French clarity and precision, he notes, are directly reflected in the rigid rules of French syntax.[70] And his related comment on the result of writing philosophy in Germany—"Once that is accomplished, it will be infinitely more difficult to give shallowness the appearance of truth"—finds an echo, with the same oppositions between French and German at work, more than a hundred and fifty years later, in a comment by Martin Heidegger, not long before his death in 1976: "The French assure me of this truth again today, when they begin to think they speak German."[71]

The eighteenth-century distinctions between the French and German languages thus helped to disseminate a larger cultural opposition of French and German cultures throughout the nineteenth and into the twentieth centuries. But the importance of those eighteenth-century distinctions in later European cultural and intellectual history extended far beyond their simple reiteration. Those terms had an influence not just in their repetition but also in their dynamic transformation into other terms, a transformation that might, at one extreme, greatly extend the cultural significance and range of the terms and, at the other, ironically nullify their cultural force and influence. Both of these possibilities appeared in one of the most compressed moments of intellectual history, in Switzerland in the early 1870s, in the defining work of the young Friedrich Nietzsche. Trained in philology in Germany and teaching at the University of Basel, Nietzsche approached language using the philological focus on the derivation of words and grammar, and in this sense, he exemplifies Foucault's description of the study of language in the nineteenth century. But *contra* Foucault, Nietzsche also thought in terms of how language functioned as representation, and he not only took over eighteenth-century debates; he extended them, conferring on them an enormous significance.

Writing as a late nineteenth-century German Romantic, Nietzsche inflated the provenance of terms, turning the distinction between national languages and cultures into two universal human conditions, which he called the Dionysian and Apollonian impulses. Displaced and generalized into these new categories, eighteenth-century distinctions exerted an enormous influence on the thought of the *fin de siècle*. Notwithstanding his training as a philologist, Nietzsche continued to think in eighteenth-century terms and conferred on those terms a new, broadened importance. What was even more extraordinary was that while others followed Nietzsche's thinking, Nietzsche himself chose not to. In a remarkable intellectual development, within a couple of years after expanding the opposition of France and Germany into the opposition of Apollonian and Dionysian, Nietzsche turned on all those distinctions, offering a powerful critique that is one of the clearest markers of his shift away from Romanticism to a style of ironic, deconstructive thinking that we now identify as "poststructuralist."

At the beginning of the 1870s, Nietzsche showed a strong allegiance to late nineteenth-century German Romanticism, which upheld the opposition between French superficiality and German profundity, a view for example propounded by the nationalist and Romantic figure whom Nietzsche idolized, Richard Wagner.[72] Nietzsche's German Romantic and cultural nationalism and his adoration of Wagner are readily apparent in his first book, *The Birth of Tragedy* (1872), which offers a Romantic radicalization of eighteenth-century stylizations of French and German culture. Nietzsche generalizes characteristics once understood as distinctively French—clarity of reasoning and a culture of artful appearance—into a universal human impulse, which he calls the Apollonian, and he expands the depths of German interiority into the opposing universal impulse, the prerational, still-instinctual Dionysian will and intuition, which directly communicate the essence of the world.[73] Nietzsche's Romanticism refigures the dichotomy of France/Germany into a dualism of generalized traits of human psychology, and in a related work he underwrites that move with a generalized version of the late eighteenth-century critique of the French language.

In his contemporaneous essay "On Truth and Lying in an Extra-Moral

Sense" (1873), Nietzsche asserts that all language suffers from the particular communicative defects that eighteenth-century critics attributed to French. As we have seen, those critics, both French and German, believed that the ever-increasing refinement of the language—following the imperatives of French civility—ended up undercutting the logical rigor of the language. Metaphor turned what was designed to be a language of logic into a wayward rhetoric, which in its accumulation of self-regarding metaphor departed from its reference, the original sense perception that the language was to describe. Nietzsche applies this particular eighteenth-century criticism to all languages: "The various languages . . . show that words are never concerned with truth, never with adequate expression. . . . The 'thing-in-itself' . . . is also absolutely incomprehensible to the creator of language and not worth seeking." What generates this swerve of language away from the primary truths of the world is a narcissistic urge to produce metaphor. The creator of language, Nietzsche tells us, "designates only the relations of things to men, and to express these he uses the boldest metaphors." These metaphors function for Nietzsche in precisely the same way that they functioned for eighteenth-century critics of French: they separate the mind from the sense-perception of the "thing-in-itself." Nietzsche explains: "First, he [the creator of language] translates a nerve impulse into an image! That is the first metaphor. Then, the image must be reshaped into a sound! The second metaphor." Metaphor accumulates on top of metaphor in the workings of the mind, until the mind is lost in its own self-created, metaphorical world: "When we speak of trees, colors, snow, and flowers, we believe we know something about the things themselves, although what we have are just metaphors of things, which do not correspond to the original entities."[74] And in Nietzsche's most daring turn of argument, he adds that rational reasoning is also just metaphorical activity in that it produces intellectual abstractions and generalizations removed from and standing in place of one's specific concrete experience of things. Thus, in terms that sound exactly like those of Rousseau criticizing French civility, Nietzsche concludes that "the intellect develops its main powers in dissimulation. . . . Here deception, flattery, lying and cheating, slander, false pretenses, living in borrowed glory, masquerading, conventions of concealment, playacting before others and before oneself . . . is so much the rule and the law." Here, human beings "are deeply immersed in phantasmagoria; their eye merely glides around the surfaces of things and sees 'forms.'" As the most powerful source of metaphorical addition, the reasoning intellect disables human sense experience, so that "perception," Nietzsche concludes, "leads nowhere to the truth."[75]

Some interpreters have jumped to the conclusion that Nietzsche's essay on language shows a poststructuralist recognition of the slippages of language and how they jeopardize the possibility of attaining a clear, fixed truth. But what these commentators have not noticed is that Nietzsche does all this not to endorse but to criticize the slippage of language, and thus he does not reject but is implicitly affirming the conventional notion of truth. Faulting language for failing to live up to the "truth," Nietzsche writes the essay on language as a late Romantic who deplores the loss of proximity to, as he puts it, "things-in-themselves."[76]

In Nietzsche's radicalized late nineteenth-century Romanticism, the flaws of the French language and civility become those of language in general, so that language per se is illusion. In *The Birth of Tragedy* he calls the general psychological impulse that produces illusion the Apollonian, and he opposes to it the Dionysian, which is the human impulse that always remains in close proximity to things-in-themselves, the essences of the world. This latter impulse cannot express itself in language, German or otherwise, but it still manages to find expression in a distinctively German medium. In the terms of nineteenth-century century Romanticism, music manifests a prerational will and intuition that directly manifest the primary forces at work in the world, and Nietzsche identifies the purest Dionysian music in the modern period as German—the music from Bach through Beethoven to the composer whom he sees as the savior of German culture, Richard Wagner. In this tradition of German music, Nietzsche imagines a return to an authentic accurate proximity to primary experience.

The epistemological directness accorded to the German language by eighteenth-century German theorists thus becomes in the hands of Nietzsche, the late Romantic, the defining quality of German music. His work of the early 1870s generalizes the terms of eighteenth-century debate and translates them into the idiom of late nineteenth-century German Romanticism, all in a fashion that, as we see in the next chapter, exerted considerable influence on European culture. But what was even more remarkable than this transformation of eighteenth-century terms was that shortly after accomplishing it, Nietzsche begins to repudiate it, and he does so by now using the same eighteenth-century terms of the German/French antithesis in a way that undercuts precisely the identity that they were meant to produce.

The pro-Germanism of Nietzsche's Wagnerite Romanticism veiled doubts that Nietzsche had concerning not just Germany's political mission—which Wagner also questioned—but also its cultural mission; and because, for Nietzsche, Wagner was the newest embodiment of that mission, Nietzsche's ironic excavation of the conventional opposition of Germany to France also signaled the beginning of his separation from Wagner. In 1874, two years after *The Birth of Tragedy*, Nietzsche published the second of his "untimely meditations," an extended essay titled *On the Advantage and Dis-*

advantage of History for Life. This book showed its "untimeliness" in a number of ways. It rejects, as the title suggests, the German historical thought of the nineteenth century.[77] It refuses to endorse the recent Bismarckian unification of Germany. And it repudiates German cultural identity—and with it late German Romanticism—by ironically deconstructing its foundational terms in the opposition of Germany to France. The logic of that opposition, according to Nietzsche, issues not in a self, spiritually superior to the superficial self of French culture, but in a self no less empty and stymied in its emptiness.

In *On the Advantage and Disadvantage of History for Life,* in the course of a general survey of what he considers the intellectual exhaustion of the West, he expresses his particular disappointment with a German unification brought about by Bismarckian *Realpolitik* rather than by an authentic cultural coalescence. This leads him to reflect on the inadequacy of German cultural identity, which he defines in a formula already familiar to us: "More than another people," Germans suffer "from that contradiction of content and form."[78]

Germans, he tells us, consider themselves a people of unique substance and depth, of profound character, so that their hope for a "national culture" is "nourished by the belief in the genuineness and immediacy of German feeling, by the belief in an unharmed inwardness." The complete reliance on inner content renders all external form untrustworthy, something to be loathed and feared as a "convention, a costume and disguise." Stylized appearance makes the German anxious, and that fear of sensuous form causes the German to leave "the school of the French."[79]

Nietzsche's analysis of the German character restates the emergence of German identity over and against the dissembling surfaces of French civility. But unlike the Germans of the late eighteenth century who believed that the rejection of form would allow a stable identity to come into being, Nietzsche points ironically to a different result. He considers the privileging of interiority to be not the way out of an epistemological impasse but a new way into one. In grounding identity on a "sense of content," this "famous people of inwardness," he derisively writes, run into the "famous danger in its inwardness." The German commitment to depth and profundity, predicated on a complete rejection of surface appearance, means that no sensuous act or form can ever be counted as a necessary or adequate display of inner character. Absolute interiority can never be definitely known by an external sign. For the German, Nietzsche writes, "the visible deed is not the deed of the whole and a self-manifestation of his inner being." "The German," he says, "cannot be judged at all by an action and remains hidden as an individual even after this deed." German identity, to use Nietzsche's elegant image, is confined "to its inaccessible little temple."[80]

An interiority that can never definitively be known by its appearance, that is unintelligible to sense perception or empirical experience, produces an uncertainty about establishing when or how interiority shows itself or even, ultimately, whether it exists at all: "The content itself, of which it is assumed that it cannot be seen at all from the outside, may at some time or other evaporate; externally one would not detect a trace of this nor of its earlier presence." That uncertainty, Nietzsche concludes, corrodes one's confidence in inwardness, makes it feel "counterfeit," or causes it to disappear altogether, leaving "as the distinguishing mark of the German" only his external form, "his outer being, that arrogantly clumsy and meekly ineffectual outer being."[81] That empty form, according to Nietzsche, is the cultural presupposition of German unification. German identity, originally fashioned as the opposite of a French civility that fails to make itself transparent, does not, according to Nietzsche, overcome that problem of representation but reproduces it in other terms. That derisive conclusion, which reverses the logic and aim of German cultural identity, marks the beginning of Nietzsche's departure from late German Romanticism. It is the first clear indication of a thoroughgoing ironic, deconstructive strategy of thinking—Nietzsche's "transvaluation," or reversal of values—that defines his subsequent writings.

After his full break with Wagner in 1878, Nietzsche enjoyed antagonizing the latter by assuming a new pro-French posture as he tried on different cultural personae. But the conclusion of *The Advantage and Disadvantage of History for Life* does not opt for France over Germany. It offers a different solution, another phantasy of cultural identity that Nietzsche believed transcended the dualism of French and German cultures and their problems with uncertain representation. At the end of his essay, he asks Germans to accept a conception of "external culture" that "can be something other still than *decoration of life*, that is, fundamentally and always only dissimulation and disguise." Against this "Romance concept" of culture, but also against the German idea of a sealed-off inner nature, Nietzsche points to a third possibility, to "the Greek concept of culture as a new and improved nature, without inside and outside, without dissimulation and convention, of culture as the accord of life, thought, and willing."[82] Nietzsche's turn to ancient Greece as a way of transcending the impoverished terms of the French-German dualism directs us to another strategy in both France and Germany of constructing cultural identity, one that again had its source in the eighteenth century, and that again yielded, notwithstanding Nietzsche's optimism, its own instabilities of identity.

CHAPTER THREE

Strange Classicism

Aesthetic Vision in Winckelmann, Nietzsche, and Thomas Mann

In Peter Gay's interpretation of the Enlightenment, classicism and classical texts played a vital role; Enlightenment writers, according to Gay, turned to the ancients to free themselves from Christianity and traditional belief. Adopting from the "pagans" critical rationality and this-worldliness as its fundamental orientation, the Enlightenment engineered a breakthrough to "modernity." Since Gay published *The Enlightenment* in the 1960s, the role of classicism in eighteenth-century intellectual life has been shown to be much more complex than Gay allowed. Civic republicanism, which drew on classical models of republican virtue and polity, exerted, according to J. G. A. Pocock and others, an "antimodern" influence on political thought as it advocated an ethos of independence and communitarianism at odds with the egoistic self-interest of putatively "modern" sensibilities, such as commerce. And more recent cultural histories have pointed out other far-reaching consequences of civic republicanism, in particular how it reshaped notions of gender at the end of the eighteenth century.

Although these more recent studies have yielded a more nuanced historical understanding of the political uses of classicism in the eighteenth century, Gay's association of classicism in the eighteenth century with the formation of a rational identity remains valid in one important sense. The neoclassical revival in art and literature in the second half of the eighteenth century offered a movement of sensibility and intellect that recommended a model of well-functioning rationality. Neoclassicism in art sought to express a self of harmonious, developing rationality, one that carefully modulated its passions and desires.

The turn to neoclassicism in mid-eighteenth-century Europe was di-

71

rectly tied to the cultural developments and stresses described in the previous chapters. Beginning around 1760, French and German intellectuals began to emphasize the problematical aspect of the French discourse of civility—its dubious reliance on pleasing sensuous form to communicate an underlying moral sensibility. To these critics the alluring appearances of civility signified not virtue but moral confusion and a weakness for sensuous gratification. Both French and German artists and writers looked to the neoclassical revival as a remedy. For these critics of French civility, classical models offered a self that resisted the false appeal of the senses. Self-contained in its autonomous reason and moral clarity, classicist selfhood or subjectivity imagined a rehabilitated, autonomous self, free of the corrupting influence of aristocratic French civility.

Classicism offered an alternative identity to French and German artists and writers, but it did so in ways as multiple, complex, and contradictory as other discourses of identity. In France, the turn to neoclassicism was one of a number of attempts to infuse a new morality into society, and a neoclassical ethos worked hand in hand with an increasingly popular Rousseauian civic republicanism into and through the Jacobin period of the French Revolution. In Germany, neoclassicism was also important in the reconstruction of identity, but a different kind of identity was at issue. While an answer to the problem of French civility, classical revival in Germany had other functions as well. It provided inspiration to a national culture that was reshaping itself and an alternative to the better-known characterizations of national cultural identity employed by Herder and Fichte. For writers such as Johann Joachim Winckelmann, Johann Wolfgang von Goethe, Johann Christoph Friedrich von Schiller, and others, classical values and principles—a classical self—offered a model of identity that was preferable to the folk-mindedness of other cultural nationalists, such as Herder.[1] Classicism in Germany, in other words, served the project of constructing a distinctive German cultural identity. Unlike the radical civic republicanism of the French Revolution that came to be associated with classical revival in France, German classicism remained nationalist and cultural in form. Indeed, its contemporaneous formulation in terms of tropes of identity and interiority left German classicism fixated on certain aesthetic rather than political issues, and, when confronted by the French Revolution, it tended almost reflexively to rehabilitate what the Revolution attacked—namely, the aristocratic sociability of the old regime.

From a common starting point in general principles of classicism, writers and artists in Germany and France constructed different phantasies of autonomous identity—one politicized and rigidly gendered, the other culturally nationalist and aesthetic. But though following different paths, both forms of classicist identity displayed stresses and desires that actually worked to undercut those identities. The attempt to perform each self ultimately showed other, problematic urges. In Germany and France, the phantasy of being a classical subject curiously veiled, in different ways, a desire for extinction.

The emergence of German classicism out of a common European-wide classical revival and the peculiarities of German classicism's subsequent development can be seen in three key texts: Winckelmann's *History of Ancient Art* (1764), which provided the foundational view of classicism in Germany for the next hundred years; Friedrich Nietzsche's *Birth of Tragedy* (1872), which defined the romantic reorientation of classicism; and Thomas Mann's *Death in Venice* (1912), which brought eighteenth- and nineteenth-century classicism to a close.[2] These texts demonstrate a deep otherness or strangeness in classicism, a strangeness discernible if not fully explainable in the metaphors and visuality—in the prescribed manner of seeing—of an orthodox classicist view of rational subjectivity. From Winckelmann through Nietzsche to Thomas Mann, the complex and problematical character of classicism becomes ever more explicit, issuing in Mann's conclusion that classicism is an impossible project, at once enabling and disabling the projection of a rational autonomous self as a model of German identity.

EUROPEAN CLASSICAL REVIVAL AND THE REGULATION OF PERCEPTION

The French discourse on civility, with its institutional sources in the court and the salon and dominating European culture in the seventeenth and eighteenth centuries, prescribed a beautiful graciousness in every word, appearance, and action. Founded on the assumption that moral character necessarily showed itself in pleasing sensuous forms, that discourse was immediately recognized as unable to ensure that the beautiful appearances of civility signified properly. No less than virtue, corruption also made use of pleasing form, a use that was unsettling because its efficacy was parasitical on the conventional expectations of civility's moral signification. Civility, in other words, provided corruption with an especially effective disguise and weapon, a way of surreptitiously insinuating itself into the company of virtue. Thus, even as the discourse of civility disseminated its doctrines, it produced accompanying uncertainty and criticism—uncertainty about civility's ability to make moral intentions transparent; and criticism that civility in fact displaced virtue, producing instead a weakness for sensuous gratification. The conflicted nature of the French discourse on civility manifested itself in a variety of cultural forms—in views of language, as we have seen, and in views of gender and politics, as we shall see. The problems of French civility were also evident in the aesthetic discourse of the period, and in focusing on that discourse, one can see that the problems of French civility in fact reiterated a long-standing anxiety in the history of aesthetics concerning the potential immorality of beautiful images.

Not far from the numerous common aesthetic claims that beautiful images and figures signify an intellectual or moral content, there has been an accompanying fear that those images, because of their reliance on a pleasing sensuousness, undercut whatever moral message they are supposed to convey. The conventional foundational statement of this anxiety is found in Plato's notorious banning of poets and painters from his ideal republic. According to Plato, artists destroy virtue by displacing its authority with emotional and physical responses that passively follow external stimuli. "If you grant," Socrates says, "admission to the honeyed muse in lyric or epic, pleasure and pain will be lords of your city instead of Law.[3]

This issue of the inherent moral slippage of sensuous images recurred periodically throughout Europe in different forms, sometimes exacerbated by specific historical conditions. In the eighteenth century, while many European writers and artists were aware of the issue, Germans seemed particularly anxious about the moral slippage that art appeared to invite.[4] The German strategy of establishing identity on tropes of moral depth and interiority—explicitly and implicitly opposed to the dissembling pleasing surfaces of French civility—seemed to rule out the use of all forms of sensuous appearance to signify cultural identity. What was deeply interior—spiritual and moral character—could not be fully represented by pleasing appearance, behavior, and speech. Some Germans, such as Kant and Hegel, thus argued for the ethical and intellectual supremacy of pure forms of interiority (in Hegel's case philosophical self-consciousness; in Kant's a moral will that refuses any reliance on sensory stimulation).[5] But no German writer or intellectual, particularly in a period of cultural revival, could entirely repudiate the conventional view that inner character showed itself in aesthetic representation, because such a response would have amounted to a repudiation of most of the enabling means of the cultural revival, of art in general. The problem was how, after rejecting civility's misleading beautiful surfaces, Germans could go on producing beautiful appearances in various forms of art. Germans wanted to place art and literature in the service of remaking cultural identity, but would doing so not then expose one's identity to the deceptions and instabilities of pleasing, sensuous appearances?

This fundamental impasse at the heart of German cultural revival—that a pure German interiority disallowed pleasing sensuous manifestation—did not stop most Germans from asserting that the highest form of a German identity was both best fashioned and best expressed in the beautiful surfaces of art and literature. But the contradiction between moral inwardness and corrupting sensuous form showed itself nonetheless. In the midst of the strongest German affirmations of the value of art there appeared odd, disruptive expressions of the anxiety that beautiful forms did not express the morality of Germans but undercut it.

In a 1751 essay defending the moral uses of art, the critic Johann Adolf Schlegel, for example, abruptly overturns his argument with the contradictory admission that the "vices" also "know how to use the beautiful arts to their advantage, especially those that have their origin in sensuousness." Wilhelm von Humboldt, in his famous essay "On the Limits of State Action" (1791–92), advocates the cultivation of "the aesthetic feeling, in virtue of which the sensuous is to us the veil of the spiritual." But in the same essay he makes a contradictory admission: "the feeling for the beautiful seems as if it would impair the purity of the moral will." In an unchecked appreciation of sensuous beauty, he says, "human pleasure becomes degraded to mere animal gratification, and taste disappears, or becomes distorted into unnatural directions." The same anxiety about the displacing and distorting power of beautiful forms is particularly striking in Schiller's *On the Aesthetic Education of Man in a Series of Letters* (1795), because it seemingly contradicts the work's purpose of establishing the crucial role of aesthetic appreciation in the formation of a moral personality. Schiller writes, assuming the voice of the ethical critic of art: "'it is by no means contrary to [the] nature [of art] to have, in the wrong hands, quite the opposite effect [from that of virtue. Art may put its] soul-seducing power at the service of error and injustice. Precisely because taste is always concerned with form, and never with content, it finally induces in the mind a dangerous tendency to neglect reality altogether and to sacrifice truth and reality to the alluring dress in which they appear. . . . How many men of talent . . . are not deflected by the seductive power of beauty from serious and strenuous effort?'" In his lectures on the history of aesthetics, given at the University of Berlin in the 1820s, Hegel begins with a gesture similar to Schiller's. He questions the conventional linking of morality to art. Art, Hegel says, may sometimes serve moral purposes, but it is just as likely to encourage moral "vacuity" and "frivolity." Art cannot be a trustworthy medium of morality, because it labors "under a defect of form." It may sometimes be subordinated to noble intentions, but we must always remember, Hegel writes, that "the means of art is deception." "For beauty," he explains, "has its being in appearance."[6]

In eighteenth-century art, a particular and dominant French style seemed to embody all the moral waywardness that Europeans—and especially Germans—feared. With its soft, intimate coloring, playful themes, and lightness of mood, the art of the Rococo seemed unencumbered by moral or intellectual content. Rococo focused attention on a "delicate play on the surface," and that emphasis on refined, pleasing surfaces linked it to French civility. In the words of one of its interpreters, Rococo was "essentially French in its grace, its gaiety, and its gentleness."[7] An art that foregrounded smoothly accessible surface impressions, unimpeded by semiotic content that pointed to putatively "deeper" moral lessons, allowed Rococo's many representations of sensuality "to speak," as Norman Bryson puts it, "directly to desire." Soft, sensual bodies resting on clouds or delicately portrayed nobles engaging in charming play in a garden offered, according to Bryson, a hallucinatory eroticism that could be apprehended by the viewer in the most immediate way, with the slightest effort: in a glance.[8]

The Rococo tableau's all-too-easy seduction of the eye activated all the period's sensitivities to the problem of moral slippage in art, and, in this period of intensified criticism of civility, European artists and writers sought a moral alternative, an art that disciplined the eye. What many turned to, including the German and French, who also followed their own specific concerns and anxieties, was the revival of classicism.

Positioning itself against Rococo as a style of transparent moral representation, neoclassicism gained popularity first in Italy, then spread to the rest of Europe. Neoclassical art revived ancient values of moral seriousness, civic grandeur, and a loftiness of personality, virtues that were to be portrayed in a reinforcing style of clarity, simplicity, and restraint. The playful and sensual bodies of Rococo were replaced by noble figures of warriors, lawgivers, and philosophers. Sobriety, abstinence, self-renunciation, and duty were moral lessons conveyed in deathbed scenes, in solemn scenes of oath-taking, and in acts of heroic patriotism.[9]

In theme and style, neoclassicism offered a first line of defense against the potential immorality of beautiful surfaces. As a second line of defense, reinforcing and underwriting its claims to moral and intellectual transparency, classicism entailed a further theory and prescription of aesthetic reception or recognition. Rendering moral themes, as Bryson puts it, in "an askesis"—a rigorous discipline—"of formalist description," the classicist artwork was intended to produce an effect in the viewer far different from that of the easily appropriated sensuality of Rococo. Functioning properly, the classicist artwork regulates the viewer's vision, so that, while the image is still pleasing to sight, that apprehension in sense perception is immediately sublated; it passes automatically into a rational contemplation of how beauty is constituted out of abstract principles. In a founding statement of this idea in Plato's *Symposium*, Socrates acknowledges that the appreciation of sensuous form draws one into an absorption in the beautiful surfaces of physicality, an absorption, he says, that would tie one to a love of the body. Beginning with the sight of the sensuous form, Socrates urges another response. In a favored metaphor of classicism, he advises the viewer to scan "beauty's wide horizons," for as one turns "toward the open sea of beauty," one comes to recognize other beauties—the beauty of law and institutions, the beauty of science, and ultimately the beauty of knowledge. The proper apprehension of the image necessarily passes, in other words, from a sensuous appreciation of physical, empirical particulars through increasingly mediated, abstract, and rational recognitions to reach "the very soul of beauty" in a philosophical contemplation of timeless, universal forms. This coming to aesthetic appreciation is represented as a *paideia,* an education of the soul; but, as Socrates makes clear as well, the *paideia* is a prophylaxis, the regulation of aesthetic response in order to forestall the possibility of moral corruption. When this "vision of the very soul of beauty" has been attained, Socrates says to Phaedrus and others, "you will never be seduced again by the dream of gold, of dress, of comely boys, or lads just ripening to manhood, you will care nothing for the beauties that used to take your breath away and kindle such longing in you." Sense perception turns into what Socrates calls "inward sight," a transformation that provides assurance that pleasing beautiful forms will no longer be able to deceive the viewer. "And remember," Socrates goes on, "that it is only when he discerns beauty itself through what makes it visible that a man will be quickened with the true, and not the seeming virtue—for it is virtue's true self that quickens him, not virtue's semblance."[10]

This classicist transformation of vision—the passage from sensuous appreciation to a rational contemplation of abstract universals—was often reiterated as the ideal aim of art in the classical revival of the eighteenth and early nineteenth centuries. For Winckelmann, a proper appreciation of beauty begins with the sight of a figure taken from nature, and it concludes when one sees in that figure "concepts which seek to transcend nature itself."[11] He repeats this view in his description of the statue in the Uffizi of Niobe (see fig. 1), whose "beauty is like an idea conceived without the aid of the senses."[12] According to Hugh Honour, Goethe made this idea of classicist transformation the keystone of his understanding of art. "The artist," Honour explains, "should begin by studying the differences between individuals and then by a leap of imagination subsume each individual in one act of vision or intuitive synthesis and, thus, rising from abstraction to abstraction, finally represent the type or universal seen in its indivisible harmony and purity *sub specie aeternitatis.*"[13]

The prophylactic function of the *paideia* of classicist vision was also frequently reiterated. Speaking still of the *Niobe,* Winckelmann says that its

Fig. 1. *Niobe with Her Youngest Daughter.* Uffizi, Florence, Italy. Copyright Alinari/Art Resource, New York.

creator "ventured into the kingdom of incorporeal forms . . . he became a creator of pure spirits and heavenly souls, which, exciting no desire of the sense, produced a contemplative . . . consideration of beauty of every kind" (*H*, 3:136). Humboldt puts the same point more succinctly when he says in a letter to Goethe that art should attain "a pure aesthetic pleasure without desire."[14] The most influential eighteenth-century sculptor of neoclassicism, the Italian Antonio Canova (in words imputed to him), shares this sentiment:

> The nude, when it is pure . . . with exquisite beauty, takes us away from moral perturbations and transports us to those early days of blessed innocence: all the more so because it comes to us as a spiritual and understood thing, and lifts our soul to the contemplation of divine things, which since they cannot be made manifest to the sense by their spirituality can only be indicated to us by excellence of forms, to kindle us with their beauty and detach us from the imperfect and fleeting things of this earth.[15]

When Canova refers to "exquisite beauty" transporting us to "those early days of blessed innocence" during which our souls perceive a divine image, he is invoking another trope of classicism, one that shows that *paideia*, the education of the soul, is not just a progression but also a return. In the ultimate state of aesthetic recognition the viewer comes to see again a primordial rational form, unchanging in its perfection and given in the mind of God. Winckelmann uses this same trope of a return to the vision of original perfection when he says that ideal "beauty is like an essence extracted from matter by fire; it seeks to beget unto itself a creature formed after the likeness of the first rational being designed in the mind of the Divinity" (*H*, 2:200). In this return to a vision of an *Ur*-rational form, the viewer has developed through time to reach a condition that frees the viewer from temporality. In the presence of properly perceived classical art the viewer attains the "fullness of time" and comes to dwell among abstract, unchanging universal concepts.[16]

For classicist aesthetic recognition to operate properly, a visual circuit must be established in which the viewer cannot help but see the universal moral content and rational nobility of the artwork. Guided by the artwork, this aesthetic seeing constitutes or confirms the viewer's own sense of rational and moral integrity; in the presence of the classicist artwork, seeing it the way it demands, the viewer feels as well the presence of a serene moral reason.[17] Winckelmann's description of the beauty of the object—"the forms of such a figure are simple and flowing, and various in their unity, and for this reason they are harmonious" (*H*, 2:200)—constitutes an equivalent state of mind in the viewer: "Just as the perception and enjoyment of ourselves and true pleasures are to be achieved with peace of mind and body, the perception and enjoyment of beauty must be delicate and gentle, coming like a mild dew, rather than a sudden downpour of rain."[18]

When the object of perception is a flowing harmony of signified and signifier or content and form, the process by which the viewing subjectivity is formed is also one of a flowing, seemingly natural harmonization. But the apparent naturalness of this harmonization should not obscure the fact that the process is one of careful regulation—a regulation to forestall the potential deflections of sensory experience. Paradoxical as it may seem for a consciousness concerned with appreciating sensuous surfaces, classicist subjectivity might still be characterized as ultimately defined by its ability to resist the influences of the changing, multitudinous physicality of the material world in order to attain a state of a totally rational self-possession. The overcoming of materiality is represented by different tropes—as a short-circuiting of desire or as the transcendence of temporality. Another characteristic trope of the classicist subject's attainment of rational self-possession against the materiality of the world is found in Winckelmann's description of the *Laocoön* in the Vatican, a description that made Winckelmann famous and was repeated mantralike by Germans for the next hundred years.[19] The figure of Laocoön (see fig. 2), ensnared by a crushing and biting serpent, experiences excruciating pain. But although the pain seems to ripple through the muscular body, it is never registered, Winckelmann says, "with violence either in the face or in a gesture." The priest suppresses his agony—at most, the stomach muscles contract—and that stoic suppression of facial expression and gesture is enough to convey an overall impression of "noble simplicity and still grandeur."[20]

According to Winckelmann, the imperative of signifying serene self-possession is so strong in ancient art that, even in representations of the human body in situations of extreme pain and constraint, the artist will still manage to convey a sense of repose. The *Laocoön* is still inscribed with the features of rational subjectivity, but whereas in the descriptions we have just considered, that subjectivity was of a piece with the unified harmony of the figure's form and seemed to flow from it, in the case of the *Laocoön* the attainment of rational subjectivity appears as an *agon*, a hard-fought struggle against the physicality of the body. When the aesthetic figure is the body at rest or ease, it is pleasing to the viewer, whose vision is then gently, almost unnoticeably regulated to constitute the viewer as a rational subject. But when the represented figure is in pain and arouses unsettled feelings in the viewer, rational subjectivity becomes more clearly an exertion of regulative will. Here, because the figure must establish rational form over and against the impressions of overtly external and coercive stimuli, classicist identity comes about according to a model of domination and self-mastery.

Fig. 2. *Laocoön*. Vatican Museums, Vatican State. Copyright Alinari / Art Resource, New York.

This more aggressive version of subjectivity also appears in an array of classicist writings. Schiller's plan for aesthetic education as a program for creating a rational, harmonious self is, for example, explicitly represented as an *agon,* a conflict against the entropic physicality of a material world that "flatters our senses in immediate sensation" and "can manipulate our susceptible and labile psyche." Art, for Schiller, is an exercise in mastery over materiality: "Here then resides the secret of the master in any art: *that he can make his form* consume his material; and the more pretentious, the more seductive this material is in itself, the more it seeks to impose itself upon us . . . then the more triumphant the art which forces it back and asserts its own kind of dominion over him." And this classicist artwork, marked by rational freedom and power, inscribes the same qualities in those who receive it: a "lofty equanimity and freedom of the spirit, combined with power and vigour, is the mood in which a genuine work of art should release us, and there is no more certain touchstone of true aesthetic excellence."[21]

This aspect of classicist rational subjectivity—that it fashions itself as a powerful mastery over external threats—suggests one further aspect of classicism that has been much commented on by recent interpreters, namely, that classicism results in a rigid system of gender differentiation. George Mosse has argued that ever since Winckelmann's time, his ideal of beauty as a noble, soulful stillness suggesting rational control and emanating from the muscular male body has served as the model for Western masculinity, a model that precluded women from being identified with qualities of rational control and endurance.[22] A complex suppression of the feminine, according to Alex Potts, is implied in Winckelmann's focus on masculine beauty.[23] In the French neoclassicism of the last years of the old regime the glorification of masculinity was especially apparent in the paintings of Jacques-Louis David, and his images of masculine power and gender separation were at one with those of Jacobin civic republicanism.[24]

DISARTICULATION

Ideally the classicist self is a subjectivity defined by its sense of self-sufficient rational plentitude, the feeling of rational self-possession, of being in control of oneself because one's physical responses to external circumstances have been rationally mastered. The classicist subject regulates and overcomes the self's natural passivity before changing sensory experience, whether that experience is in the form of pleasure or pain. The mastery of the classicist subject also overcomes the physicality of the external world in that it transcends the vicissitudes of time when it attains its highest state in a rational appreciation of eternal principles of beauty. Ideologically, the stability of classicist subjectivity is reinforced by overlapping discourses of gender differentiation, cultural nationalism in Germany, and republican politics in France. All these come together to produce what should have been the most stable and most self-assured of identities, one represented in Winckelmann's suffering but stoic Laocoön or in the classical heroes of David's paintings.

But although the classicist self was often projected in these triumphalist modes, it was surprisingly difficult for this subject to enact itself in the prescribed manner. From the beginning, classicist subjectivity was characterized by contradictions, self-generated impediments, and seemingly inevitable backsliding. The most grandiose moment of classical subjectivity—its achievement of complete self-mastery in the regulation of sensation and the overcoming of time—was, for example, often experienced not just as an apotheosis but also as an affliction.

Even as German writers raised up this monumental self, they also acknowledged how their own creaturely selves failed to live up to it, a feeling registered in the widely held view that Greek accomplishments would never be duplicated. And if their own, German accomplishments were inevitably inadequate to classical exemplars, then the Germans would be at best living in a shadow of greatness or in an era of decadence when greatness was no longer possible. Winckelmann's call to imitate the Greeks becomes, from this perspective, an impossible, enervating burden. E. M. Butler's study of Germany's adoration of Greece emphasizes this theme of debilitating latecoming as a consequence of the Greek "tyranny" over Germany. In his last years, Goethe, according to Butler, suffered from a sense of failure in his hope of becoming Germany's Homer, the writer, that is, of a foundational national epic, which Goethe thought necessary for the cultural revival of his country.[25] Unaware of Goethe's self-doubts, Schiller suffered from his own sense of not living up to the perceived classical greatness of Goethe's accomplishments, a concern that Thomas Mann, expressing yet further fears of latecoming, made into a short story.[26]

The rational regulation of the senses and the overcoming of time also produced another unintended complication. As commentators have often noted, the apparently serene self-sufficiency of the classical figure, manifested in its nobility and stillness, particularly in sculpture, summoned up connotations not just of vigor and life but also of coldness and death. Winckelmann himself acknowledges that this was how the work of the Renaissance's greatest imitator of the Greeks, Raphael, was often perceived (*H*, 2:257). For Romantics especially, the foregrounding of a sense of control in classicist representations conveyed an impression of lifelessness.[27] The colorless contour inscribed in marble that Winckelmann considered the ultimate source of beauty is to the modern commentator Mario Praz "like a trace in the soil of a corpse that has wasted away."[28] In a poem of 1816, Heine, rebelling against what he felt to be an overbearing classicist legacy, associates cold marble with death and death with Goethe—thereby conflating the theme of morbid classical rigidity with Heine's anxieties about his own latecoming.[29] Goethe's contribution to a retrospective volume on Winckelmann celebrates Winckelmann's aesthetics and their basis in a Greece populated by beautiful young men appreciative of beauty, a place where "feeling and reflection were not yet fragmented." In speaking of Winckelmann's life, Goethe makes no mention of his death at the hands of a thief; he seeks to recover Winckelmann's positive spirit; yet in speaking of Greek art he cannot help but invoke the connection between classicism and death—a connection that is at once noted and disavowed by declaring it hygienic: "we can detect, not only in the supreme moment of enjoyment but also in the darkest moment of self-sacrifice—or even extinction—an indestructible health."[30]

The cold rigidity of classicism was identified with death; yet, paradoxically, the same classicist figures produced the opposite effect: a sense of a living sensuality, so intense that it escaped reason's regulation of sense perception. Where one nineteenth-century critic saw in Canova's *Cupid and Psyche* group in Rome all the passion of the arms of a windmill, Gustave Flaubert is overcome with erotic fascination: "I looked at nothing in the rest of the gallery: I came back to it several times, and the first time I kissed, under her arms, the swooning woman who reaches out towards her long marble arms. And the foot! The profile! May I be pardoned for it: it was my first sensual kiss in a long time. It was something more: I kissed beauty itself."[31]

Notwithstanding the often-repeated claim that classicist art produced a contemplative appreciation of timeless rational principles of beauty, its works were often accused of displaying the same dissolute sensuality as that of Rococo art. As Norman Bryson points out, when neoclassicist art first began to establish itself in France in the 1760s and 1770s, it appeared to many as scarcely less "decadent" than the Rococo art that was its putative antithesis, particularly as it was introduced under the patronage of the king's mistress, the notorious Madame Du Barry. Connected to this figure of bad reputation, the new style, Bryson concludes, was "discredited as the frivolous style of expensive mistresses."[32] In even the most politically didactic and radical republican period of the French Revolution, neoclassicism was never able to reconcile its abstract concept of ideal beauty with "images redolent with the pleasure of looking at a beautiful body," a point that Potts makes in his analysis of the sensual androgynous figure of David's unfinished painting of the martyred boy Bara. According to Hugh Honour, by the Napoleonic period neoclassicist art had overtly revived in mood and theme all the erotic sensuality it had theoretically repudiated.[33]

Classicism thus generated seemingly opposite responses of morbidity and excessive sensuality, both of which undercut claims to rational subjectivity. Perhaps most strangely, these opposing states could come together in scenes of sadomasochism. Heine, for example, offered this derisive rewriting of Winckelmann's by-then-canonical response to the *Laocoön:*

> Now come and embrace me sweetly,
> You beautiful bundle of charms;
> Entwine me supply, featly,
> With body and feet and arms!
>
> She has coiled and twisted around me
> Her beautiful sinuous shape—
> Me, the most blest of Laocoöns,
> She, the most wonderful snake.[34]

When the cold rigor of classicism and its intense sensuality were simultaneously foregrounded, the effect was a psychologically unsettling sense of perverse obsession. As Mario Praz shrewdly notes, classicist description oscillated between the Platonic and the fetishistic.[35] And this fetishistic aspect undercut as well an autonomous, rational subjectivity, as Baudelaire recognized when he condemned classicism in his essay "The Pagan School" (1852): "His [the classicist connoisseur's] soul, constantly excited and unappeased, goes about the world . . . like a prostitute crying: Plastic! Plastic! The plastic . . . has poisoned him and yet he can live only by this poison. He has banished reason from his heart; and as a just punishment reason refused to return to him. . . . Infatuated with his tiring dream, he will want to infatuate and tire others with it." Baudelaire concluded that in the case of classicism, art had no justification for its own sake: "The danger is so great that I excuse the suppression of the object."[36]

General and critical reception of classicism was thus often at odds with the claims of classicist subjectivity to a serene rational plenitude. The problems of classicism in projecting rational subjectivity were not the result of external obstacles or events but of some weakness in classicism itself, and throughout its history, even in the foundational work of Winckelmann. What seems to change is not classicism's strange, afflicted character but the willingness, on the part of classicists, to acknowledge it, to foreground its tendency to undercut the very identity it was designed to project. This deconstructive recognition is particularly evident and given systematic form in Germany, in part, I suspect, because Germans more than any other people counted on a classicist subjectivity to provide one of the foundations of a new national culture. They seemed to experience the strangeness of classicism more intensely than others, an intensity that seems to go along with an odd fact in the history of European classicism. Commentators have noted that unlike admirers of classicism in Britain and France, the first great German admirers of classicism—including Winckelmann, Lessing, Goethe, Schiller, Friedrich Schlegel before he turned Catholic, Humboldt, and Hegel—never showed any interest in actually visiting Greece itself.

They in fact avoided, even refused, to go. And they justified—or failed to justify—their refusals with enigmatic responses and silence. As Goethe, for example, wrote to a friend, after turning down an invitation to visit Greece while he was in Italy: "Once one takes it upon oneself to go into the world and enters into close interaction with it, one has to be careful not to be swept away in a trance, or even to go mad. I am not able to speak a single word at this moment."[37] The realization of Goethe's fears did not require a visit to Greece itself, but could take place simply in the presence of the beautiful classical object.

WINCKELMANN: AESTHETIC RECOGNITION
AND DEFLECTION

Winckelmann's *Reflections on the Imitation of Greek Works in Painting and Sculpture* (1755) and his later *History of Ancient Art* (1764) achieved literary success throughout Europe. According to Diderot, French neo-classicism began in earnest when David brought back from Rome the influence of Winckelmann.[38] Winckelmann's writings were translated into French during the last decades of the old regime and republished during the French Revolution as a direct result of public debates in the Legislative Assembly. Napoleon reputedly kept a copy of the *History of Ancient Art* displayed on a table in an antechamber.[39]

That Winckelmann was welcomed by the French seems natural enough given the conjunction of values described above. His writings even appeared to endorse a connection to the radical republicanism of the Jacobins, as he asserts in his *History* that great art could flourish in Greece only during the era of the political freedom of the Greek republics.[40] But despite being made a source for French refashionings of cultural identity, Winckelmann throughout his life loathed the French, identifying them as the people of a lying decadent civility. French sensibility made the French precisely the modern people least capable of imitating Greek antiquity; the two, he said in a letter to a friend, "contradict each other."[41]

Winckelmann's German contemporaries believed that he had directed his writings to them, calling them to the special German destiny of imitating the Greeks.[42] As Friedrich Schlegel wrote in *The Athenaeum:* "The first among us who . . . recognized and announced the original image [*Urbild*] of fulfilled humanity in the form of art and antiquity was the holy Winckelmann." It was the mission of the Germans to imitate the Greeks and thereby become the people of the modern world who could attain full humanity. This humanist project, by way of imitating the Greeks, was at the heart of Wilhelm von Humboldt's conception of *Bildung*, a conception that became the basis of the reform of the German *Gymnasium* and university.

In a memorial volume entitled *Winckelmann and His Century,* Goethe's contribution summed up Winckelmann's importance for German intellectuals: "We learn nothing reading Winckelmann, we become something."[43]

Winckelmann's *Thoughts on the Imitation of the Painting and Sculpture of the Greeks,* with its arresting and often-repeated characterization of the *Laocoön,* first earned him recognition throughout Europe; but his *History of Ancient Art* was the more substantial and important study. It presents a comprehensive view of the emergence and decline of ancient Greek art, one that both demonstrates classicist subjectivity at work and seeks to instill in the prospective viewer of classical art the proper path to aesthetic recognition. Winckelmann thus asserts and reasserts the function of art in the self's *paideia,* that is, how classicist art should lead the viewer to rational subjectivity. But while he repeatedly asserts that this is art's purpose, he also repeatedly shows something else at work, the deflection of the viewer from classicism's ideal closed circuit of sensuous perception and rational recognition. This insistent swerving away from ideal subjectivity is evident not just in the contradictory aesthetic responses that Winckelmann actually shows himself experiencing but also in a striking slippage in rhetoric. As he reiterates the key metaphor that is to establish a stable classicist subjectivity, that metaphor slips into other meanings that undo the possibility of stability.

Throughout the *History* Winckelmann states the key assumption of classicist aesthetics and subjectivity, namely, to master and overcome materiality in abstract appreciation: "For the mind . . . has an innate tendency and desire to rise above matter into the spiritual sphere of conceptions, and its true enjoyment is in the production of new and refined ideas" (*H,* 2:210). A rational mind produces art that reflects and enhances the mind's rationality; matter must be fashioned in a way that will engage the mind's *paideia.* Such art, according to Winckelmann, displays and furthers its rationality in a characteristic manner. "Art," as Winckelmann puts it, "expresses her own peculiar nature only in stillness." Rational subjectivity shows itself in a condition of thoughtfulness that is represented phenomenally as a condition of calm, in which the figure's expression is serene and its gestures are restrained. Winckelmann uses a particular image to concretize this association of rationality, equanimity, and stillness; the serene surface of the beautiful figure, he writes, is like the surface of the sea. "Stillness," he says "is the state most appropriate to beauty, just as it is to the sea" (*H,* 2:246). In the "beautiful style" of Greek art, "the soul manifested itself only, as it were, beneath a still surface of water, and never burst impetuously forth."[44]

The stillness of the figure, expressing and emphasizing the figure's harmony and simplicity, allows the figure to be easily grasped as a unity. The ease with which the viewer rationally apprehends the still figure does not mean that the work lacks complexity or interest; rather, it points to the directness and efficiency of classicism's epistemological circuit: in a glance, the mind of the viewer fully recognizes the rational idea in the figure's still form, and that recognition directly ennobles the mind. Ideal beauty, Winckelmann says, "is not more strictly circumscribed, nor does it lose any of its greatness because the mind can survey and measure it with a glance, and comprehend and embrace it in a single idea; but the very readiness with which it may be embraced places it before us in its true greatness, and the mind is enlarged, and likewise elevated by comprehension of it." If the viewer has to strain at an appreciation of the artwork, the very necessity of such effort suggests that the work is of a diminished quality: "Everything which we must consider in separate pieces or which we cannot survey at once . . . loses thereby some measure of its greatness" (*H*, 2:200).

The simple, rational unity of the still figure presents itself without mediation—all at once and in a glance—to the mind's eye; and that vision of the object effortlessly carries the mind to the rational appreciation of timeless universal principles that classicism holds as the telos of *paideia*. This, at least, is how aesthetic perception and recognition should operate as a direct epistemological circuit; but what is curious about Winckelmann's prescriptions is that at the same time he asserts them, he undercuts them in his examples and elaborations. And he does so using the same imagery: the metaphor originally meant to establish a proper aesthetic recognition thus ends up signifying the impossibility of such a recognition's ever coming into being.

Ideal beauty, Winckelmann argues at one point, is found in beautiful male youth, which presents itself in the unified simplicity of the still form.[45] But this still form, he proceeds to tell us, turns out to be something of an illusion, an effect ultimately of the fact that one sees it from a distance. Winckelmann suggests in another trope of the sea that the still surface is not quite what it appears to be: "The forms of beautiful youth resemble the unity of the surface of the sea, which at some distance appears smooth and still, like a mirror, although constantly in motion with its heaving swell" (*H*, 2:202). Thus stillness and motion, two supposedly mutually exclusive states, are connected, stillness being a paradoxical illusion given by one's distance from the flowing object. Moreover, to identify this now-paradoxical relation between the viewer and the object viewed, Winckelmann has also implicitly refocused the viewer's vision: the original, immediate glance of reason must have passed into a firmer kind of looking, into a steadier, analytic gaze that has clarified as moving what initially was perceived as still.

Elsewhere in the *History*, Winckelmann says more explicitly that what he has first privileged as an initial and fully adequate form of seeing—the glance—is not in fact one of a stabilizing rationality; rather, the glance immediately calls up in the viewer a second, supplementary kind of vision. Here the still form, which is at the same time constant mobility, unsettles the initial glance and locks it into a studying gaze. Winckelmann says all this using yet another analogy of looking at the sea: "The first view of beautiful statues is, to him who possesses sensibility, like the first glance over the open sea; we gaze on it bewildered, and with undistinguishing eyes, but after we have contemplated it repeatedly the soul becomes more tranquil and the eye more quiet, and capable of separating the whole into its particulars" (*H*, 2:154).

The initial glance proves inadequate to the beautiful object, and to attain the required state of ideal contemplation of the object, to attain rational mastery over what it sees, the glance must pass into another way of looking. But this second, supplementary gaze, even if it might attain the prescribed aim of rationally seeing a stable object, has also in a sense compromised the object. For Winckelmann has now prescribed that the analytic eye looks at the ideal beautiful object in precisely the way he has earlier described as the mark of defective beauty—namely, that the eye should pass from the whole to the parts.[46]

Winckelmann's shift from the glance to the gaze emphasizes his difficulty in assuming the rational subjectivity of the viewing mind. He would like to assume that the mind has an inbuilt, natural tendency to see conceptually, to move automatically from sense perception to the abstract ideas that underlie it. The "naturalness" of this quality is confirmed in the viewer's ability to grasp the rationality of the sensuous object in a "glance." But as the object confuses the glance, Winckelmann must give up this assumption of a natural harmonization of rational cognition and sense perception and move to the other possible explanation of how the classicist subject is related to the external world. Winckelmann moves from the harmonization model of classicist subjectivity to the agonistic model, in which a rational seeing becomes a struggle of the mind to master sensory stimuli.

This shift from the naturalistic glance to the masterful gaze does not, however, stop the slippage of subjectivity. As the analytic gaze focuses on the parts of the beautiful object, what especially attracts its attention, as the source of the beauty of those parts, is their undulating lines. The gaze follows the shape of a line, which, as it flows, undergoes imperceptible shifts, until the gaze, originally focused on distinguishing between parts, is no longer able to do so: "From this great unity of youthful forms [of the ellipses that form the ideal body], their limits flow imperceptibly one into another, and the precise point of height of many, and the line which bounds them cannot be accurately determined. This is the reason why the delineation of a youthful body, in which everything is and is yet to come, appears and yet does not appear, is more difficult than that of an adult or aged figure" (*H,* 2:203). The undulating line, produced by the focused gaze, makes the outline of the beautiful figure in a crucial sense indeterminate, and this indeterminacy has a decentering effect on artistic production. Contrary to Winckelmann's injunction that Germans should imitate the Greeks, the undulating line renders imitation impossible in the fullest sense, an impossibility represented in yet another image of the sea. "The artist may admire in the outlines of this body [the *Belvedere Torso* (see fig. 3)] the perpetual flowing of one form into another, and the undulating lines which rise and fall like waves, and become swallowed up in one another. He will find that no copyist can be sure of correctness, since the undulating movement which he thinks he is following turns imperceptibly away, and leads both the hand and the eye astray by taking another direction" (*H,* 4:265).

Ideally inscribed as the stillness of the figure, a unified image of rational subjectivity is one that is immediately recognized in a glance by the viewer, who is then also constructed or confirmed as a rational subjectivity. This is Winckelmann's initial model of a harmonious aesthetic recognition, which, as he shows it at work, keeps sliding into its opposite—into demonstrations of destabilizing ambiguities in the beautiful image or figure. The viewer glimpses rational unity in a still figure, but only at a distance. And even that still beauty confuses one's vision, forces it to look more intently so that one sees the swelling motion beneath the stillness, now recognized as illusory. This gaze, a compensatory response that seeks to draw out the stability still supposedly inherent in the figure after vision has been unsettled, is decentered only further as it follows the figure's undulating lines. For the constant subtle shifting of those lines makes impossible the cultural imperative of imitation. Classicist subjectivity requires that aesthetic recognition see the presence of reason in ideal beauty, and that means it must see a stable image; hence the first requirement that the figure show stillness in expression and gesture. But Winckelmann's vision keeps encountering not stable forms but ambiguities that deflect the viewer's seeing from attaining rational vision and that lead the viewer away from rational subjectivity.

Strangely enough, although the complete figure is to present an image of stillness and stability, that unified image is ultimately constructed out of a blurring of surfaces, out of liminal meetings of conventionally opposed states. The ideal beauty of the youthful male body is marked by a line that reflects what "is and is yet to come." It stands, as Winckelmann puts it, "suspended between growth and maturity" (*H,* 2:203); it is a "combination uniting the robustness of mature years with the joyousness of youth" (*H,*

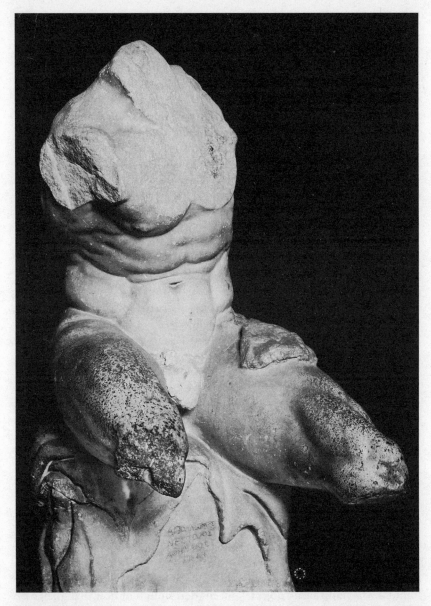

Fig. 3. *Belvedere Torso* (front view). Vatican Museums, Vatican State. Copyright Alinari/Art Resource, New York.

2:222). Beauty emerges out of a condition of equivocal temporality that produces not a clearly etched figure but an ambiguous flowing line.[47] The ambiguity of that line—its combination of softness and rigor—also suggests to Winckelmann another constitutive ambiguity, the liminal meeting of opposing gender characteristics: "This ideal [of achieved beauty] consists in the incorporation of the forms of prolonged youth in the female sex with the masculine forms of a beautiful young man, which they [the artists] consequently make plumper, rounder, and softer" (*H*, 2:208). The blending of the masculine and the feminine is found not just, as one might expect, in the representation of divinities of pleasure, such as Bacchus, whose face "exhibits an indescribable blending of male and female beautiful youth, and a conformation intermediate between the two sexes."[48]

More surprisingly, the ambiguity of gender is constitutive as well of figures that are usually perceived as masculine figures of power; the *Apollo Belvedere*, for example, unites "the strength of adult years" with "the soft form of the most beautiful springtime of youth" (*H*, 2:215), a blending which results in a face that leaves "the sex doubtful." The same constitutive ambiguity of gender is evident in the representation of Greek heroes. Achilles is said to have "from the charms of his face, assisted by female dress, lived undetected with the daughters of Lycomedes, as their companion" (*H*, 2:228). "Beauty of the same equivocal kind" is found in the story of Theseus, who, arriving in Athens dressed in a long robe, was thought by workmen in the temple of Apollo to be a "beautiful virgin" (*H*, 2:229).

The uncertainty of gender in ideal beauty does not result in clear, rationally regulated perception. The distinct form seemingly captured in a rational glance dissolves into the fluctuating perception of a discerning gaze that follows the flowing lines of a figure. And this gaze is dependent not just on the characteristics of the figure but also on the angle of vision.

The conventional, fully rational gaze of idealist aesthetics assumes, as Bryson has noted, that it extends as a geometrical perspective from an ideal objective standpoint, behind the retina, from something like a Cartesian *cogito*. The object is focused at the center of the far side of a cone of light emanating from the eye—a focusing that supposedly guarantees a view of how the object actually appears in nature. This kind of centering of the object is implied in Winckelmann's initial association of the rational glance that all at once recognizes ideal, rational beauty (which is presumed to be found in the naturalistic object); but his description of how that glance of the whole must pass into a gaze at the parts and then into a gaze at undulating lines implicitly repudiates a single naturalistic perspective. For the indeterminacies of the undulating line ensure that what one sees changes with the position one sees from.[49] The result, as Winckelmann tells us in his description of the figure of Telephus in a frieze, is a further compounding of uncertainty: to the inherent ambiguity of the line is added the ambiguity that results from the position of the viewer: "The face of the young hero [Telephus] is perfectly feminine, when looked at from below upwards; but viewed from above downwards, it has something masculine blended with it" (*H*, 2:229).

Winckelmann's remarkable demonstration of the constitutive ambiguities of beauty must modify the increasingly conventional view that he in particular and classicism in general produced reified images of powerful masculinity that have come to serve as models of subjectivity, at least in the case of Germany. Although he and other classicists often made such assertions, what they just as frequently showed in their writings and in their art was a different process at work—that the most rigorous form of male subjectivity is strangely predicated on ambiguities that also seem on the verge of undoing that subjectivity. And this is a tension that is inscribed both on the artwork and in the vision of the viewer. Thus as Winckelmann reflects on the gender ambiguities that constitute an object of ideal beauty, he is led to a striking speculation: that not the strong virile male but its opposite is the true source of classical art. He suggests that forms like Apollo and Bacchus may have been derived from the figures of eunuchs, "those equivocal beauties," as he says, repeating a favored phrase, who combined "masculine characteristics" with the "softness of the female sex."[50]

There is a powerful paradox in Winckelmann's characterization of ideal beauty in the figure of the youthful male. The image of stable rational form can sometimes be captured by a glance from a distance, but when studied up close by the gaze, the clarity and stability of the natural form give way to ambiguous undulating lines that suggest uncertainties of age and gender. In the presence of the ideal beautiful form, the viewer should be brought to a rational recognition of eternal and universal principles of beauty. Ideal beauty, in other words, should automatically engage the soul's *paideia*. But the close-up recognition of ambiguous surfaces produces a different result: it engages not a rational recognition but a diversion into a meditative pleasure that guides the mind to other kinds of seeing. Discussing the ambiguity of statues of Greek gods, which are represented as youths on the threshold of maturity, Winckelmann wants to conclude that this representation is a way of illustrating a higher order, a principle of eternity—"it was conformable," he says, "to their [the ancients'] idea of the immutability of the godlike nature." But instead of following the path of the *paideia* to pure contemplation, Winckelmann allows himself to be deflected onto another path, as he puts it: "and a beautiful youthful form in their deities awakened tenderness and love, transporting the soul into the sweet dream of rapture, in which human happiness . . . consists" (*H*, 2:210–211).

In a couple of instances Winckelmann shows us what is entailed in this "sweet dream of rapture" to which he is transported. It causes him to hallucinate. He tells us that his imagination has several times plunged him into a "reverie" of being back in Greece at its most beautiful: "I imagine myself, in fact, appearing in the Olympic Stadium, where I seem to see countless statues of young, manly heroes, and two-horse and four-horse chariots of bronze, with the figures of the victors erect here on, and other wonders of art" (*H,* 2:190).

In his description of the *Apollo Belvedere* (see fig. 4), Winckelmann first presents the statue as the instigation of the soul's *paideia.* He starts to describe the statue's beauty, mentioning in particular the ambiguous temporality that produces it: "An eternal spring, as in the happy fields of Elysium, clothes with the charms of youth the graceful manliness of ripened years, and plays with softness and tenderness about the proud shape of his limbs." He then eloquently asserts that this sight of perfect beauty should elevate the viewer, lifting the observing mind up to a pure and universal contemplation. "Let your spirit penetrate into the kingdom of incorporeal beauties, and strive to become a creation of a heavenly nature, in order that your mind may be filled with beauties that are elevated above nature; for there is nothing mortal here, nothing human necessities require" (*H,* 4:312–313, translation modified).

But even as he prescribes the ideal passage into contemplation, his description of the figure swerves onto a deflected path. Winckelmann now ecstatically personifies the statue, investing it with its own vision: "His lofty look, filled with the consciousness of power, seems to rise far above his victory and to gaze into infinity." And this seeing deity is then endowed with life, power, and sensuality: "scorn sits up on his lips, and his nostrils are swelling with suppressed anger . . . his eye is full of sweetness as when the Muses gathered around him seeking to embrace him." As Winckelmann thus describes the figure, the implied relationship between the viewer and the figure is reversed; rather than the form's "spirit," as Winckelmann put it, carrying the mind "into the kingdom of incorporeal beauties," the personified god—"his lofty look, filled with consciousness of power"—takes possession of the viewer. Winckelmann writes: "In the presence of this miracle of art I forget all else. . . . My breast seems to enlarge and swell with reverence, like the breasts of those who were filled with the spirit of prophecy; and I feel myself transported to Delos and into the Lycean groves—places which Apollo honored by his presence—for my image seems to receive life and motion, like the beautiful creation Pygmalion. How is it possible for one to paint and describe it?" (*H,* 4:313).

Looking upon the work of art does not produce a rational subjectivity, which is then presumed to be the culmination and regulation of all seeing. Seeing ideal beauty yields instead a strange displacement and dispossession of self, a hallucination in which Winckelmann comes to see himself

Fig. 4. *Apollo Belvedere.* Roman marble copy of a Greek original, fourth century B.C.E. Museo Pio Clementino, Vatican Museums, Vatican State. Copyright Alinari/Art Resource, New York.

seeing under the eyes of Apollo, a point of view that makes him feel physically transported back into ancient Greece. In this phantasmatic dislocation of ideal seeing, the visual field is not rationally centered by Winckelmann's eye; on the contrary, what he sees is felt to be subsumed and reoriented into a field of vision that seems to emanate from the beautiful object.[51] And when Winckelmann sees himself seeing from this position as the image in the eye of another, he has no independent subjectivity; he is the creation and servant of another, and this is a condition that because of its remarkable sensation of intensity and submission cannot be represented, cannot be rationally regulated and imitated.

Deconstructing tensions in Winckelmann's *History* are found in a further way, one that concerns what Alex Potts calls Winckelmann's innovative contribution to the writing of art history. Classicizing histories of the ancient period before and in Winckelmann's time regarded the development of a classical tradition of art as a finite ascension, a path from an archaic roughness to a perfection of form that accurately reproduces the natural object. When classical art attains a final ideal form, it comes to a close, having attained "the fullness of time"; purveyors of the fulfilled ideal are now expected to reproduce it. Winckelmann adds to this classicist temporality a stage that gets history moving again. The period of accomplished ideal art is inevitably followed by a period of decline, when the perfected style becomes increasingly decadent; in the case of classicism, increasingly refined, ornate, and decorative.[52]

The development of ancient art, for Winckelmann, is an arc whose uppermost curve defines a period of achieved style that appears in two successive forms: first a grand or "high classic style" of complete austerity, and subsequently a "late classic beautiful style" that is more refined, gracious, and sensuous. The beautiful style then slopes into a decline marked by excessive refinement and sensuality. These styles are homologously coordinated with contemporaneous cultural phenomena and with the liberty of the Greek republics. The exemplary artist of the grand style, Phidias, is associated with Aeschylus and Pindar; the sculptor of the beautiful period, Praxiteles, with Xenophon and Plato.[53]

What is striking about Winckelmann's periodization is how little it corresponds to his reactions to specific works of art. As Potts has observed, Winckelmann's period of an austere grand style is almost devoid of examples. Winckelmann is able to point to only a couple of artworks in the high or grand style, the statues of Niobe (see fig. 1) and Athena.[54] And although he admires those works, particularly the statue of Niobe, his response to them does not differ from his response to art of the later and putatively decadent periods of ancient history. Indeed, some of Winckelmann's most ecstatic descriptions are of figures that he believes were created in periods when Greece had lost its independence and dignity. The *Laocoön,* he thinks, was made in the time of Alexander the Great, when the Greeks had surrendered themselves to "indolence and love of pleasure" (*H,* 4:226, 228). Winckelmann's comments on the decentering sensuousness of the undulating line stem mainly from an analysis of the *Belvedere Torso,* which was fashioned when Rome had come to dominate Greece. The complete submission of autonomous subjectivity in the beautiful hallucinatory phantasy induced by Winckelmann's contemplation of the *Apollo Belvedere* is brought on by a work that appeared during the reign of Nero, an emperor conventionally identified with one of Rome's worst periods of decadence and who had an "insatiable craving" for Greek statues (*H,* 4:312). Although Winckelmann says that the greatest art should have appeared at the height of ancient Greece's political liberty and cultural activity, what he shows is that the works that most move him appeared in periods of Greece's political domination by outsiders and of its putative cultural decadence.

Winckelmann wants to establish rational subjectivity as a sealed circuit of recognition, signification, and history. The rational subject comes into being because it sees itself inscribed in the beautiful figures that appear in periods of healthy political freedom. But what Winckelmann demonstrates is that the showing forth of beauty defeats the attainment of rational subjectivity. The beautiful figure decenters and disorganizes the viewing self, diverts it away from the telos of the *paideia;* and this deflection is produced by works associated with periods identified as ones of general cultural decadence and political submission. For most of the eighteenth and nineteenth centuries, writers would reiterate what Winckelmann says; but in the latter part of the nineteenth century, paradoxically at a time when German power and unity was at its height, some Germans moved to an explicit recognition of what Winckelmann shows: that subjectivity collapses before the beautiful figure and that the appreciation of beauty comes again to be linked to a society's presumed decadence.

NIETZSCHE: THE INELUCTABLE MODE OF THE VISUAL

Already exerting a wide effect on a variety of writers and artists, Winckelmann's ideal of a classicist identity enormously broadened its influence on the German middle class once it obtained institutional form in the Prussian pedagogical and academic reforms that followed Prussia's collapse before Napoleon's armies in 1806. The new Prussian minister in charge of reforming education and an admirer of Winckelmann, Wilhelm von Humboldt, established classicism as the basis of secondary and university education in Prussia. Taught in the *Gymnasium* and tested in the

Abitur, or university entrance examination, classicism was turned not just into a subject of broad study but also into the basis of the generalized ethos of neohumanist *Bildung.*[55] As the *Gymnasium* and universities expanded in the nineteenth century, admitting more students from the middle class, classicist subjectivity came to provide one of the principal models of bourgeois selfhood. At the same time that it increasingly served as a constitutive element of bourgeois identity, the study of classicism was turned over to a more systematic and academic scrutiny in the universities, producing an empirically more rigorous and specialized study of ancient Greece, an *Altertumswissenschaft* of philology and archaeology.

Through the nineteenth century, the systematic study of classicism thus became an academic specialization, guided by positivistic methods and rooted in institutions that were in the service of both the German bourgeoisie and the Prussian, then German, state. In 1872 a young classical philologist at the University of Basel rebelled against this trend and what he saw as its slide into a narrow academicism and an official philistinism. What specifically inspired Nietzsche to write *The Birth of Tragedy,* as he himself noted in the preface to a later printing, was the event that he thought consolidated this process of reification: the completion of German unification.[56] In *The Birth of Tragedy,* German decadence—at once political, cultural, and academic—is condensed into a familiar classicist trope of affliction. Nietzsche first identifies latecoming, the sense of being an epigone, as an inevitable effect of admiring the Greeks: "Nearly every age and stage of culture has at some time or other sought with profound irritation to free itself from the Greeks, because in their presence everything one has achieved oneself, though apparently quite original and sincerely admired, suddenly seemed to lose life and color and shriveled into a poor copy, even a caricature" (*BT,* 93). He then points out how the problem of latecoming is doubled for modern Germans—in the failure of Goethe and Schiller to equal the Greeks and in the failures of contemporary Germans to equal the Weimar classicists: "If heroes like Goethe and Schiller could not succeed in breaking open the enchanted gate which leads into the Hellenic magic mountain . . . what could the epigones of such heroes hope for?" (*BT,* 123).

Nietzsche's disaffection with his own discipline and with German culture and the German state was reinforced by his association with Richard Wagner, who lived nearby and to whom Nietzsche had developed a strong attachment.[57] *The Birth of Tragedy* concludes with a ringing endorsement of Wagnerian opera as a way of liberating Germany from its current decadence and, by implication, from the debilitating burden of classicism. Nietzsche's later characterization of his book as a product of mid-nineteenth-century Romanticism, inflected with the pessimism of Schopenhauer (*BT,* 24–26), places Nietzsche's views of classicism in a tradition of thinking about ancient Greece that differed considerably from the tradition of Winckelmann. That there was more to classicism than the idealized rationality of its official pronouncements had already been explicitly recognized and analyzed in writings by others, even during classicism's greatest popularity from the eighteenth to the first part of the nineteenth century. *Sturm und Drang* writers, other idealists, Romantics—especially those who had moved from a youthful appreciation of classicism to a later Christian and Catholic loyalty—all pointed to the narrowness of classicist readings of Greek culture and art and offered other construals of classicism that foregrounded the sensuality, violence, and seemingly irrational fate of Greek stories.[58] Nietzsche's emphasis in *The Birth of Tragedy* on a fundamental "Dionysian" element of intoxicated sensuality and violence in ancient Greek culture places him in this tradition. The notoriety of the book and its eventual, if not initial, influence on both academic classicists and German intellectuals in general mark the shift of this alternative tradition of thinking about classicism into the mainstream of middle-class culture.

The Birth of Tragedy is a text that seeks to do justice to the unsettling strangeness of classicism; its definition of this issue and how it approaches it draw on a general Romantic critique of Enlightenment reason and "modernity" and continued to be influential long after Nietzsche repudiated the book.[59] But although this Romantic attempt to address the complex character of classicism has generated a significant stream of interpretation, it has also proved limited in its ability to account for the strangeness of classicism. Nietzsche fashions a privileged primordial Dionysian condition that explains rational classicist subjectivity by rendering it derivative or epiphenomenal, but even in that state classicist subjectivity continues to present itself as an enigma, one that the positing of a prior Dionysian condition cannot explain or contain. Nietzsche's distinction between conditions fails to hold up, and despite an attempt to translate classicism's otherness into the idiom of Romanticism, the former continues to show itself on its own terms. This is particularly evident in Nietzsche's strategy of aligning otherness with Romanticism's privileged form of putative original perception—hearing (and then listening) to music. Notwithstanding this Romantic stylization of classicist otherness, that otherness continues to deploy itself in displacements of visuality.

The young Nietzsche's strategy of dealing with rational classicist subjectivity begins with an inversion—what classicism regarded as essential and transcendental is turned into something secondary and derivative; and what classicism identified as meaningless excess is identified as essential and generative. This reversal of the terms of a binary opposition immediately produces a new set of issues, the most obvious of which is how and why such an inverse relationship had to occur in the first place. Or, put in the terms of *The Birth of Tragedy*, why did the Greeks, when representing a fundamental reality of irrationality and violence, do so in association with aesthetic forms of clarity, balance, and harmony?

Rational classicist subjectivity appears in *The Birth of Tragedy* under the well-known appellation of the "Apollonian." Nietzsche describes the attributes of this impulse in terms that could have been drawn from Winckelmann. The Apollonian is characterized as "measure," "nothing in excess," "self-knowledge" (*BT*, 46); it constitutes a program of restraint and control designed to fashion a clearly articulated subject, "the *principium individuationis*," as Nietzsche calls it. And like the classicism of Winckelmann, Nietzsche's balanced, harmoniously formed figure of the Apollonian shows itself phenomenally in a condition of serenity: "For Apollo wants to grant repose to individual beings precisely by drawing boundaries between them and by again and again calling these to mind as the most sacred law of the world" (*BT*, 72). The most accomplished form of Apollonian expression is plastic art, whose "climax and end" is to produce a closed circuit of visuality that seamlessly joins the beautiful figure and its viewer to produce a rational subject. In good classicist fashion, the Apollonian figure induces in the viewer a state of "contemplation" and "the justification of the world of the *individuatio* attained by this contemplation" (*BT*, 130, 131, 50).

Nietzsche's Apollonian restates the ideal self-description and teleology of classicist identity. This entire classicist apparatus is then displaced into a secondary, derivative status and given a different valence as Nietzsche puts it in the service of another, prior condition. Preceding rational consciousness and individuation is the Dionysian impulse of pure, irrational will, an original condition of sensuality and violence, as Nietzsche indicates by referring to it variously as "pure primordial pain," "primordial being itself," "the infinite primordial joy in existence" (*BT*, 50–56, 102–105). The *Ur*-condition of Dionysian intoxication and presubjectivity can be best recognized in the medium that, according to Nietzsche, reproduces its qualities of preindividuation, of being nonrepresentational, nonfigural, and emotionally enveloping. Following the conventions of nineteenth-century Romanticism in general and of Schopenhauer in particular, he identifies the medium of the Dionysian in music and, by implication, privileges hearing or listening as the form of perception that provides access to the primordial and essential.[60]

The relation of the Apollonian to the Dionysian reverses the traditional claims of classicist identity to rational transparency and plenitude. The classicist vision of eternal truth is turned, in Nietzsche's schema, into a kind of blindness—or, as Nietzsche puts it, "a beautiful veil," "mere appearance," an "illusion" (*BT*, 34, 35, 40). The Apollonian exists only to make one blind to the prior Dionysian. The emergence of this particular opposition is the source, as Paul de Man has noted, of the view that Nietzsche was an early existentialist.[61] The Dionysian's intoxicating sense of unity with nature is also, Nietzsche says, a direct experience of the "terror and horror" of existence, an experience that must leave one with a disabling, pessimistic view of the meaninglessness of life.[62] Such pessimism is of course incompatible with life, either personal or social, as Nietzsche dryly adds that this kind of knowledge probably "caused the downfall of the melancholy Etruscans" (*BT,* 42). To save themselves from a similar extinction, the Greeks invented fictions of meaning, their gods and myths of an "Olympian divine order of joy"; for how else, Nietzsche concludes, "could this people, so sensitive, so vehement in its desire, so singularly capable of *suffering,* have endured existence, if it had not been revealed to them in their gods, surrounded by a higher glory?" (*BT,* 43). The need for "metaphysical comfort" thus produced the tragedies of Aeschylus and Sophocles, which unite Dionysian suffering with beautiful, mitigating Apollonian form (*BT,* 59). When the Apollonian comes to be excessively emphasized over and against the Dionysian in the era of Socrates and Euripides, tragedy declines, displaced by a new, thoroughgoing rationalistic ethos, the extension of which is the exhausted culture of modern Europe.

As Paul de Man has argued in *Allegories of Reading,* Nietzsche's interpretation, predicated on an inversion of terms, is no less essentialist and problematic than the ideal of rational, regulated selfhood that it inverts.[63] Following and extending some of de Man's analysis will help to clarify how the young Nietzsche's Romantic interpretation fails in particular to account for classicism's otherness. The logic of *The Birth of Tragedy,* according to which the Dionysian is related to the Apollonian as original being to secondary appearance, is complicated by what turns out to be Nietzsche's equivocal descriptions of the Dionysian. Sometimes it appears to be primary and fundamental, the will itself; but at other times it is described in the same way as the Apollonian. Nietzsche also calls it an "appearance," "an immediate copy" of a prior will, a will that, now removed from the Dionysian, he refers to as the "metaphysical thing-in-itself" and the "unaesthetic-in-itself" (*BT,* 102). In these characterizations, the difference between Dionysian and Apollonian is no longer one of copy and original but of their respective distance, to paraphrase de Man, from the will.[64]

The instability of the distinction between the Apollonian and the Dionysian is disseminated throughout Nietzsche's discussion in successive oppositions that follow from the first distinction between the Apollonian and Dionysian. The most obvious of these is Nietzsche's identification of the rational Apollonian with form in general and the Dionysian with formlessness, as when he describes the latter as "the inmost kernel which precedes all forms in the history of things." This distinction between the form of the Apollonian and the formlessness of the Dionysian also proves impossible to maintain. In the first and simplest sense, the distinction collapses because Nietzsche contradicts himself. He acknowledges, for example, that music, the supposedly pure expression of the Dionysian, has form, and that in its form music displays a quality that orthodox classicist form strives for: abstract universality. "Melodies," Nietzsche says, "are to a certain extent, like general concepts, an abstraction from the world" (*BT*, 102).

The slippage from formlessness to form is evident as well in another, subtler way. Here the problem lies in the discrepancy between Nietzsche's claims (that music has no form) and the fact that he must make those claims linguistically, in a rhetoric that is mainly devised to describe form. Consider, for example, the semantic incoherence of his description of the Dionysian as "the inmost kernel which precedes all forms." In what sense can formlessness be a "kernel"; does not the word-image "kernel" belie the meaning of formlessness? Or, to put this more generally, how can Nietzsche describe formlessness in a language that makes pervasive use of metaphors of form?

Without himself recognizing it, Nietzsche's language readily slips into a rhetoric of form, and what is even more interesting is that in many cases the particular rhetoric of form that he uses to describe Dionysian formlessness turns out to be Winckelmann's rhetoric of disturbed visuality. To recognize this, we should first note how visuality is caught up in the binary structure of *The Birth of Tragedy*. Visuality is the negative term of a third conceptual opposition, homologous to and following from the Dionysian/Apollonian and form/formlessness dualisms. This third opposition is between Apollonian visuality and Dionysian hearing or listening to music.

As one might have noticed in the preceding analysis, Nietzsche, following orthodox classicism, frequently describes classicist subjectivity in metaphors of visuality. It is "appearance," "illusion," a "dream" (*BT*, 35, 38). Apollo is "the deity of light" (*BT*, 35). "The plastic artist," Nietzsche says, "is absorbed in the pure contemplation of images" (*BT*, 50). When the Apollonian operates harmoniously with the Dionysian, complementing it without suppressing it, the result is a "beautiful" image. When the Apollonian is taken to an extreme and becomes Socratic and suppresses the Dionysian, that process is still represented as a visual one. As Nietzsche puts it: "under the stern, intelligent eyes of an orthodox dogmatism, the mythical premises of a religion are systematized as a sum total of historical events." Under this demystified vision, "the feeling for myth" and thus life's vitality expire (*BT*, 75). And later, incensed at the Socratic suppression of the Dionysian, Nietzsche confers on the Socratic the form of a vision become monstrous: "Let us now imagine the one great Cyclops eye of Socrates fixed on tragedy, an eye in which the fair frenzy of enthusiasm had never glowed" (*BT,* 89).

The Apollonian in all its forms (both benevolent and malicious) enacts itself in visual terms. The Dionysian, by contrast, is explicitly named as the nonvisual.[65] The Dionysian musician, Nietzsche says, is "without any images" (*BT,* 50, 33). Nietzsche points out that all attempts to describe Dionysian music figuratively, that is, in images—as, say, in calling a Beethoven symphony "pastoral"—inevitably fail to do justice to the music (*BT,* 54). Music, for Nietzsche, is the will itself, incapable of being fully apprehended in vision. In archaic Greece, it is the chanting of the worshipers of Dionysus that returns them to a primordial swirl of pain and sensuality (*BT,* 62–67). When the chanting bacchants evolve into the Dionysian chorus of Greek tragedy, the chorus discharges its energies into Apollonian images of tragedy; but the result, as Nietzsche is careful to point out, is not a classicist affirmation in visuality; there is no Apollonian "redemption through mere appearance." Rather, the effect of a still-powerful Dionysian impulse in Greek tragedy is "the shattering of the individual and his fusion with primal being" (*BT,* 65).

We should recall that in Winckelmann's *History* rational classicist subjectivity comes into existence along a visual circuit: seeing the austere, harmonious form fashions the viewer into a rational subject. But although Winckelmann repeatedly asserts this ideal circuit, what he shows is that the analytic gaze behaves differently as it beholds the beautiful object. Vision comes to be taken over, and subjectivity is expropriated as Winckelmann's seeing slips into hallucination. He sees himself seeing from the point of view of another. What for Winckelmann takes place entirely within vision, as both ideal projection and errant deflection, is split by Nietzsche into two seemingly different modes. Vision, in its orthodox classicist form, issues in rational individuation; the mode of disarticulation, of a return to presubjectivity, is hearing or listening to music. Nietzsche asserts and reasserts this opposition between different modes of perception, but that opposition is never actually deployed. In fact, the appeal to the power and primacy of Dionysian music turns out to be a false and misleading start.

At one point, for example, Nietzsche reiterates his contention that Dionysian music returns a person to a primordial condition. But immediately afterward he shows that he cannot be satisfied with a description of that condition in terms of listening or hearing alone. To apprehend the Dionysian, the loss of subjectivity, he immediately slips back into a rhetoric of disturbed visuality. He tells us that the person in attendance at a Greek tragedy, caught up in the performance, felt "himself exalted to a kind of omniscience, as if his visual faculty were no longer merely a surface faculty but capable of penetrating into the interior, and as if he now saw before him, with the aid of music, the waves of the will, the conflict of motives, and the swelling flood of the passions, sensuously visible, as it were, like a multitude of vividly moving figures and lines, and he felt he could dip into the most delicate secrets of unconscious emotion" (*BT*, 130).

In his most substantial section on the processes of the Dionysian, Nietzsche describes how the ancient Greeks, attending a tragedy and hearing the chorus, are plunged back into the primordial Dionysian. That transition, predicated by listening to music, is then described as a remarkable *visual* transformation. The Greek experiences "a force of vision . . . strong enough to make the eye insensitive and blind to the impression of 'reality'" (*BT*, 63). This vision "overlooks" reality as the audience and chorus experience a double hallucination. First they see themselves transformed into satyrs; then they see before them the appearance of the deity, Dionysus himself. "In the magic transformation," Nietzsche writes, "the Dionysian reveler sees himself as a satyr and *as a satyr, in turn, he sees the god*, which means that in his metamorphosis he beholds another vision outside himself" (*BT*, 64).

In this transformation of vision, as in Winckelmann's, the seeing subject is expropriated: he sees himself seeing from the point of view of another. In the most heated moment of Dionysian frenzy, Nietzsche, without himself noticing, slips from a discussion of the effects of music into a discussion of visuality at its strangest, of how subjectivity can be lost in visual experience. Music, in this development, is no more than a catalyst precipitating changes in visuality.

As he speaks of the crucial role in the Dionysian of hearing music, the form of Nietzsche's words suggests that something else is even more important, the medium of vision that Dionysian hearing presumably should exclude. Remarkably, Nietzsche does not recognize that how he speaks of the Dionysian belies what he says about it. This is a slippage, a mixing of metaphors, that he performs yet again when he seeks to describe the overwhelming power of Dionysian music played by the ancient lyrist. Without noticing it, his description of the harsh otherness of the Dionysian lyrist becomes a harsh image of visual subjection: the lyrist "is the pure, undimmed eye of the sun" (*BT*, 55).

Notwithstanding Nietzsche's Romantic splitting of classicist subjectivity into Apollonian and Dionysian conditions, what he ultimately shows is that classicism never wanders far from the Apollonian realm of visuality. What the splitting does affect is the content of disturbed visuality. In Winckelmann's reveries, he phantasizes himself transported back to ancient Greece; he sees himself at an athletic game or as Pygmalion. Those images are clearly attuned to Winckelmann's personal desire; they are disruptions of Winckelmann's ideal classicist identity, bent by the pressure of desire.

Their strangeness is communicated by an excess of idealization or personification, by Winckelmann's changed position in relation to them (he sees himself seeing them), and by the intensity of the affect that surrounds them. Even while denying the visual otherness of classicism, Nietzsche operates within it. He registers the otherness of classicism's visual forms, but his Romanticism impoverishes the content of those forms. Nietzsche's description breaks down either into meaningless ambiguity—he sees "a multitude of vividly moving figures" or "waves of the will"—or into a scene, both lurid and clichéd, of a collective transformation into satyrs. The unlikeliness of this scene reminds one of what de Man points out as the unlikeliness of Nietzsche's claims about music.

Nietzsche asserts that the primordial Dionysian in the form of music is unbearable in itself, and he concludes that it is Apollonian form that makes the Dionysian tolerable. The same relation is found, he goes on to say, in Wagner's operas, which offer the hope of a revival of the vitality of Greek tragedy. Nietzsche, as de Man points out, then reaches an absurd deduction, one posed as a rhetorical question that both heightens its melodramatic quality and helps to conceal its improbability: "can [one] imagine a human being who would be able to perceive the third act of *Tristan and Isolde* without the aid of word and image, purely as a tremendous symphonic movement, without expiring in a spasmodic harnessing of all the wings of the soul?"[66] Nietzsche presents expiring in the unmediated experience of Wagnerian music as a real, literal possibility, knowing full well that the reader can accept it only metaphorically or rhetorically. The same can be said of what Nietzsche maintains is the content of Dionysian visuality. Nietzsche does not mean that the participant in a Greek tragedy metaphorically sees himself transformed into a satyr but that he literally sees himself transformed into one. Would the equivalent happen at a Wagnerian opera, which, according to Nietzsche, operates in the same way as a Greek tragedy?[67]

The difference between Nietzsche's and Winckelmann's displays of the disturbed vision of classicism is a difference, we might say, between two different construals of the unconscious. Nietzsche's Romanticism conceives of the irrational as a mental state repressed by rational consciousness; to recognize the irrational means going "beneath" or "behind" consciousness to some specific, alternative set of phenomena. The problem is that Nietzsche has no vocabulary with which he can name this unconscious. He cannot describe it, as Winckelmann does, in quotidian language or images; in fact, given the "formlessness" of the Dionysian, Nietzsche cannot ultimately describe it at all. The formlessness of the Dionysian forecloses a description in images. The consequence is that by default Nietzsche ambiguously refers to seeing lights, "waves of the will," or to a stock scene of satyrs, none of which can be joined to an Apollonian world of appearance in any believable way. Wagnerian music by itself would not kill us; nor would it make us see ourselves physically turned into satyrs. Nietzsche's Romantic splitting of classicism into a series of unstable binary oppositions ultimately leaves the Dionysian disconnected in its hyperbolic description, its improbable relation to ordinary life. Put another way, the problem with Nietzsche's characterization of the Dionysian is that it is impossible to take seriously.[68]

What Winckelmann shows in the recurring deflections of classicist vision is another view of how the unconscious operates. It is not at a level below consciousness but is part of the same surface, manifesting itself in rational consciousness as a deflection or distortion of what that consciousness prescribes, as a slipping away of rationality or as a stain on its surface.[69] On this view there is no set of forms characteristic of the unconscious—no flashing lights or satyrs—but distortions of prescribed forms, unsettling and uncanny because those distortions are all too close to familiar expectations.

Nietzsche's extravagant Dionysian imagery will also appear in the work of other writers and artists, as we shall see in the specific case of Thomas Mann's *Death in Venice*. But there as well, the legacy of Winckelmann will also exert its influence, showing that the strangeness of classicism is to be found not in a make-believe underworld, but on the distorted and distorting surface of the beautiful Apollonian object.

THOMAS MANN: CLASSICIST *LIEBESTOD*

Nietzsche's *Birth of Tragedy* roughly marked the beginning of a long "crisis" of German and European intellectuals, one that intensified into *fin-de-siècle* culture and extended well into the twentieth century. Conventionally linked to social changes brought on by full industrialization and the increasing democratization of institutions, this crisis has been identified as a questioning and rejection of liberal and humanist ideals and their displacement by a new or revived concern for the irrational and passionate elements of individual and social life.[70] And as we have seen in *The Birth of Tragedy*, this critical rethinking in Germany could assume the form of the problematization of what was perhaps that country's most important manifestation of liberal humanism—classicist subjectivity.

To understand the thought and culture of this period of crisis, historians and interpreters have often taken over certain terms of explanation that were used in the period itself and that we have seen deployed in *The Birth of Tragedy*, namely, that the suppression of the irrational by an ultra-rationalist conception of the self gives way to a return of the repressed. This view, predicated on the assumption that human nature is divided into two characters at war with each other, does not abandon the liberal and classicist notion of subjectivity but merely reverses its valences. And in retaining the dichotomous structure of liberal identity, this view also preserves many of that structure's problems, notably, as in the case of *The Birth of Tragedy*, the problems of maintaining distinctions that follow from the rational/irrational split.

Death in Venice, published in 1912, carries all the conventional marks of *fin-de-siècle* anxiety. The story of the decline and death of the German writer Gustav Aschenbach is couched in terms of biological decay, evolutionary degeneration, social decline, cultural decadence, the usurpation of the West by the "Orient," and the dissolution of gender distinctions. And, like other cultural products and events of this period, the novel has often been interpreted in terms of a return of the repressed irrational or unconscious against rational control. But, as in Nietzsche's *Birth of Tragedy*, this method of interpreting *Death in Venice* does not adequately address what goes on in the novel, notwithstanding the fact that Mann himself sometimes endorses the method. In addition to and against this dichotomy of the rational and irrational, *Death in Venice*, like *The Birth of Tragedy*, presents the case that those putative opposites are not separate, antithetical conditions, but from the beginning are inseparably implicated. More specifically, the novel shows again that the origins, trajectory, and effects of rational identity do not simply operate in the manner prescribed by reason itself. In this sense, Mann incorporates not just the early Nietzsche's Romantic view of classicist subjectivity as a repression decreed by reason. The novel also, and in tension with that repression hypothesis, incorporates the kind of classicist subjectivity performed in Winckelmann's *History*. *Death in Venice* is a remarkable summation of the different themes and rhetorics of German classicist subjectivity, a summation that ends in a striking, explicit recognition of the dislocating strangeness at work—both beside and through—classicism's projections of rational subjectivity.[71]

The novel was composed under the sign of a characteristic classicist affliction. Thematically, the story continues the concerns of Mann's first novel, *Buddenbrooks* (1901), with working out the implications of the cultural "exhaustion" of the German middle class. Mann's great success in elaborating that theme left him feeling exhausted, thus illustrating in his life the theme of his art. After *Buddenbrooks*, he was unable for more than a decade to write another novel. Under the shadow of *Buddenbrooks*, he suffered from perhaps the most common sort of latecoming, the anxiety of being his own epigone, and many of the stories he wrote during this time are concerned with the problems of latecoming and of how art militates against the satisfactions of ordinary life.[72] In *Death in Venice*, Mann's working through of these personal, thematic, and cultural concerns takes the form of an intensely self-conscious consideration of the contradictions and ambivalences of classicism.

As a young man, the German writer Aschenbach was an iconoclast, driven by "a passion for the absolute" to find the answer to difficult questions. His was an art of the "problematical."[73] But at a certain point at the end of his youth, he put those questions aside. "Turning away from all moral skepticism, all sympathy for the abyss," Mann writes, Aschenbach experienced a "'miracle of reborn ingenuousness.'" He now put his writing in the service of teaching morality, and this writing, characterized by "a discriminating purity, simplicity, and evenness of attack," gave his work the "stamp of mastery and classicism" (*DV*, 17). Aschenbach became the complete classicist. He placed art in the service of achieving a rational subjectivity that asserted its autonomy against internal and external forces of domination. And this identity fashioned out of "self-conquest" was ideally coded, as we might expect, in a specific gender: it showed a dedication, Mann says, that Aschenbach "might well call masculine" (*DV*, 74).

As a classicist concerned with disciplined form and moral teaching, Aschenbach wrote inspirational work easily accepted by the German public and the German state—such as a piece on Frederick II. Mann tells us that Aschenbach was the appropriate hero of his era; his writings were widely read; he received honors, including a knighthood (*DV*, 15, 74). The one-time iconoclast had become the classicist writer of the people and the state. This close supportive relationship between Aschenbach and authority resulted in writing that became increasingly routinized and sterile: "Gradually," Mann says, "something official and didactic crept into Gustav Aschenbach's products, his style in later life . . . inched toward the fixed and standardized, the conventionally elegant, the conservative, the formal, the formulated" (*DV*, 18).

At the age of fifty, feeling tired and restless in his work, Aschenbach feels a compulsion to go to Venice, where he sees the Polish boy Tadzio, who is visiting Venice with his mother and sisters. Aschenbach is immediately struck by the boy's "perfect beauty," which, as a writer of classicist sensibility, he processes within the appropriate mode. His first sight of Tadzio recalls for Aschenbach "Greek sculpture of the noblest period" (*DV*, 34). Tadzio is figured in forms drawn from classical myth and art: he looks like "the ancient statue of the boy pulling out a thorn" (*DV*, 34); Aschenbach is reminded of "the head of a statue of Eros" (*DV*, 38); in his daydreams, Aschenbach places Tadzio in classical scenes, among others, as Hyacinth (*DV*, 65) and Narcissus (*DV*, 67, 41); and Tadzio inspires Aschenbach to imagine Socrates speaking to Phaedrus (*DV*, 59, 95). The lessons that Aschenbach initially draws from these encounters also follow a classicist circuit of perception and recognition: the images of Tadzio induce a contemplative state designed to attain a level of universal understanding. After he first spots the boy, Aschenbach is led, Mann says, "to occupy himself with abstract or even transcendental things; he pondered on the . . . alliance which must be contracted between universal law and the individually distinct for human beauty to result, from this he passed into general problems of form and content" (*DV,* 36).

And later, as Aschenbach watches Tadzio on the beach, he reflects on "the intellectual beauty of the boy." Seeing the figure of the boy carries his mind to the recognition of a familiar topos of classicist doctrine—that ideal beauty re-presents an original image, perfect and divine. Aschenbach felt "he was grasping the very essence of beauty, form in the thought of God, the one pure perfection which lives in the mind, and which, in this symbol and likeness, had been placed here quietly and simply as an object of devotion" (*DV,* 58). This recognition leads Aschenbach to fashion his own classicist metacommentary as he daydreams for the first time of a dialogue between Socrates and Phaedrus, a dream in which the former teaches the latter the classicist doctrine that beauty is the education of the soul; it is "the only form," Mann has Socrates say, "of the spiritual which one can receive through the senses" (*DV,* 60).

These characterizations of aesthetic sensibility—that it is disciplined, masculine, contemplative, a subsuming of the particular into the universal, a vehicle to a higher spirituality—reiterate ideas we have seen advanced in orthodox classicism, which are now, in the sensibility of the mature Aschenbach, condensed into what Mann considers a conventional, state-sponsored German understanding of beauty. But although this official discussion is asserted and reasserted, there are indications from the beginning that it does not fully or adequately describe what Aschenbach experiences. Immediately after dreaming of Socrates speaking with Phaedrus, Aschenbach feels inspired to write "on a certain large human issue of culture and taste," and he writes a text that sounds distinctively "classicist," since it is destined "soon to kindle the acclaim of many through its clarity, its poise, and its vibrant emotional tension" (*DV,* 60–61). But although the form of the text is conventionally classicist, the affect associated with it is not. Mann himself explicitly indicates this disjuncture when he says: "Certainly it is better for people to know the beautiful product only as finished, and not in its conception, its conditions of origin." Writing in Tadzio's presence, Aschenbach is intensely aware of the presence of "Eros," and far from being an exercise in rational mastery over his topic, the experience of writing before Tadzio is for Aschenbach deeply unsettling: "Strange hours!" he says, "Strange enervating effects!" (*DV,* 61).

The result of these peculiar feelings is that when Aschenbach finishes writing and starts back from the beach, he feels "exhausted, or even deranged, and it seemed to him," Mann says, "that his conscience was rebuking him, as if after a debauch." Even though Aschenbach calls this writing a "rare creative intercourse between the spirit and body" (*DV,* 61), what he shows us is a dissociation between the feelings that he experiences from writing in Tadzio's presence and the trained contemplative response that dictates that writing's classical form.

The gulf between what Aschenbach officially presents as rational subjectivity and what he actually feels widens ever more as his interest in Tadzio intensifies into obsession, one so powerful that even after learning that cholera has arrived in the city, Aschenbach chooses to stay in Venice, and in that choice consigns himself to dying from the disease. The collapse of orthodox classicism is thus enacted as Aschenbach's deteriorating dignity, overwhelming obsession, and willing sacrifice of his life; his initial recognition of Tadzio as a muse for classicist contemplation reveals itself as an illusion that, succumbing to other forces, is reduced to a pretext for an erotic and deadly fascination.

This view of the collapse of classicist subjectivity supports the model of analysis outlined above as the explanation in terms of repression. On this view and model, Aschenbach's repressed homosexual drives finally break through the surface of his official aesthetic identity. Harvey Goldman's influential book on the idea of "calling" in Mann and Max Weber argues, for example, that Aschenbach is an artist who is caught in an artistic "calling" that demands a repressive "puritanical soldierly" duty, one that severs him from what Goldman refers to as "life." The result of the loss of a vital reality is madness, Aschenbach's infatuation with the boy.[74]

Mann himself suggests that Aschenbach's collapse is to be understood in terms of repression; in fact Mann suggests a repression so powerful that in Aschenbach's fate can be seen the fate of all humanity. Repression is both phylogenic and ontogenic. The rending of official identity is manifested not just in how Aschenbach feels and behaves; the shattering of repression is also represented as a species regression, enacted in a series of hallucinations. When Aschenbach is still in Munich and overcome with the desire for travel, his "yearnings" take on "visual form": he sees "a tropical swampland under a heavy, murky sky, damp, luxuriant and enormous, a kind of primeval wilderness of islands" (*DV,* 7). When Aschenbach sees Tadzio playing in the water at the edge of the Lido, the boy appears to him "as some slender god" who emerges "out of the depths of sky and sea," who rises and separates from "the elements." This "spectacle," Mann says, "aroused a sense of myth . . . like some poet's recovery of time at its beginning, of the origin of form and the birth of gods" (*DV,* 44). And not long before his death, Aschenbach experiences his most striking altered vision.

In a "frightful dream" he sees himself in an ancient Dionysian bacchanal described in terms similar to those in *The Birth of Tragedy*.[75] Beginning with "anguish and desire," Aschenbach sees himself surrounded by men dressed as satyrs; bacchants are chanting, and an obscene wooden symbol is brought into the gathering; all are anxiously awaiting the appearance of "the strange god!" Aschenbach sees himself seeing this Dionysian scene, and as the participants fall in a frenzy on sacrificial animals, he sees himself joining them: "Yes, he and they were one, as they hurled themselves biting and tearing upon the animals, devoured steaming bits of flesh, and fell in promiscuous union on the torn moss, in sacrifice to their gods" (*DV*, 88–90). Aschenbach thus regresses through Apollonian images, through the phenomenal appearance of classicist and classical forms, to a primordial Dionysian unity. As Apollonian form turns out to be a thin and useless veil over more powerful Dionysian urges, Apollonian tropes of classicism slip into the imagery of the early Nietzsche's Dionysian Romanticism.

These strong indications of a repression breaking apart, in terms drawn from Nietzsche's *Birth of Tragedy*, constitute key elements in the usual interpretation of the disintegration of Aschenbach's classicism. Aschenbach, on this view, has become delusional because of repression or an excess of repression. But although there is considerable evidence to support this view, it does not fully address how Aschenbach's Apollonian, classicist self is described and how it collapses. Beside the Romantic, early Nietzschean characterization of Aschenbach's collapse is another view that cannot be explained by a Dionysian shattering of Apollonian repression. On this other view, the disintegrative features of classical beauty are not what is below it, in what it suppresses. Rather, classicism's deconstruction takes place entirely on its surface, in the very deployment of its principles and tropes of rational subjectivity. *Death in Venice* contains not only a radicalized Nietzschean argument about the repression of the Dionysian,[76] but also the ambivalent discourse of Winckelmann's classicism, which, even as it asserts the rational stability of beautiful form, reveals to us its uncertainties.

Early in the story, for example, after saying that Aschenbach's work carried the mark of "mastery and classicism," the narrator lapses into a reverie on how "ethical resoluteness" might result in "a strengthened capacity for the forbidden, the evil, the morally impossible"; and that thought leads him to consider the morally equivocal nature of aesthetic form. "And does not form," he asks, "have two aspects? Is it not moral and amoral at once— moral in that it is the result and expression of discipline, but amoral, and even immoral, in that by nature it contains an indifference to morality, is calculated, in fact, to make morality bend beneath its proud and unencumbered scepter?" (*DV*, 17).

That form can sever itself from any putative moral signified, that it can in fact aesthetically reshape any moral content into its opposite, is an issue that recurs in the story, culminating in a final, ironic classicist recognition that explicitly returns us to the original anxiety in Western philosophy about the deceiving nature of pleasing sensuous surfaces. Aschenbach does not die after his sleeping dream of a Dionysian bacchanal; there is another intervening hallucination—one even more unsettling because it is a subtle, waking disturbance of vision that Aschenbach calmly experiences while sitting on the beach, watching Tadzio playing in the surf. As Aschenbach's illness gets the better of him, he again sees before him Socrates speaking to Phaedrus on the nature of beauty. In this, the story's second Platonic dialogue, Socrates begins by reiterating the official classicism of the first imagined dialogue:[77] "For beauty, Phaedrus . . . beauty alone is both divine and visible at once; and thus it is the road of the sensuous; it is, little Phaedrus, the road of the artist to the spiritual." But immediately after stating this conventional starting premise of classicist aesthetics, Socrates swerves onto another path: "But do you now believe . . . that they can ever attain wisdom and true human dignity for whom the road to the spiritual leads through the senses or do you believe rather . . . that this is a pleasant but perilous road, a . . . wrong and sinful road, which necessarily leads us astray?" (*DV,* 95).

To this Platonic question, Socrates provides an answer that explicitly states what Winckelmann showed: "form and innocence . . . lead to intoxication and desire, lead the noble perhaps into the sinister reaches of emotion which even our beautiful rigor rejects as infamous." That conclusion about the ambiguous nature of classicist form leads Socrates to overturn one by one the principal tropes of classicist identity:

> For you must know that we poets cannot take the road of beauty without having Eros join us . . . as our leader. Indeed, we may even be heroes after our fashion, and hardened warriors; and yet we are like women, for passion is our exaltation. . . . You now see, do you not, that we poets cannot be wise and dignified? That we necessarily go astray, necessarily remain lascivious. . . . The mastery of our style is all lies and foolishness, our renown and honor are a farce, the confidence of the masses in us is highly ridiculous, and the training of the public and of youth through art is a precarious undertaking which should be forbidden. For how, indeed, could he be a fit instructor who is born with a natural leaning toward the abyss? (*DV,* 96)

In the Nietzschean set piece of the dream of the bacchanal, the Dionysian urges and images break through repressive classicist form; but in another demonstration of strange classicism, in the repudiation of Socrates, the form itself is the source of transgression, inverting its own terms, turning the masculine into the feminine, mastery into servitude, aesthetic education into sensual corruption, and the articulation of identity into its disappearance in an abyss. And from this cascade of reversals, Socrates arrives at the judgment of Baudelaire: the danger is so great that we may excuse the suppression of the object.

The collapse of classicist subjectivity in *Death in Venice* takes place as a deconstruction of the tropes of classicism, and this deconstruction is enacted in ways that are similar to procedures found in Winckelmann's *History*— that is, in terms of metaphor and visuality. The instabilities of classicist beauty are registered in Winckelmann's *History* in the shifting meaning of a repeated image of beauty. The sea, for Winckelmann, ambivalently signifies both stillness and undulating motion, clear form that can be captured in a glance of reason and shifting form that unsettles the glance and leads the gaze into heteronomous sensuousness. The sea, in other words, is the image of both the stability of rational subjectivity and its instability. For Mann, as well, the sea is identified with classical beauty, and, as a metaphor of classical beauty, it obtains the same ambivalent signification that it carries in Winckelmann's *History*.

In one extraordinary passage, for example, Mann converts the classicist ideal of surpassing the constraints of empirical existence in the serene contemplation of ideal beauty into an ideal of dissolution: "He [Aschenbach] loved the ocean for deep-seated reasons: because of that yearning for rest, when the hard-pressed artist hungers to shut out the exacting multiplicities of experience and seek refuge on the breast of the simple, the vast, and because of a forbidden hankering . . . after the inarticulate, the boundless, the eternal, sheer nothing." And this conflation of transcendence and dissolution allows Aschenbach to add an ironic commentary to the classical notion of perfect cultural achievement: "To be at rest in the face of perfection is the hunger of everyone who is aiming at excellence; and what is nothingness if not a form of perfection."[78]

The deconstruction of Aschenbach's classicist subjectivity is enacted in yet another way that recalls the instabilities of Winckelmann's *History*. As we have already seen, Aschenbach's classical recognitions manifest their instabilities as disturbances of quotidian vision.[79] From the beginning, Aschenbach is guided by dreaming and waking hallucinations. The most extravagant of these is the Nietzschean set piece of a Dionysian bacchanal, but there are also scenes of the jungle that set him on his journey to Venice (*DV*, 6), scenes of Tadzio transplanted into classical settings, and scenes of Socrates speaking with Phaedrus. And what often instigates these disturbances of vision is the intersecting looking that goes on between Aschenbach and Tadzio.

Other commentators have noticed the role of looking in *Death in Venice* and have argued that Aschenbach's looking at Tadzio is the way he constructs, as Goldman puts it, a "fantasy of himself as master and possessor of the beautiful." Aschenbach's "voyeuristic" gaze, on this account, turns Tadzio, the real boy, into an object of obsession.[80] This interpretation of Aschenbach's looking derives, of course, from a conventional view of the gaze as a medium of subjugation. But as we have seen in the case of Winckelmann, something more complicated takes place in looking at classical beauty; the aesthetic gaze does not fashion a masterful subjectivity but in fact breaks it down, allows it to be taken over by the gaze of another. This also occurs in *Death in Venice;* Aschenbach's gaze is always returned.

On one of their first encounters, as Tadzio is leaving the hotel dining room, Mann tells us that "for some reason or other he turned around before passing the threshold, and since no one else was in the lobby his strange dusky eyes met those of Aschenbach" (*DV,* 36). Later, passing Aschenbach, Tadzio "lowered his eyes modestly before the man with gray hair and high forehead, only to use them again in his delicious manner, soft and full upon him" (*DV,* 49). On the beach, Aschenbach sometimes avoids catching Tadzio's eyes, but "at other times he would look up, and their glances met." And the narrator makes a point of adding that "they were both in earnest when this occurred" (*DV,* 66). Tadzio and Aschenbach are identified as "people who knew each other only with their eyes" (*DV,* 65).

What ultimately emerges is that Aschenbach's gaze is not exerting his will over Tadzio's; on the contrary, Aschenbach's looking is first returned and then led by the look in Tadzio's eyes. As the boy and his family walk through Venice, Aschenbach follows; but wanting not to be seen, he is "driven to disgraceful subterfuges," such as hiding behind other people. Knowing that Aschenbach is following, the boy walks apart from the others and offers Aschenbach a look: "sauntering alone, he would turn his head occasionally to look over his shoulder and make sure by a glance of his peculiarly dark-gray eyes that his admirer was following." Aschenbach is "lured forward by those eyes" (*DV,* 93). What happens to Aschenbach is what happens to Winckelmann before the *Apollo Belvedere:* autonomous subjectivity gives way to subjection; Aschenbach's vision is taken over by a visuality that emanates from another.

The arguments that Aschenbach is overcome by delusions of his own aesthetic mastery or by his repressive separation as an artist from life ignore the ambivalences that have always surrounded the classicist aesthetic and that in this period of liberal crisis are explicitly acknowledged and played out as a kind of suicide of subjectivity. The orthodox allegory of classicism—the *paideia* of the soul initiated by the vision of sensuous beauty—yields to a counterallegory of the soul's deflection and loss. We might say in fact that Aschenbach is never a free subject but from the beginning is caught in the dissemination of classicism's deconstructing tropes. The beautiful form that signifies clarity, rigor, and rational subjectivity is the same form that does away with those characteristics.

All the equivocal signs of classicism—the beautiful figure's double and ultimately deadly meaning, the ambiguous sea, the visuality of the other that overturns subjectivity—come together in the final moment of Aschenbach's life, a moment that, with good classicist ambivalence, is represented as both transcendence and extinction. At the end of the book, shortly after his second hallucination of Socrates and Phaedrus, Aschenbach is again on the Lido. He sees Tadzio, crossing the shallows of the water to a sandbar. Separated by an expanse of water and with water before him, Tadzio appears to be walking out into the sea. As he seems about to vanish, Tadzio "glance[s] over his shoulder to the shore," and Aschenbach lifts his head "as if to meet the glance." Tadzio, "the pale and lovely summoner," raises his hand from his hip, as if "calling" Aschenbach "to cross over, vaguely guiding him," in Mann's words, "toward some prodigious fulfillment." And Aschenbach, we are told, "rises as if to follow" (*DV*, 98). At that moment, following the glance of the pagan god drawing him into the sea, Aschenbach expires.

CHAPTER FOUR

Classicism and Gender Transformation

David, Goethe, and Staël

In Jacques-Louis David's 1784 painting *The Oath of the Horatii* (see fig. 5), the strong, noble figures of the brothers Horatii swear an oath to sacrifice their lives in battle defending Rome. Staring straight ahead, they raise their arms toward a set of swords held upright by their father, while receding to the edge of the painting are the women of the family, averting their eyes as they collapse, unable to bear witness to the terrible resolution of men. Since its initial display in Rome, the *Oath* has provoked powerful and particular responses. The painting seizes the attention of the viewer, bestowing a sudden, dramatic sense of riveting clarification. Hugh Honour offers a vivid version of this standard view: "With the *Oath of the Horatii* David suddenly reached full maturity. Completely emancipated and completely in command of a new and rigorously purified style, he now achieved a perfect fusion of form and content in an image of extraordinary lucidity and visual punch."[1]

As Honour points out, the sense of a forceful, clarified recognition that the painting induces in its viewers derives as much from its content as from its austere, controlled style. Contrary to Rococo's scenes of pleasure and play, the *Oath* presents a classical scene that is "a clarion call to civic virtue and patriotism";[2] the painting in other words, makes one recognize one's duty, the overwhelming claims of a higher moral order. The reason these claims exert such an arresting force is that the men's desire to sacrifice themselves for the state is represented as an act of exaltation, of transcendent heroism; and the viewer feels directly addressed by the painting because it seems to draw the viewer to a higher form of self.

Given the events that soon followed the presentation of the *Oath*—the final crises of the old regime and the explosion of the French Revolution—

Fig. 5. Jacques-Louis David (1748–1825). *The Oath of the Horatii,* 1784. Oil on canvas. Louvre, Paris, France. Copyright Giraudon/Art Resource, New York.

the painting's announcement of commitment to a new moral order seemed prescient, and it has often been interpreted as a foreshadowing of the Revolution. In these interpretations of the *Oath,* the trope of recognition passes into one of prolepsis: the painting's classical austerity and sense of moral imperative are recognized as anticipations of Jacobin republicanism and its cult of civic virtue; and here, of course, commentators have pointed out how David became a prominent Jacobin, ally of Robespierre, deputy of the National Convention, and official organizer of republican festivals. When David first thought of the *Oath,* he conceived of it as contributing to an art of reform that would serve as an impetus to what he and many others thought was a much-needed renovation of a decadent society.[3] An active and enthusiastic participant in the Revolution, David himself came to endow the *Oath* retroactively with even more proleptic significance, believing that it inspired the Tennis Court Oath of the embattled Third Estate.[4]

The *Oath* as prolepsis is a galvanizing recognition of self-sacrifice, austere virtue, and moral commitment that seems to look forward to the overthrow of monarchy, aristocratic sensibility, and the refined culture of civility—in a word, to Jacobin Revolution. The painting represents all this in heroic and moralistic terms, but recent historiography, critical of the message of the *Oath* and of Jacobin Revolution, has shown that the painting involves other terms as well, ones that can be regarded as proleptic in a different fashion.

Consider one of the first important transfixed recognitions brought on by the painting and reported by the German classicist painter J. H. Tischbein in a famous review of the painting when it was first displayed in Rome. Looking on the painting, he imagines himself transposed to early Rome, witnessing the oath and appreciating its significance: "we should find ourselves transported back to Rome's first youth and realize that the descendents of such warriors must have become rulers of the world."[5] As Tischbein makes clear, there is conveyed, along and through this representation of selfless moral commitment, an overwhelming sense of power, and, as critics have pointed out, this sense is identified with the male figures and dissociated from the female ones. In recent historiography, the *Oath* has come to be seen still as a prolepsis but now as one that focuses on the representation of gender differences and differentials of power during the Revolution. Classicist revival in French culture, on this interpretation, was in the service of a powerful phantasy of gender separation, male supremacy, and the suppression of the public role of elite women of the old regime. This classicist phantasy of masculine assertion and feminine submission had become prominent in late eighteenth-century France, was implemented in the radical French Revolution, and continued into the nineteenth century. In David's *Oath,* it found its idealized, emblematic, proleptic representation.[6] The recent historiographical revisiting of David's *Oath* links it to a realignment of gender relations that suppresses the idealized traditional role of the elite public woman. Here I seek to deepen and refine that point of view by considering in greater detail the cultural choices and elisions of classicist masculinity and recapturing thereby some of the critical pathos that was, for a time, associated with it.

In *Death in Venice,* Gustav Aschenbach identifies his mature art in the mode of David, as one of "mastery and classicism" and an "ethical resoluteness"; but at moments of unrest in the story, he wonders if there is not another side to this classicism's desire for "simplicity, greatness," and a "new rigor" of form. This desire for the "reborn innocence" of moral clarity and power, he recognizes, suggests more to him than it typically admits to: "But ethical resoluteness beyond knowledge, the knowledge that corrodes or inhibits moral firmness—does this not in turn signify a simplification, a reduction morally of the world to too limited terms, and thus also a strengthened capacity for the forbidden, the evil, the morally impossible?"[7] Aschenbach's suspicion of hidden meanings in classicist ethical subjectivity is, I argue, the elided truth of David's *Oath:* that the clarified ethical resoluteness of its classicism is based on a suppression of the recognition that its ethics are an affliction. As an affliction, David's high-minded, moralistic rendering of heroic transformation differs from Aschenbach's in that it is set as a gender conflict, a sacrifice of women and the family. To paint the *Oath* as he did required the intentional suppression of this sense of affliction that was always recognized by earlier classicisms, including the aristocratic classicism of the seventeenth-century baroque, which was still active in eighteenth-century culture.

This older classicism, its appreciation of the affliction of masculine transformation, and its affirmation of female agency were revived and given "modernized" form in the classicist work of Johann Wolfgang von Goethe, who serves as an alter ego of David; Goethe's career and work in the late 1780s and 1790s serve as a direct refutation of the masculinist classicism of David and the Jacobins. Because of his attachment to an older, aristocratic order, Goethe attempts to keep alive what he regarded as the best of aristocratic civility in a classicism that would offer a critical alternative to David's. But notwithstanding the cogency of his critique, his desire to recuperate the female figure and the sociability of civility is ultimately stymied as his conception of a post-Revolutionary social and political imaginary offered that figure no viable location.

Goethe's recognition of the ambivalences of classicist masculine transformation and his affirmation of women in aristocratic classicism and sociability are carried on by one of his admirers and a direct heir of the institutions of the old regime—Germaine de Staël—as she negotiates her way in Revolutionary and Napoleonic Europe. In key writings of the early nineteenth century, she seeks to sort through and reorder the terms of cultural and gender conflict into a formula viable in a new society.

Whereas the previous chapter attempted to show how the enactment of classicism undermined its prescribed subjectivity, this chapter is concerned with the interplay of binary formulas that arrange and rearrange various cultural terms—namely, the terms of French civility and its conventional criticisms, those of French and German identity, and the terms of classicist revival and gender differentiation. David in the late 1780s sought to arrange these terms into binary oppositions that would spell the end of French civility and the elite public woman of the old regime. Against that cultural strategy, which was realized in the French Revolution, Goethe and Staël attempted to rearrange the same terms into structuralist formulae that would recuperate what they identified as the best of the old regime—in particular, the ideal figure of civility, the elite public woman. For Goethe this attempt at cultural rehabilitation proved to be extremely difficult not just to bring about but even to conceptualize in a post-Revolutionary world, a world identified with institutions that were defined as incompatible with the elite public woman. For Staël, the problems of incompatibility could be surmounted by taking into account what she believed were the lessons of her travels in exile—the putative differential character of different national cultures.

THE CULTURAL CRISIS OF THE OLD REGIME
AND THE RECONSTRUCTION OF GENDER

Setting out for Rome in 1783 to paint the *Oath* in a location of classical inspiration, David conceived of his journey and painting as responses to a putative generalized condition of cultural and moral decline in France. Since the defeats of the Seven Years' War and the resulting disarray of the French economy, the monarchy had been injured by criticism of its fiscal and political incompetence. The early 1770s witnessed the outbreak of another intense conflict between the monarchy and the Paris *Parlements*. In the mid-1770s the accession of Louis XVI installed a reformist government, but its plans for economic revival soon collapsed in the face of popular resistance. Thereafter through most of the 1780s, successive political scandals eroded respect for the government and the elite of society, giving rise to a wide range of political and cultural tracts denouncing government "despotism," pointing to the moral decay of the aristocracy, and warning of the general physical enfeeblement of the entire French population.[8] In the representations of legal *mémoires* and in writings such as Choderlos de Laclos's *Les Liaisons dangereuses,* France before the Revolution seemed to have fallen into a state of complete decadence, an apparent condition that reinforced the message of Rousseau and his followers about the debilitating defects of aristocratic civility. The turn against Rococo art in France was largely inspired by this reaction against what was believed to be the luxurious, corrupting sensuality and idleness of elite France.[9]

In the discourse of French civility, the ideal virtues of pleasing appearances and refined, gentle behavior had always been identified as "feminine" characteristics. The feminine character of civility was not just metaphorical; elite women played prominent roles in the institutions of civility. As conspicuous figures at court and as salonnières, these women exercised considerable social and cultural influence, operating as arbiters of good taste and creators of refined sociability. Teaching middle-class men aristocratic manners and discourse, the salonnières of the seventeenth and eighteenth centuries turned their salons into conduits for the middle class into the aristocracy.[10] In the second half of the eighteenth century—particularly in the grand salons of Marie-Thérèse Geoffrin, Julie de Lespinasse, and Suzanne Necker—the salonnières expanded their traditional role of educator in aristocratic social mores and assumed the functions of organizing and judiciously expediting the fluid intellectual discussion that characterized the Enlightenment salon. As Dena Goodman has recently argued, these grand salons functioned as centers of Enlightenment philosophy.[11]

When aristocratic civility seemed to perform according to prescription, as a discourse of gracious, harmonious appearances and behaviors that reflected and produced goodwill, its feminine character and the elite women who implemented civility were looked on in a favorable, idealizing light. But when civility seemed to malfunction, when pleasing appearances were taken as an instrument of evil manipulation, the feminine coding of civility was linked to dissemblance and moral corruption.[12] Thus the aporia of civility was condensed into the figure of the elite public woman, and the indeterminacy of that figure meant that elite public women could be perceived in directly contradictory ways, as virtuous civilizing influences and as agents of moral corruption.[13]

In the broad criticism of aristocracy and its culture of civility in the second part of the eighteenth century, the figure of the elite public woman fell under attack. In his *Letter to M. d'Alembert* (1758), Rousseau asserts that "the ancients had, in general, a very great respect for women," a respect they showed "by refraining from exposing them to public judgment." In contemporary France, the opposite obtains: "With us, on the contrary, the most esteemed woman is the one who has the greatest renown, about whom the most is said, who is the most often seen in society, at whose home one dines the most, who most imperiously sets the tone, who judges, resolves, decides, pronounces, assigns talents, merit, and virtues their degrees and places, and whose favor is ignominiously begged for by humble, learned men."[14] Linking the salonnière to the actress and to a conventional stereotype of the domineering woman in plays, Rousseau plays on every feminine trope of the conventional criticism of civility: its ability to generate pleasing appearances that are in the service of manipulation and vice. The contradictions of civility are condensed in the figure of the elite public woman, and men who succumb to these female implementers of civility, who give way to luxury and pleasure, are themselves feminized, as Rousseau put it notoriously, referring to the salonnière: "Every woman in Paris gathers in her apartment a harem of men more womanish than she."[15]

Rousseau's writings foreshadowed and fed an escalating attack on elite women in the last decades of the old regime. In the pamphlet literature of the late eighteenth century, the mistresses of Louis XV were freely associated with pretense and excess; Madame de Pompadour in particular was identified as the champion of Rococo and corrupt luxury. Parlementarians and other enemies of the monarchy portrayed the ascent of Madame Du Barry in the early 1770s and her association with the failed reformer chancellor Nicholas-Charles-Augustin de Maupeou as a political takeover by a woman who was no more than a prostitute. The anxieties about the untrustworthy gracious woman of civility were given exquisite literary form in Laclos's infamous Marquise de Merteuil of *Les Liaisons dangereuses*. The popular literature just before and into the Revolution subjected Marie Antoinette to pornographic caricature and ridicule.[16]

Accompanying the widening criticism of monarchy, aristocracy, and civility were a variety of programs for reform that ranged from projects for economic and political revival to cultural measures that would improve morals and alter aesthetics.[17] One of the strongest and farthest-reaching movements for reform was that of classicist revival and civic republicanism. Rousseau and other critics of civility looked to classicist republicanism as an answer to the lax morals and dissembling appearances of his era. A return to ancient values of simplicity and austerity, of self-sacrifice and civic obligation, served as a Rousseauian formula for the establishment of a society of transparent morality.[18] We have already seen that this call for a restoration of classical values was invested in images of masculine rationality, power, and self-mastery; the expression of classical self-restraint and patriotism slipped seamlessly into representations of male heroism and exertion, even if the projection of this subject could be strangely undone as it was enacted. This projection and undercutting of a masculinist classicist project was evident in works of both German and French classical revival, but there was also in French neoclassicism a complication directly connected to and given emphasis by changing events. In a period of political agitation and fear of cultural decadence, the urge for reform and masculine transformation in late eighteenth-century France was more intense, radical, and oriented toward far-reaching social change. Whereas projections of classicist masculinity in Germany seemed to center on phantasies of the male subject as a self-sufficient aesthetic being, the idea of classicist masculine emergence in France went hand in hand with a social and political program, central to which was a redefined role for women and a strong rejection of the putative corrupting world of decadent, dissembling aristocratic civility. French classicist reformers were engaged in a campaign against what they saw as the deceiving and corrupting public women of the old regime.[19]

Just as austere classicism sought to recall men to a vigorous republican tradition, so it sought to return women to their putatively "natural" roles—

as republican wives and mothers, paragons of simple virtue, nurturers, and silent supporters of men.[20] The Rousseauian view of the classical woman received a particularly strong formulation in the *Encyclopedia*. As Desmahis wrote in his contribution "Femme (*morale*)": "Her happiness is to know nothing of what the elegant world [*le Monde*] calls *pleasures;* her glory is to live in obscurity. Confined to the duties of wife and mother, she devotes her days to the practice of unheroic virtues: occupied with running her family, she rules her household with indulgences, her children with gentleness, and her servants with kindness. Her home is a haven of religious sentiment, filial piety, conjugal love, maternal affection, order, inner peace, sweet slumber, and health."[21]

During the Revolution, Jacobins saw themselves as republicans seeking to resurrect the civic virtues of the Roman republic, elevating men to moral duty while restoring women to republican motherhood. Initially in the Revolution, women were active in street demonstrations and political clubs, but as the Jacobins gained power, female political participation was discouraged. Jacobin propaganda disseminated a Rousseauian vision of natural feminine domesticity and passivity that was then enacted in the Terror. In 1793 the Jacobins included women's clubs and associations in their ban of political associations; in October of the same year, they executed the feminist activist Olympe de Gouges. Elite public women of the pre-Revolutionary period were led to the guillotine—notably Marie Antoinette in October 1793 and Madame Roland, the distinguished liberal of the old regime, in November 1794.[22]

When the Bastille fell in 1789, David was still a member of liberal intellectual circles,[23] but he readily embraced republicanism as the Revolution took a more radical turn. Becoming an ardent Jacobin, he was instrumental in the suppression of the French Academy as a privileged corporation. In 1794 he was elected as a Jacobin deputy to the National Convention. David loyally followed Robespierre, who put him in charge of organizing Jacobin festivals. On the eve of Thermidor, when Robespierre's arrest was expected, David is supposed to have called out, in what Norman Bryson nicely identifies as an attack of hysteria, "If you drink the hemlock, I will drink it with you." After Thermidor, because of this outburst and his work for the Jacobins, David was put in prison for two years.[24]

The close connection between David and the Jacobins has contributed to the view that the *Oath* is an anticipation of Jacobin aims and ideals. The painting seems to announce emphatically the Jacobin phantasy of male rejuvenation and the replacement of the elite public woman who dominates men with the subsidiary, domestic republican wife and mother. Both the painting and the radical Revolution demanded an exaggerated stylization and separation of gender identities, a reification of male and female character and the distance between them. Set in an austere classical space and rendered in a style of acute visual clarity, the powerful forms of the brothers Horatii portray, as Dorothy Johnson puts it, "regenerate men."[25] Their coming into masculine power is directly associated with their resolve to sacrifice themselves in the service of the state and is implicitly associated with their detachment from the world of republican women. The Horatii constitute an exalted male sphere of self-sacrificing duty and heroic power, an emergence that takes place as—in fact, because—the men separate themselves from a passive and feminine domestic realm that shrinks in significance to the side of the painting. In the visual logic of the painting, women recede into domesticity as men assume a position of public power and achievement. The *Oath* redefines the cultural and gender terms of the old regime. It splits a realm inhabited by men and women into private and public spheres, defines men by their ability to leave the private for the public, while women are consigned to the former. In eighteenth-century classicism, the capacity for self-sacrifice in a necessary obedience to duty was gendered male and was often called "sublime," opposed to the more pliable female sympathies, designated as "beautiful."[26]

The transformation of men, their separation from the private and their passage into the public, is marked as an emergence into power, an assertion of a deep masculinity that is so invested with lofty nobility that it seems less an affirmation of self than its transcendence, a surpassing of prosaic human limitation. In the painting the men's glorious transcendence of the everyday commands the assent and admiration of the viewer, but the fact that it is a transcendence enmeshes it in problems that extend beyond the painting itself. David was aware of these problems; indeed, there was a strong classicist tradition of such an awareness. To paint the *Oath* in the manner he did, he had to suppress that awareness, eliding the traditional aristocratic recognition that hypermasculine emergence, as a form of transcendence, was also a form of affliction. The traditional recognition of the double and deadly nature of masculine transformation would issue in a classicist alternative to David's masculinist conception, an alternative that attempted to return classicism to the aristocratic civility and sensibility of the old regime.

AFFLICTION AND THE SUPPRESSION
OF THE FEMALE VOICE

According to one of his students, David first thought of painting something about the story of the Horatii after attending a performance of Pierre Corneille's *Horace* at the Comédie Française in late 1782. Popular and repeatedly performed in the eighteenth century, Corneille's play was the specific inspiration of the painting, although David then imagined a scene that does not appear in the play. In one sense, as Thomas Crow has argued, David's invented scene is a fitting extension of Corneille. As Crow points out, in the eighteenth century, in the conventional opposition between Racine and Corneille, the former was regarded as superior in his refinement, elevated taste, and appreciation of amorous feeling. Corneille was regarded as surpassing Racine only in his ability to capture the spirit of an uncultivated, more impulsive, martial people, such as the early Romans. David's Horatii are Corneillian creations in that they embody an explosive, primitive power.[27] But the rest of David's invented scene is a striking departure from Corneille's play *Horace*. The play is in fact unserviceable for David's single-minded adoration of heroic masculine emergence.

The story of Horace concerns the dilemmas of two families, linked by marriage, from warring states. One of the Roman Horatii, the young Horace, is married to a sister of the Curatii. Likewise, one of the Curatii, the young Curiace, is engaged to a sister of the Horatii, Camilla, who sits closest to the edge of David's painting. The brothers Horatii are chosen by Rome to represent the city in combat, while the opposing state has of course chosen the brothers Curatii. Only the young Horace survives the fight, and when he returns to Rome he is cursed by Camilla for killing her beloved. In a rage, Horace kills his sister. Arrested and put on public trial for murder before an angry crowd, he is defended eloquently by his father, and he is acquitted.

The story of the Horatii is thus not simply the epic story of the separation and elevation of heroic men from a state of passivity identified with women. The painting monumentalizes one act of an ongoing tragedy in which the exaltation of the heroic male results in the destruction of the family: brother kills sister, a father chooses his son over his daughter, a sister marries into the family that slaughters her brothers. In the full story of the Horatii, which the viewers of the painting would have known, the message or moral is more complex than what is communicated in David's reductionist painting.

The play affirms the transformation of the young Horace into a hypermasculine hero who, in his zeal to serve the state, looks forward to and is unapologetic about killing his wife's brothers and his sister's fiancé. Indeed, Horace tells us that the ability to sever those ties only shows how much the greater is his valor; the disavowal of those claims in the service of the state offers the prospect of "fame" to which few men "dare to aspire."[28] But the play also points to the unhappy consequences of Horace's determination; the story of the Horatii is one of both heroism and tragedy, and as such one can no longer turn the story into simple, straightforward

Fig. 6. Jacques-Louis David (1748–1825). *Horatius the Elder Defending His Son.* Drawing (study). Black chalk, ink, and wash on paper. Louvre, Paris, France. Photo: Michele Bellot. Copyright Réunion des Musées Nationaux / Art Resource, New York.

privileging of hypermasculinity. The determined, aggressive male is glorified, but he is also put in question, and in that sense the ultimate meaning of the story is at least conflicted and possibly even indeterminate.[29]

Although on different occasions David seemed to be sensitive to the tragic outcome of male severity and heroic assertion, in the period when he worked on the *Oath,* those sensitivities appear to have receded. He completely overlooked the play's deep ambivalence about the results of heroic emergence. In a preparatory drawing for the painting (see fig. 6), he conceived a scene that portrays the story of the Horatii entirely from the viewpoint of the aggressive young Horace, who brutally and blindly welcomes all sacrifices. The drawing shows a defiant Horace being defended by his father before an angry crowd, while at their feet lie the lifeless body of his slain sister and the prostrate weeping mother. When David showed this drawing to his friends, they criticized the painting on both aesthetic and moral grounds. His patron Michel-Jean Sedain is supposed to have said, with some sarcasm: "Will our French custom allow for the fearsome authority of a father who pushes his stoicism so far as to excuse his son for the murder of his own daughter? No, no, we are not developed enough for such a subject."[30]

What David, in his extremism, did not notice is that, in his original conception of the painting, the appalling result of male valor is difficult to look on sympathetically: the men in fact appear loathsome in their disdainful disregard for the fate of women. In the final version of the *Oath*, David has removed the offending scene of a murdered woman and her weeping mother, but he shows no more sympathy for the tragic results of Horace's actions and for the fate of the women. In fact he devises a way of letting masculine assertion prevail while minimizing to the point of suppressing those aspects of the story that put male glory into question, aspects that viewers would have known from the play.

This strategy of concealing the implied horror of the oath accounts for a peculiar aspect of the painting. All commentators point to the strong contrast in the *Oath* between the powerful, assertive men and the crumpled female figures, and, recognizing that the collapsing figures of the women are a result of the terrifying action of the men, some go on to describe the women as deeply troubled, "quaking," or evoking "an atmosphere of deep sorrow."[31] The collapsing female figures indeed create a striking contrast to the male figures, but the descriptions of terrified women belie the oddness of the stylization. Women are confronted with a sublime and frightening scene of assertion and sacrifice on the part of the men, a scene that should leave them disturbed in some way. Yet the female figures convey no sign of fretfulness, no suggestion of the terror that they must feel in such a situation. They are in a state of total passivity, which may be read as a kind of sorrow; but if so, it is of a peculiar somnambulent sort. Rather than being overwrought or downcast, the women seem to be asleep.[32]

This peculiar stylization of the women is an answer to a problem identified in David's first conception of the painting and points to the extremism of his masculinist views at the time. It suggests the tragic result of the oath of the Horatii in the most innocuous way. The imminent demise of the family and the death of the sister are suggested by the collapsed female figures. But rather than seeming overwrought or anguished, their distraught and mournful feelings have put them into what seems, oddly, like a state of sleep. One effect of representing or suggesting the outcome of the *Oath* in this way is that the tragedy is almost abolished, turned into gentle allusion. One might say that while the men continue to be represented in what, following Crow, one might call a stiff Corneillian register, the soft, drooping women are offered in Racinian register; their terrible fate is made into a decorous sleep.

The *Oath* asks its viewers to forget a common lesson of these ancient parables—that male heroism is both exaltation and affliction—and in this sense it skews the complex reception of ancient tragedy in the eighteenth century. David's *Oath* cleverly elides the consequences of the transformation of the Horatii, allowing the viewer, such as the rhapsodic Tischbein, to admire without qualms the transformation of men. This elision, moreover, serves a double purpose. The play not only shows us the problems of heroic male transformation in showing us the tragic consequences of Horace's actions; it also emphatically and repeatedly tells us to expect those problems and, once they have unfolded, condemns them. The play contains explicit, eloquent criticism of masculine emergence. The young Curiace, fiancé of Camilla, follows his duty and defends Alba in combat with the Horatii, but only after lamenting the cost. He is appalled by the young Horace's easy resolution, which he calls barbaric; he declares that he is glad not be a Roman, since that means he might conserve something human. The young Curiace recognizes the unhappy results of his dutiful action, but the strongest and most extended challenge comes from Camilla, who condemns, both before and after the battle, the transformation of the young Horace and his appeal to Roman glory.[33] The representation of sleeping women in he *Oath* thus accomplishes a double elision. Their sleep not only mitigates the associations of the actions of the Horatii with the tragedy of women; it also silences criticism. The bitter, angry Camilla is rendered mute and passive.

This silencing of Camilla points to an aspect of the painting that has not been much discussed but is central to its story of masculine transformation and gender separation. Conventionally, when speaking of the painting in terms of divided gender identities, commentators point to the painting's split visuality, to the fact that the men in the painting define themselves by their strong steady gazes, while the women are defined by the failure of their vision, by their inability to look.[34] This is an important and much-discussed dichotomy (about which more could be said),[35] but there is another that is equally important and almost always ignored. This other dichotomy is important because it is in fact what predicates both male emergence and gender separation.

Men enter into a condition of exalted masculinity when they come together to swear an oath. Masculine emergence, in other words, is predicated on a speech act and one with particular characteristics. We can imagine that at the moment represented in the painting the men are speaking directly and decisively, in a few resolute words that allow for no ambiguity or equivocation. The words are a clear, direct commitment to action, and in saying the words, the men bring on the action; an oath is one of the simplest and strongest examples of performative speech.[36]

The significance of the oath in the painting is that it transforms men into superhuman beings, capable of acts of extraordinary bravery and self-sacrifice; but the other side of that transformation is that the men are implicitly disavowing their quotidian lives, their everyday pleasures and loyalties. All this is represented in the painting. As men speak in the militant, performative, and confrontational language of the *Oath,* they separate themselves from the quotidian domestic sphere of women, whose diminishing importance, whose disavowal by men, is registered in forlorn muteness. Women droop into a somnambulent silence, which innocuously—because it is sleep and not death—marks feminine passivity and its secondary, superseded significance.

This dichotomy of speaking and mute figures, along with the dichotomy of seeing and nonseeing, contributes largely to the effectiveness of the painting. The binary oppositions give the scene a simple and direct force. But although the dichotomies are stylized as opposites, the stylization is tendentious: the opposites reinforce rather than contradict each other. The opposition of male and female principles is constructed in such a way that the principles come together to produce a nearly seamless endorsement of male exaltation.[37]

In Corneille's play *Horace,* Camilla's strong vocal opposition to the heedless young Horace indicates a sharper and less skewed opposition than the one David represents in his painting, an opposition that does not complement but contradicts. The antithetical opposite of men speaking an oath is not women who are silent but women who speak and who speak in a way that seeks to undercut performative male speech. Opposed to militant performative speech is a fluent female speech that would halt action, that seeks to produce more speech and reflection. Unlike the severe masculinist classicism of David, the older aristocratic French classicism of the baroque seventeenth century, which still thrived in eighteenth-century theater and opera, was profoundly ambivalent about the transformation of men into would-be Horatii. This aristocratic classicism had no qualms about identifying that emergence not just as a transcendence but also as an affliction. And often the classical figure who pointed out the ambivalent character of male transformation and who attempted to stop it was an elite woman who spoke. Camilla is one example of such a woman, but there were also others, and these models of female agency would be remembered and rehabilitated throughout the period when the extremist gender politics of David's *Oath* were being implemented.[38]

GOETHE: IPHIGENIA AGAINST THE HORATII

After painting and exhibiting the *Oath* in Rome, David returned in 1785 to France, where the work would be elevated into the emblem of the arrival in aesthetics of an austere classicism, whose pendant cultural and political values were those of an assertive masculine regeneration and gender separation. In the same year that David left Rome, Johann Wolfgang von Goethe set out on his now-famous trip to Italy. Eventually arriving in Rome, which he made his home base, he remained in Italy until 1788. Goethe's trip to Italy was a much-needed change from what he had felt was a physically exhausting and intellectually limiting position as a senior civil servant in Weimar.[39] A trip to Italy was for Goethe a visit to the source of the kind of culture he had come to revere.

In the early 1770s Goethe had made a literary reputation on the basis of works of intense emotionalism, most famously his *Sufferings of Young Werther* (1772). But by the mid-1770s he had put aside that work for a classicist view of the world. His classicism can be considered part of the general classicist revival in European culture at the end of the eighteenth century. But in its social allegiances, it was of an entirely different persuasion from David's or Winckelmann's. Goethe's turn to classicism roughly coincided with a critical change in his life. Befriending the new duke Carl August of Saxe-Weimar in 1778, he moved to Weimar, where he wrote and served in the duke's administration, rising to the eminent position of privy councilor.[40]

In his early work, Goethe strongly criticized aristocratic values and institutions, mounting, for example, in *The Sufferings of Young Werther,* a particularly negative characterization that drew on conventional criticisms of aristocratic civility and sociability as cruel, unnatural deception.[41] After his move to Weimar and his insertion into the center of courtly and aristocratic life, his interactions with the nobility and Carl August were not always smooth;[42] nor did he become unaware of the abuses of aristocratic privilege. But notwithstanding those qualifications and the tensions they suggested, from the mid-1770s Goethe had arrived at a *modus vivendi* with aristocracy and monarchy, and the writings of this, his classicist period, reflected those loyalties.

His new connection to the prince and aristocracy were only strengthened by the attacks on those institutions in France. In the mid-1780s Goethe followed the rising political tensions in France. His recent major biographer, Nicholas Boyle, tells us that Goethe read Necker's justifications of his unsuccessful economic reforms and that he was especially alarmed by reports of the Diamond Necklace Affair, which, in its attack on Marie Antoinette, challenged the authority of the French monarchy.[43] Goethe's commitment to the aristocratic culture of the European old regime in this period is strongly evident in his first work of his Italian visit, the prose version of his play *Iphigenia in Tauris.* Here he offers, cast in classicist allegory, a defense of aristocratic values against the new masculinity and gender separation given emblematic form in David's *Oath. Iphigenia in Tauris* reasserts the values of civility, in particular the role of the elite public woman. After Goethe's return to Weimar and as he followed the events leading up to and into the French Revolution, his figure of Iphigenia reappears in other important works to constitute a major aspect of his response to the Revolution. *Iphigenia* initiated what turned out be a concerted campaign against the dissemination of the hypermasculine classicism found in late eighteenth-century France. Goethe offered an alternative classicist view of gender, one that sought to recuperate endangered principles and institutions of the old regime.

That Goethe's classicism of the late 1780s and the 1790s seeks to preserve the aristocratic culture of the eighteenth century is already evident in even a simple outline of the events of *Iphigenia*. The story was widely disseminated in the culture of the European old regime. Multiple published versions were available throughout the century in Europe; by one estimate eighteen different versions were published between 1697 and 1779. Plays about Iphigenia by Euripides and Racine were part of the standard and much-performed theatrical repertoire in the eighteenth century.[44] Besides Christoph Gluck's two famous operas, *Iphigénie en Aulide* (1773) and *Iphigénie en Tauride* (1779), there were at least thirty operatic settings of the Aulis story between 1632 and 1819 and more than fifteen of the Tauris story between 1704 and 1802.[45] Gluck's *Iphigénie en Aulide,* according to James Johnson, "revolutionized" Parisian opera, marking a turn away from the playful *tragédie lyrique* to more serious drama that focused on internal states and intensity of emotional expression.[46]

The critical light that the story of Iphigenia casts on an ethos of masculine emergence was particularly evident in the early French Revolution. In those years Gluck's *Iphigénie* operas continued to be performed, but the performances now inflamed and polarized political loyalties, resulting in shouting matches and fights. *Iphigénie* was identified with the elite public woman of the old regime, sometimes with the most elite; Johnson tells the story of how the Duchesse de Birn, at a performance of *Iphigénie en Aulide,* to the horror of the Revolutionaries in the audience, cried out, "Chantons, célébrons notre Reine" ("Let us sing, let us celebrate our queen").[47] In 1793 the National Convention imposed various censorship restrictions and ordered the production of patriotic plays and operas. *Iphigénie* plays and operas were withdrawn from repertoire in September 1793, not to be restaged until after Thermidor. But notwithstanding its suppression in France by the Jacobins, the story of Iphigenia continued to operate throughout the Revolutionary period as an inspiration for a view of gender relations alternative to the increasingly dominant representations of heroic male emergence, an alternative view that recuperated the ideal social function of the elite public woman of the old regime.[48]

Iphigenia in ancient Greek legend is the daughter of Agamemnon, the king of Mycenae and the acknowledged leader of the Greeks. Assembled at Aulis and ready to sail for Troy, the Greek ships are becalmed. The Greeks learn that only if Agamemnon sacrifices his daughter to the goddess Diana will their army receive the wind that will carry their ships to Troy and to glory. The story of Iphigenia involves themes strikingly similar to those in the story of Horace. It shows in particular the two sides of heroic male emergence, but here, more emphatically than in the story of Horace, affliction presents itself as an overwhelming problem, a huge blockage to the transformation of men. Agamemnon, unlike the young Horace, agonizes over his choices. That he is required to sacrifice Iphigenia to initiate heroic transformation makes that sacrifice seem not, as in *Horace*, an unintended and unfortunate consequence, but here a necessary precondition or a condition of possibility. And when Agamemnon chooses to kill Iphigenia, he sets in motion the full destruction of his family—his murder by his wife, Clytemnestra; and hers by their son Orestes, who is then cursed by the persecution of the Furies.

The plays and operas of Iphigenia at Aulis concern her sacrifice; the sequel, *Iphigenia at Tauris,* takes place after all the murders in the family and seeks to resolve them. The Tauris story not only shows that Iphigenia has been spared but also makes her into the agent of healing who restores Orestes. At Aulis, all the Greeks believe that Agamemnon has sacrificed Iphigenia; but just as he is about to strike the death blow, the goddess Diana invisibly spirits away Iphigenia to the island of Tauris, where she is installed as high priestess in Diana's temple. This is no happy fate, as she continues to be enmeshed in the barbaric ways of men. The island's brutal leader, Thoas, forces her to preside at the sacrifice of all strangers who happen to land on the island. Eventually, after years on the island—after the Trojan War and the events that have befallen her family—Iphigenia is faced with the prospect of having to kill Orestes, who has landed on Tauris.

In Goethe's *Iphigenia at Tauris,* the militant, action-oriented male is still powerfully evident in the figure of Thoas, who in making Iphigenia sacrifice foreigners believes that he is obeying a higher duty, a divine law, and that Iphigenia's revulsion is merely a sign of womanly weakness.[49] The infirmity of women, as in David's *Oath,* renders them incapable of committing themselves to a "social bond." Initially seeming to confirm this view and lamenting her own weakness—"Oh, if I only had a man's heart in me / Which when it harbours some bold resolution / Closes itself to dissuading voices"—Iphigenia, like Camilla, comes to strongly question hypermasculine assertion, and she does so pointing out that every act of male glory is also an affliction that befalls women and families. "Forbear your swords!" she calls out. "Consider me and what must be my fate. / Fights are soon fought, and they make men immortal: / But does posterity count the endless tears / Of the forsaken women who survive?"[50]

Corneille's *Horace* recognizes an inescapable quandary in masculine emergence—that it necessarily issues in tragedy; its assertion of transcendent heroism goes hand in hand with an admission that it also destroys quotidian life. The tragedy of *Horace* is that tightened knot of aspiration and loathing, which makes the play indeterminate in its judgment of heroic transformation. In Iphigenia plays and operas, the condemnation of masculine assertion is clearer and stronger, but traditionally the resolution and ultimate meaning of the stories were still left indeterminate. In all previous versions of Iphigenia, from Euripides to Racine and Gluck, the escape of Iphigenia and her brother from Tauris is sprung on us as a special intervention of the gods, as if the tragic quandary of heroic transformation could not be resolved by human judgment or action alone, as if in some sense human tragedy was a destiny that human beings could not change.[51] The innovation of Goethe's *Iphigenia*—as critics have noted—is that he dispenses with these formulaic, classical, and old-regime endings to the story and, in doing so, does away with the residual uncertainty of their views about heroic transformation. Goethe's condemnation of masculine posturing overwhelms all its possible justifications, including appeals to destiny.[52] Goethe makes Iphigenia fully into a humanist actor. In his play she is the author of her own rescue and of her brother's. And she accomplishes all this by engaging in intense, sympathetic speech that not only questions the rationale of masculine assertion[53] but ultimately changes the behavior of men, so that by the end of the play she has lifted the curse from Orestes and has convinced Thoas to give up human sacrifice and to allow them to leave the island. Iphigenia's words overturn heroic male emergence. She returns males, who have been driven by their sense of higher duty, to a more quotidian humanity, a humanity defined as familial and domestic.[54]

This figure of Iphigenia is the answer to David's Horatii, and she reappears strongly in Goethe's works that are written in nervous response to the events of the French Revolution. Following the escalating radicalism of the Revolution and the invasion of southern Germany by the Revolutionary army, Goethe composed a long epic poem in 1792. In *Hermann and Dorothea*, a small German town is unsettled by a stream of southern Germans who have been driven from their homes by the advancing French army. When the good burgher's son Hermann sees what is happening, he becomes angry and aroused, so that as he speaks to his mother he feels himself taken over by a powerful sense of duty. Hermann speaks in a militant performative language, and as he speaks he is transforming himself into a patriot and warrior, into a Horatius: "This I feel in my innermost soul," he says, that "my spirit has moved me / To this undaunted desire: To live for my fatherland and to / Die for it, and to give others a worthy and noble example." The mother, however, knows better; she knows that Hermann's "lot in life is to be here / Quietly tilling [his] fields."[55] And when she questions him about his sudden transformation, she finds that his militant declaration conceals a deeper, uncomfortable attraction for the German refugee girl Dorothea. Hermann's mother leads him to clarify his desire and to forget his patriotic declaration. Hermann's invocation of overriding civic duty, instead of producing hypermasculine transformation, unravels into an admission of domesticity and quotidian desire, of wanting a life with, rather than against, women.

In *Iphigenia* and *Hermann and Dorothea* fluent female speech halts the precipitous transformation of men, which is marked or occasioned by the few militant words of men. In David's implied elision of this same opposition in *The Oath of the Horatii*, the opposition refers to representations of women's public role in the aristocratic institutions of the old regime, a connection that helps to explain an otherwise peculiar reference in *Iphigenia*. At one point in the play, Thoas's retainer says that Thoas "thinks little of fine speech. . . . He is accustomed / Only to giving orders and to acting: / He does not know the art of delicately / steering a conversation to its point."[56] Thoas speaks minimally, in a simple and direct fashion; his words bluntly and fully express his feelings; they are oriented to decisive action. Thoas's speech is the language of direct, militant command, the speech of heroic male emergence. And this powerfully performative speech is contrasted with, as Goethe puts it, "the delicate art of steering a conversation," a reference that is implicitly and oddly associated with Iphigenia, oddly because no part of the dialogue resembles what one would expect of conversation. The reference to conversation and its association with Iphigenia is ultimately a reference to the social function of the elite public woman of the old regime, who mediates between transformed men and, in mediating, returns them to a quotidian humanity.

As we have seen, eighteenth-century anxieties about the deceiving power of civility circulated around the figure who was identified as the impresario of civility, the salonnière. In the conventional discourse of civility, that figure assumed a highly idealized form. As Dena Goodman describes her, the salonnière occupied the position of coordinator of discussion because of her putative ability to mitigate the conflictual, aggressive character of men, and in doing so fostered a refined and well-functioning sociability.[57] The medium she used to create that sociability was a pleasing and fluent oral discourse—in a word, conversation. The characteristic medium of the salonnière is the direct opposite of the medium of the hypermasculine Horatii. Whereas swearing an oath is a speech act that is directly performative, issuing in a certain kind of immediate action, the conversation of the salon, carefully regulated by the salonnière, is performative in a highly mediated and self-reflexive fashion. The conversation of the salon seeks to produce not action separated from speech, but thought and more speech, a process that involves carefully regulating one's behavior to avoid offending the other interlocutors. David's *Oath* is a rejection of that refined world of civility and sociable speech for one of minimal militant speech and decisive male action; Goethe's answer to heroic male emergence reminds us of that world of careful, refined speech acts and of how it ideally functioned. Iphigenia's language functions in the same manner as the conversation of the Enlightenment salon: it calms tumultuous men, forestalls precipitous action and hypermasculine transformation, and creates shared understanding. This figure of the mediating woman who overturns masculine transformation gives Iphigenia and Hermann's mother a power over men. In the agitated years of the Revolution, Goethe would continue to turn to this ideal figure, as she now seemed to him all the more necessary given the rise of even-more-bellicose men.

Goethe's *Conversations of the German Refugees* (1794–95) begins with the recent expulsion of the invading French Revolutionary army from southern Germany, allowing a group of German aristocrats to return to the estate of a baroness. Two of the men in the company, one disposed toward political reform, the other reactionary, fall into excited argument. Each man frankly and inflexibly asserts his views, contradicting, then taunting the other, forcing the other to take an even more extreme position, until the reactionary calls for the hanging of all reformers, and the reformer for the guillotining of all reactionaries. This argument is conducted according to the terms of militant male speech—the direct, inflexible, and committed speech of the *Oath* and of Thoas—and it results again in an unhappy rupture of human relations. This, precisely, is *not* conversation.

After the reactionary has angrily left, the baroness rebukes the remaining would-be reformer and Revolutionary sympathizer. Like Iphigenia, she ridicules the pretext for his extremism, the invocation of higher principle that overrides day-to-day relations. And she makes clear what we might now call the paradox of militant male speech. As an austere and direct expression of the most elevated moral sentiment and commitment, it is supposed to signify autonomy and even transcendence, but as the baroness points out, the enactment of militant male speech undercuts autonomy, lets speech slip beyond the control of the speaking subject, so that it reconstructs him into something inhuman. Against this slippage of speech and subjectivity, the baroness urges a return "to the old ways," to an older form of sociability, to the civilizing ideal speech situation of the old regime.

"Now let us agree," she says, "to restore those conversations by intention, by self-imposed rule! Try as hard as one can to be interesting, careful, and especially sociable!"[58]

GOETHE: THE ELITE PUBLIC WOMAN AT AN IMPASSE

Explicitly opposed to the kind of heroic male emergence identified in *The Oath of the Horatii*, Goethe offered an alternative classicist subject, a female figure who is a moral agent but whose ethics differ from those of militant men. Rejecting the idea of an overriding, transcendent duty or imperative that precipitates male transformation, Goethe's classicist subject halts or overturns male emergence and, in doing so, recuperates the role of the public woman of the old regime. He confers on his classicist women a "civilizing" influence, the ability to mediate between men to create a pleasing, harmonious sociability that we have seen embodied in the ideal of refined conversation. The reassertion of these aristocratic values in this period of Revolutionary upheaval may have seemed to Goethe a proper, moral position, but in the context of the aroused sensibilities of European society, it also carried with it an air of anachronism and cultural reaction. One early indication that Goethe's views were out of step with the changing time can be seen in the reception of *Iphigenia in Tauris*.

As he tells us in his memoir of Italy, when he first circulated the play among his friends in Rome in December 1788, it was warmly received, although its reception was nothing like the acclaim that fell on David's *Oath*. According to Schiller, Goethe's work was too "mannered" to be popular, a view that Goethe also seems to endorse when he writes that the work failed to sell well in Germany because of its form.[59] In its unities of time, space, and action *Iphigenia* mimics the style of seventeenth-century classical French tragedy, a dramatic genre that was the favorite of Goethe's patron, the duke of Saxe-Weimar.[60] Indeed the play was first performed in a characteristic aristocratic and courtly venue—as a private performance in which members of the aristocracy and court played different roles, Prince Constantin and Carl August sharing the role of Orestes' friend Pylades and Goethe playing Orestes.[61] Goethe's biographer Nicholas Boyle asserts that the problem with Goethe's writings in this entire period was precisely that they were directed at court tastes and not at a German "public."[62]

Goethe's associations with aristocratic and courtly life and his championing of certain of its values and institutions were isolating him from the cultural and political changes around him even as they provided him with a means to criticize those changes. What made his position more difficult, what brought him to an impasse, was that he recognized in some crucial ways that the old regime was passing as a viable social and historical era.[63]

As we have noted, the young Goethe was well aware and highly critical of the problems of aristocratic society, and he formulated his criticisms in terms of the conventional challenges to aristocratic civility as dissemblance and corruption. Going to Weimar, he set those observations aside, especially as he now appreciated other and to him positive aspects of the principles and institutions of the court and aristocracy, aspects he defended in his classicist female figures. But even as he defended aristocratic civility and the court against their critics, once the Revolution broke out he had to recognize that the critics had a point, that they pointed to evils he himself had once identified. Even if he did not think much of the idea of heroic masculine emergence, even if he wished to preserve what he thought was the best of the old regime, he also recognized in the end that that society was collapsing. In this sense Goethe was not a deluded cultural reactionary, blind to the problems of the society he wished to preserve. Rather, he was in the more difficult position of seeking to preserve aspects of a society whose time, he believed, was up; and the question now was how or where to locate the values he admired of a superseded society. How, in short, could the elite public woman of old-regime civility exist in the new world seemingly created by the French Revolution?[64] This issue and the quandary that it constitutes—the dislocation of the elite public woman of the old regime—appear as an insoluble problem in *Hermann and Dorothea* and in the play *The Natural Daughter* (1803), the latter explicitly intended to be his response to the French Revolution.

The Natural Daughter concerns a fictional, unknown illegitimate daughter, Eugenia, of the king of a state on the eve of a revolution. Goethe's embrace of the old regime is evident in his characterization of the king as a benevolent and gracious father, who intends to acknowledge Eugenia publicly and to give her a place in court. When she learns that her good father is going to recognize her at court and invest her with influence and power, she euphorically imagines a glorious presentation, and as she does she gives voice to the discourse of civility's conventional justification of elaborate, artful appearances: "What is appearance if it has no substance?" she asks, defending her enthusiasm. "Could there be substance if it is not seen?" Eugenia imagines the moment of her public presentation, in all the finery of her position and genealogy, as a triumph: "Superbly fitted out thus I am," she says to her governess. "My happiness is assured."[65]

But Eugenia's phantasy of aristocratic civility and triumph proves to be extremely fragile, pressed, on the one side, by her eventual recognition of the aporias and abuses of civility, and on the other by the coming of revolution. Eugenia eventually realizes that she is utterly naive about the court, as she comes to see that beneath and through its refined appearance conspiracies are at work. One, directed against her, is already in motion, and it eventually issues in her abduction and threatened death.[66] Eugenia is ultimately offered a choice between a treacherous world of deceptive public display, exile overseas, or a "humbler sphere of domesticity," as the wife of a provincial magistrate. She at first refuses to deny her identity, to put aside her prerogatives as an elite public woman. What finally compels her consent to a coerced marriage (overseas exile is not seriously contemplated) is the recognition that the conspiracy directed against her is but one of many forms of political activity driving the country to revolution. She recognizes that the social world of refined civility is on the verge of disappearance. To stay close to that world without endangering herself, she consigns herself to a derogating marriage with a provincial bourgeois.[67]

We do not know what Goethe ultimately intended for Eugenia, since he never wrote the two succeeding plays of the projected trilogy. We can only speculate about why he never finished those works, but what may have been a consideration was the situation in which Eugenia finds herself at the end of the play: an ideal old-regime public woman, forced to repudiate her "publicness" by both the contradictions of the old regime and the antagonisms of revolution.[68] The independent public woman of the old regime, whom Goethe obviously wants to succeed and to continue, finds herself at a cultural and historical impasse. Not wanting to abandon her cultural inheritance but recognizing that its time is past, she places herself in a state of social suspension. The same fate, though here disguised, applies to the main female character in what is perhaps the oddest work of Goethe's classicist period, *Hermann and Dorothea.*

Hermann and Dorothea is set against a background of social and political tumult; Germans from the left bank of the Rhine are fleeing before the invasion of the French Revolutionary army. When the poem opens, the refugees have crossed the Rhine and are moving deeper into southern Germany. These dramatic events provide a promising source for Goethe's epic narrative, set as it is in hexameter and elevated language.[69] But in *Hermann and Dorothea* this source of epic developments is kept at arm's length. Instead of following the flight of the Germans, most of the poem focuses on distinctly unepic characters—a small-town innkeeper, his wife and son, an apothecary, and a pastor. The poem recounts their reactions to the flight of their fellow Germans and allows only one of the refugees—Dorothea—to speak directly when she decides to return with Hermann to the town.

The poem deals not with the unfolding of social and political upheaval but with nonparticipants and a woman who chooses to leave that tumult for the security of bourgeois life. The narrative line thus works against conventional expectations, and in this sense follows the narrative trajectory of *Iphigenia* and *Conversations:* the movement from the great transformative public events of the period to the tranquil domestic sphere of the family.

This overall macronarrative schema is reiterated in individual incidents. We have already seen how Hermann, ostensibly motivated by patriotic zeal, is on the verge of abandoning his bourgeois existence to join the German army. But Hermann's mother blocks his transformation into a Horatius, and he returns to the family as he confesses that his patriotism was only a way of concealing his love for Dorothea. Later in the poem we learn that Dorothea earlier had a German fiancé who, full of reform-minded enthusiasm, left her and his family to join the Revolution in Paris. Like Hermann's encounter with his mother, this incident begins with the ostensible transformation of a man into a hero, defined by his repudiation of his quotidian world and the world of women. But again this narrative movement is immediately aborted, as Dorothea then tells us that her fiancé was imprisoned and executed and that his unfortunate death freed her from her commitment to him, allowing her ultimately to marry Hermann. Here, too, submergence in transformative public events and the possibility of masculine emergence give way to a prosaic, feminine world of the family. The only successfully "epic" character in the poem is Dorothea, who has heroically defended herself and other women against the physical assault of French troops, a development that, in a nice reversal of gender roles, makes Hermann wonder if he is worthy of her. But as soon as she receives an offer of a stable domestic existence, she gladly puts aside her heroic persona and returns with Hermann to his family's home.

Goethe's epic poem reverses the trajectory of the kind of epic development suggested by *The Oath of the Horatii* and places the epic style in the service of realizing bourgeois domesticity. But while it plainly offers a tranquil bourgeois existence as an alternative to the new world of the Revolution, it also modifies the life of the small-town German bourgeoisie so that it recuperates elements of the world the Revolution destroyed, the aristocratic civility of the old regime. The poem is not just a refusal of the conventional epic transformation of men into hypermasculine heroes: it also narrates a subtle transformation of bourgeois men.

The narrative trajectory affirms small-town Germany as a good alternative to the Revolution, but it does not entirely idealize the former. Goethe in fact readily criticizes the provincial bourgeoisie, and those criticisms are in keeping with what he says in other writings.[70] The father shows himself to be small-minded and self-centered (he regrets giving up his old dressing gown as aid to the refugees), materialistic (he is disappointed that Hermann has not already married someone wealthy), and unfair and rather bullying in his treatment of Hermann. He speaks neither in the engaging aristocratic conversation of civility nor in the militant rhetoric of the radical republican, but in homely platitudes, the linguistic form of an invincible *bürgerlich* common sense. Hermann is a kind and gentle son, held back by his mother from turning into a hypermasculine patriot. But the other side of his gentleness are shyness, awkwardness, and passivity, as his father explicitly and repeatedly points out to him. Hermann suffers from his father's domination.[71]

The male figures of *Herman and Dorothea* are the antitype of the epic's characteristic protagonist; they are the mundane, provincial bourgeois, a conventional opposite of the male transformed into the noble, hypermasculine hero. Goethe's use of the epic style to represent these characters seems to emphasize their smallness; hence the tendency of some critics to argue that Goethe intends an "ironic" epic—a parodic epic of an unepic people.[72] This view does not, however, do justice to the poem's convolutions.

The representation of men in *Hermann and Dorothea* is a low, bourgeois variant of Goethe's generally negative portrayal in his classicist writings of men asserting their masculinity. Women in the poem are also portrayed in a way consistent with how they appear in those other works, a way that does not fit with conventional representations of passive bourgeois women. The mother lacks the pomposity and smugness of the father, is more discerning about people's character, and deftly mediates relations between father and son. She soothes her son's sense of injury at his father's belittling words by showing him that beneath the father's veneer of patriarchal authority there is a more flexible heart,[73] and we have already seen how she halts the transformation of Hermann into a Horatii. The mother's resourcefulness, independent thought, and power of mediation echo the traits of Iphigenia and, before her, the elite public woman of the old regime.

Dorothea is an even more emphatic version of the same, defending herself against French troops and ministering to the weaker of her fellow fleeing Germans. And in her Goethe makes a strong, explicit connection to the culture of the old regime. Dorothea tells Hermann how she has assimilated French customs:

> For the French were our neighbors, and they in that earlier epoch
> Set much store by politeness, and not the nobility only:
> Townsfolk and peasants as well, and they made their families learn it,
> So we Germans were used to it too and practice it.[74]

The epic, in other words, shows us petty and authoritarian bourgeois men but also strong-willed, intelligent women who interact with those men and change them. Like the mediating woman of the French salon, Dorothea civilizes Hermann and his father, bringing out their noblest and most rational aspects. At the end of the play, influenced by her uplifting character and feminine grace, the father puts aside his severe manner and his petty materialism and welcomes the impoverished woman into the family with a tearful embrace. Dorothea's consent to Hermann's marriage proposal allows him to come into his own as an adult bourgeois. Addressing her (and us) for the first time "with noble and manly emotion," he makes the final speech that is a paean to the ethos of the bourgeois family in a time of political trouble:

> Then let our bond, Dorothea, be so much firmer in all this
> General chaos; let us endure and continue and hold fast
> To the fine possessions we have here.
> For in an unstable time . . .
> he who holds firmly to his purpose gives shape to his whole world.
> Let not us Germans continue this terrible present upheaval,
> Swaying uncertainly hither and thither: it does not befit us.
> Let us say rather: This is ours and so
> Let us maintain it.[75]

Hermann and Dorothea is not an ironic representation of the bourgeois but a social phantasy, an idyll of social harmony and a recuperation of aspects of the old-regime discourse of civility that had become threatened by the French Revolution. The intelligent and independent mediating woman of civility finds renewed life in provincial bourgeois domesticity, while under her influence the ordinary parochial bourgeois male is ennobled, a development that is subsumed in the epic form as an answer to more conventional and disastrous republican epics and masculine transformations of the French Revolution.

Hermann and Dorothea is a social phantasy that rescues an idealized old-regime principle of feminine cultivation and sociability by depositing it in the vessel of a German small-town bourgeois family. The fusion involves a trade: feminine aristocratic civility finds a haven in the bourgeois household, and in providing that haven, bourgeois men are ennobled. This reciprocity issues in a happy resolution and offers a social position, so the poem concludes, from which people can withstand further political disturbances. But the problem with this happy and resolute unity at the end of the poem is that it is extremely awkward or forced in different ways. Even ennobled, conventional bourgeois motivation still fits uncomfortably into the epic form. "Holding fast to the fine possessions we have," as Goethe has Hermann say, sounds distinctly flat as a heroic cause. Much as Goethe may want the social persona of the bourgeois to seem compatible with heroic poetry, their incompatibility continues to show through.

Hermann and Dorothea seeks to solve the displacement of the elite public woman of the old regime by displacing her further, depositing aristocratic femininity into the bourgeois household. But while this saves her from the

Revolution, it endangers her in another way. Her relegation to the bourgeois household cancels her public life and puts her under the authority
of the bourgeois male, however improved he might be by her presence.
This outcome is particularly clear in *The Natural Daughter*, where an anguished Eugenia, an elite public woman of the old regime, finds it difficult
to repudiate her entitlement to "eminence in the world" for "a humbler
sphere of domesticity." She agrees to marry the provincial magistrate only
when she feels the external forces of the coming revolution threatening to
crush her, and although her choice is meant to preserve her (and the culture she represents), Goethe cannot help but acknowledge that it is also a
defeat—the forceful, independent woman of the old regime must submit
to the authority of the narrower mentality of a bourgeois male. Goethe attempts to mitigate the problem of derogation and loss of independence by
having Eugenia agree to marry the magistrate only if, as she puts it, they
can continue to behave as "friends," or as "brother" and "sister," an
arrangement that would continue to allow Eugenia a measure of real if not
apparent independence and parity regardless of the customary and *de jure*
submission. Goethe's contrived ending of the play—its recognition and
disavowal of domestic patriarchy—suspends Eugenia between aristocratic
independence and bourgeois submission.[76]

In *Hermann and Dorothea*, the mother is shown to be effective in handling
the men, and presumably Dorothea will show the same talent. But notwithstanding their abilities at mediation, both women are ultimately bound by
a formal principle of patriarchal authority, one that again makes Goethe
uneasy. The father is more bluster than action, but he still exercises authority, as will Hermann after him, particularly since at the conclusion of
the play he acquires serious, adult, and bourgeois masculinity. That Goethe
is bothered by the ultimate submission of his civility-derived women in the
bourgeois family can be seen in the awkward circulation of the theme of
female servitude in the poem, which, as a literary *Verneinung,* or equivocal
denial, repeatedly broaches the theme only to disavow it. When Hermann
returns to the refugees to ask Dorothea to marry him, his words fail him—
the failed speech of the still-awkward, not-yet-adult, male bourgeois—so
that she thinks he is offering her a position as a domestic servant. Uncertain of what to do, he lets her suffer this misapprehension. This first
prospect of female servitude, explicitly aroused, is then quickly denied.
Thinking she has agreed to be a servant in the household, Dorothea immediately undoes her fate rhetorically, invoking a shopworn trope that
turns servitude into a kind of mastery: "Service is a woman's lot," she says
to Hermann, "and the sooner she learns it the better! / For it is only by
service she ends up being the mistress. / And enjoying the power that by
rights is hers in the household."[77]

As they travel to the inn, Hermann warns Dorothea about his father's desire to be shown deference in the household—a predilection that Dorothea graciously accedes to by saying that she has learned the proprieties of politeness (and therefore of deference) from the French.[78] Her link to French civility makes her required submission seem acceptable, the slippage from one cultural system to another apparently reconciled by turning female service in the bourgeois household into an act of *politesse*. When they reach the inn, the misunderstanding is finally cleared up. Dorothea is to be a wife (and presumably mother) and not a servant. Overcome with emotion because she has secretly loved Hermann all this time, she accepts the proposal and tearfully addresses the father. She tells him that the misunderstanding—that she is to serve—is, in effect, the proper understanding after all, but now made acceptable because it is adorned in sentiment rather than necessity: "for I promise, the loving and faithful / service you would have had from a maid, you shall have from a daughter."[79] Although she speaks in a moment of sentimental reconciliation and although her words are represented as an act of love and faith, Dorothea confesses a truth that Goethe regrets even as his character speaks it—that Dorothea's promise binds her to the home and to the governance of men. Threatened by heroic male emergence and the French Revolution, the elite public woman is given sanctuary in the bourgeois household; but in putting her there, Goethe in effect consigns her to the same location imagined by a masculinist classicism. Dorothea's concluding oath to the father suggests the same fate for the elite public woman as David's *Oath of the Horatii:* relegation to a secondary domesticity.

DREAMS OF COMPLEMENTARITY: STAËL, *CORINNE, ON GERMANY*

European interest in German culture, and news of its great revival since the end of the eighteenth century, were greatly broadened by the immensely popular publication of Germaine de Staël's report of her trip to Germany in 1804. Written in 1810 and published in 1813, *On Germany* was a major impetus in disseminating throughout Europe the image of Germany as a nation of poets and thinkers, less urban and urbane than the French, but more richly emotional and spiritual, with their roots in medieval culture rather than in Hellenism. Germany was "Romantic" as opposed to "classic," an opposition that governs much of Staël's analysis.

Later Germans—notably Heinrich Heine—chafed under the delivery of German culture into the hands of a medieval Romanticism. From what we have seen even in this study, Staël's characterization is very forced indeed, ignoring, for example, the strong claims of classicist revival as a possible source of a new German cultural identity. In *On Germany,* she recognizes these manifestations of classicism and does not quite know what to do with them. She is, for instance, rather disappointed to report that the Goethe she meets is not the emotional enthusiast she had imagined wrote *Werther,* and she finds the works of his classicist period rather cold—dramatic art conceived as tomblike "monuments."[80] But she forgives these lapses as she finds Goethe a pleasing conversationalist whose elegance and broad knowledge make her feel as if she were conversing with Diderot—only better, she says, since Diderot is affected—"a de vouloir faire effet"—whereas Goethe disdains pretense. Goethe pleases her but also, plainly, intimidates her.

Staël's report on Germany—from the macrocharacterization of its culture as Romantic to the microdetails of Goethe's heartfelt conversation—is written in constant dialogue with her conceptions of France, and she makes expansive use of the conventional tropes of the cultural differences between French and German culture: German profundity and sincerity versus French *bonheur* and affectation. Staël makes use of—indeed, greatly publicizes—this conventional dichotomy, but unlike others, who typically favored one term of the opposition over the other, she oscillates between the two, faulting one to affirm the other and then reversing those valences. She admires the simplicity and sincerity of German life, and she believes that German intellectuals combine that genuineness with depth and thoroughness of thought, a combination that is the meaning of German *Innerlichkeit.* And what is of particular consequence for Staël is that in German men such straightforwardness and depth make them "incapable of deceiving," producing in them a "perfect loyalty" that "renders love less dangerous for the *bonheur* of women."[81]

Staël's affirmation of Germany issues from the established criticism of aristocratic French civility and the particular controversies of the period. At the center of those controversies were the writings of Rousseau. We have seen that his aggressive and misogynist version of civic republicanism was taken over by David and the Jacobins, but there was also another Rousseau of the late eighteenth century, whose criticisms of aristocratic society were made in a softer key. In his epistolary novel *La Nouvelle Héloïse* (1761), Rousseau offers a model of self quite different from the stoic, self-denying classicist warrior of David, even if common to both is a rejection of the putative decadent, immoral, and deceiving culture of the old regime.[82] Through a series of letters, the main character, Julie, describes her sacrifice of illicit passionate love for the simple virtue of a natural wife and mother on a Swiss estate—in other words, the realization of Rousseau's ideal republican woman in a pastoral mode. What made a remarkable impression on a broad and enthusiastic readership was not just the novel's moralizing but its intense emotionalism—its "sentimentalism," or out-pouring of emotion—which seemingly allowed one human being to directly address the deepest feelings of another.[83] Yoked to an idea of natural morality, his critical sentimentalism appealed to many who were not directly drawn to the militant masculinity or politics of Rousseau's civic republicanism. Among the many who were inspired by the novel were members of the intellectual aristocracy, including the young Germaine de Staël, who first gained literary attention for her work on the sentimental Rousseau, her *Letters on Rousseau* (1788). The same Rousseauian current informs her characterization of German men in *On Germany*. In their simple, heartfelt goodness, they serve as trustworthy sentimentalists, whom Staël calls here by their new nineteenth-century appellation: Romantic.

Staël's Rousseauian sentimentalism leads her as well to reiterate the Rousseauian criticism of civility. In *On Literature Considered in Its Relationship to Social Institutions* (1800), for example, she points out that France had "in some respects" become "too civilized," so that "its institutions and social customs had taken the place of natural affections." The result, she says, was a society centered around vanity, appearance, and performance, becoming in effect a "theater in which recognition had nothing to do with real merit." Taste, she concludes, turned "effeminate rather than delicate"; politeness, instead of drawing people together, simply divided them artificially into classes.[84] In *On Germany* she establishes the honest sentimental character of the Germans by opposing them to the manipulative, performative personality of the French: "The French think and live in others, at least according to the relationship of *l'amour-propre;* and one senses, in most of their works, that their principal aim is not the object that they are dealing with, but the effect that they produce." Staël draws from this criticism the standard conclusion of the critique of civility, found in both Rousseauist sentimentalism and classicism—that in a society of *amour-propre* and refined deception, the goodness of women is always in danger, as they can be seduced by false speech and the appearance of love.[85]

The characterization of the German in *On Germany*—profound, genuine, trustworthy—is thus a stylized inversion of the characteristics of French civility, an inversion effected by combining the new image of Germans with a Rousseauian sentimentalism. But however much Staël deplores the problems of aristocratic French civility—and elevates the German—she cannot do so in the thoroughgoing way of the Germans themselves. Staël's sentimental Rousseauism exists in contradiction to her own enjoyment of the refined society that it criticizes. This contradiction becomes readily apparent when she is confronted by that other stream of Rousseauism, the classicist and hypermasculine criticism of civility. Staël moves between Germany and France according to the opposed stylizations of the two cultures and the internal, contradictory pressures of the discourse of civility. But when confronted in the Revolution with the classicist criticism of civility become Jacobin aggression she moves back toward old-regime sociability, seeking to defend her own way of life.

Born in 1760, Staël came of age in the twilight of the old regime. Her father, Jacques Necker, was an important figure in French politics. Originally a Swiss banker, he served as a popular reformist finance minister in France during the last years of Louis XVI's reign; his dismissal in 1789 resulted in rioting that culminated in the fall of the Bastille and his recall to office. Staël's mother, Suzanne Necker, had fashioned herself into one of the most prominent of Enlightenment salonnières. In the last years of the old regime, Staël not only was trained to take over the salon—filling in for her ailing mother, who died in 1794—but also established herself as a promising young writer with her well-received *Letters on Rousseau*.[86]

In the early years of the Revolution, Staël was among those public women who were slandered—in her case by no less than Antoine de Rivarol, the writer on French language. Although she took no part in the feminist agitation for suffrage, because of her prominence she was grouped with the activists and likened, unsurprisingly, to seductive courtesans.[87] After the September massacres, like other aristocrats she fled France, going first to England, then settling on her family estate in Coppet, Switzerland. She did not return to France until Thermidor, and during the Directory she became a moderate republican, even though doing so meant repudiating her family's service to the monarchy. When Napoleon became first consul for life in 1802 she was forced again into exile, returning to Coppet, from where she made trips to Germany in 1803, to Italy in 1804, and to Russia in 1812. After Napoleon's fall she returned to France, in 1814; and in the early Restoration she supported the idea of a constitutional monarchy modeled upon the English system.[88]

Staël points out in various writings that one of the most fateful consequences of the radicalization of the French Revolution and the Napoleonic empire was the suppression of aristocratic sensibility and sociability. When she writes about this lost world, she defends it, explicitly and implicitly reiterating the conventional justification of civility—its equation of refined appearances with moral character; the loss of this civility is the work of brutality and arbitrary power. "Since the Revolution," she writes in *On Literature*, "a revolting vulgarity of manners is often combined with the exercise of any kind of authority." The demand of the "republican spirit" for "more severity" has destroyed taste, and that destruction is both the result and the cause of the worst human attributes. "The coarseness victimizing us is almost always composed of vicious sentiments: crudity, cruelty, and violence in their most hateful forms." Staël notes that this republican (and, we might say, classicist) spirit was in particular directed against the prominent public woman. "Ever since the Revolution men have deemed it politically and morally useful to women to reduce women to the state of the most mediocrity." And Napoleon, "influenced from his early habits of Revolutionary days," retained a certain "Jacobin antipathy to brillant Paris society" and to its elite public women, an antipathy, she suspects, that lay behind her exile from Paris.[89]

Although Staël has adopted the sentimentalist Rousseauian critique of French civility, she rejects the classicist Rousseau's relegation of women to republican domesticity. While "modesty and simplicity," she writes, "are enough to maintain the respect a woman needs in her family . . . more is needed in society." And what is needed is precisely what characterized those aristocratic qualities lost to the Revolution: "elegance of language" and "nobility of manner," crucial parts of "a woman's dignity" that "a republic," Staël notes, "strips" away.[90]

Staël's ties to aristocratic sociability emerge strongly in *On Germany* as she switches from a consideration of Germany's advantages to a survey of its limitations. She affirms the simpler sincerity and deeper reflection of the Germans, but she also tells us that these go hand in hand with a lack of urban culture and a charmless sociability. Those deficiencies are particularly notable in relation to that defining element of aristocratic sociability—the conversation of the urban salon, directed by the salonnière. As she points out time and again in *On Germany,* the "rapidity of *esprit* that animates gatherings and places in movement all the ideas" is scarcely to be found in Germany.[91] In one breathless passage she describes the electrifying effect of Parisian conversation and ends up endorsing all the displacements of civility that she has found fault with as a Rousseauian critic of civility: form overpowering content, pleasurable performance seductively displacing ideas and values:

> The type of well-being that is the test of an animated conversation does not consist mainly in the subjects of conversation; the ideas and knowledge that one develops there are not of principal interest. It is a certain manner in which one acts on others, of creating pleasure reciprocally and rapidly, of speaking as soon as one thinks, of enjoying the moment itself, of receiving unforced applause, of showing *esprit* in all the nuances of tone, gesture, look, thus producing a will that is the sort of electricity which throws off sparks, relieving one of an excess of vivacity, while awakening others from a painful apathy.[92]

This *jouissance* called up by the memory of the salon is identified with female freedom and influence, as she applies to the salon its most idealized seventeenth-century characterization: a "paradis des femmes." Over and against this memory and image of female joy and power, Staël looks on the German woman as a plodding, intellectually deferential inferior, utterly lacking in the "quick spirit that makes conversations live and ideas move."[93]

Staël's work in general and *On Germany* are thus cleft by contradictory ideas and loyalties. As a critic of civility's deceptions and putative immorality, she elevates the German. But when she remembers the pleasures of the French salon, she deplores the German's social ineptitude and celebrates French sociability. She rehabilitates French civility in the face of the ostensible severity and coarseness of another culture, and this tendency is reinforced by her sense of how Revolutionary and Napoleonic France have undermined graceful sociability and the important cultural role of elite women.

On occasion, Staël shows an awareness of her oscillation between the positive and negative poles of the discourse of civility as she toys with ways of reconciling them. At one point in *On Germany*, for example, she imagines that the melancholic German might be enlivened by learning the practices of French conversation. But as soon as she raises this possibility, the conventional criticism of civility blocks further thought as she recognizes that bringing French refinement to the German would undercut German virtues. French pleasure and elegant sociability, she concludes, would inevitably ruin the scrupulous good faith, capacity for solitary work, and independence of thought she has so admired in the Germans; superficiality and dissemblance would come to dominate in Germany as they have in France.[94] The description of Goethe's conversation is another attempt at reconciliation, with Goethe appearing as a stimulating but sincere conversationalist, a Diderot one can trust.

On Germany displays all the cultural conflicts discussed in this and previous chapters—the arguments for aristocratic civility and those against it; endorsements of the elite public woman and her condemnation—and because Staël's views and experiences put her on both sides of the conflict, those conflicts appear in *On Germany* as a set of contradictions and dilemmas, oscillations between cultural opposites. And these contradictions, dilemmas, and oscillations within the discourse of civility take place in a highly charged atmosphere of Revolutionary and Napoleonic persecution of civility.

Staël sometimes weakly attempts to reconcile the antithetical terms of civility, its affirmations and denials. But *On Germany* can also be considered to offer an imagined resolution of the conflicting terms of civility in a different, and more far-reaching, manner, one that also seeks to deal with the French republican and Napoleonic attack on old-regime civility. This phantasy of resolution puts to use Staël's travels during her exile as she uses those travels to sort through and solve the cultural antagonisms of the era.

On Germany's characteristic mode of analysis—the binary opposition—is found in Staël's other works. When she writes about England, Germany, and Italy, she thinks about them in terms of strictly antithetical types.[95] In her work directly preceding *On Germany*, the novel *Corinne, or Italy* (1807), which she was inspired to write while in Germany, the tragic love story is cast as a collision between opposing national personality types, the Italian and the English. And like the dichotomy of France and Germany, that of Italy and England is locked in a chain of other, homologous antitheses: oppositions of "north" versus "south," "classic" versus "Romantic," "sublime" versus "beautiful," "masculine" versus "feminine." And notwithstanding sometimes different labeling, these oppositions involve the terms of the conceptual and historical conflicts of eighteenth-century classicism—between the affirmations of aristocratic civility and its conventional criticisms, a classicist republicanism and a sentimentalist Rousseauism, heroic masculine emergence and the relegation of the elite public woman of the old regime to deferential domesticity.

In the proliferation of binary oppositions in her writings, Staël seems to be not just a structuralist *avant la lettre,* but a compulsive one, seeing the world as a proliferation of oppositions, one summoning up a series of others. In the dissemination of these finely tuned oppositions, she is plainly trying to orient herself in her dislocation, as a French exile in other European countries. But in considering how these many various terms relate to one another, we can also see that she is aiming for something more—a way of configuring her cultural legacy, contradictions, and experiences of Revolutionary France and Europe, so that out of the arrangement of national cultures and gender identities a possibility of resolution emerges. The most important works of her exile, *Corinne* and *On Germany,* constitute a complex structuralist phantasy that seeks to give order to the conflicts and complexities of the time and to imagine a situation in which the elite public woman might be rescued from a damaging history and restored.

Conceived during her visit to Germany in 1804 and written after a subsequent trip to Italy, *Corinne, or Italy* was Staël's most successful literary work, one that established a receptive audience for *On Germany*, which was written the following year but not published, because of Napoleon's censorship, until 1813.[96] At the beginning of *Corinne,* the Scottish peer Oswald Lord Nevil leaves Britain in late 1794 and travels to Italy to improve his health, which, since the recent death of his father, has been impaired by "a deep sense of affliction" (*C,* 3). Weak, sick of life, and melancholic, Oswald arrives in Rome, where he witnesses a public ceremony, the crowning of the most celebrated public woman in Italy, the "poet, writer, *impro-visatrice*" known by the sole name Corinne (*C*, 19). Oswald is overwhelmed by the splendor of the event—by Corinne's unassuming grace and beauty, by her poetic improvisation on the theme of the glory of Italy, and by the enthusiasm of the crowd, which cries out "Long live Corinne! Long live genius! Long live beauty!" Oswald falls in love with Corinne. Corinne, in turn, notices Oswald in the crowd, and, struck both by his sadness and by his identifiably "English" sense of dignity,[97] she includes in her improvisation an acknowledgment of him and his emotional condition. They soon meet, and, with that encounter, Corinne is also in love.

What complicates this immediate attraction is, first of all, the cultural type that Oswald represents. Being English, Oswald, we are repeatedly told, necessarily holds certain cultural views. By nature grave and melancholic, he is "restrained and veiled" in his emotions (*C*, 49). He subscribes to a "stern and solemn religion" and believes that strict obedience to a severe duty outweighs all other concerns (*C*, 54, 68, 180–183, 237, 291). This overwhelming sense of obligation frequently prompts Corinne to comment that Oswald is harsh in his judgment of both himself and of others, but it also gives Oswald a sense of dignity, profundity, and self-sufficiency.

Corinne also knows that Englishness requires that its women be confined to a domestic sphere. While English men are active in war, commerce, and politics, English women have as their "only vocation" the maintenance of house and family (*C*, 253). Women are expected to be unassuming, silent, and deferential and to devote their lives to raising children and caring for their husbands (*C*, 96, 105, 124, 131). As the representative of the north and of England, Oswald is considered by Staël to function under the sign of the Romantic "sublime."[98] But Oswald's traits— he is grave, melancholic, dutiful, dignified, and profound—are also "sublime" in the classicist sense. And as in David's classicism, for instance, Oswald's sublimity serves as a marker for an intensified masculine identity that separates itself from (and therefore simultaneously defines) a female identity, one whose difference, whose pleasing and seductive nature, is called the "beautiful." These distinctions, though renamed and called Romantic by Staël and her interpreters, are ones that we have already encountered in the cultural conflicts of the old regime surrounding the elite public woman and the classicist ideal of masculine emergence. Notwithstanding the new appellation—like Nietzsche's "Dionysian" opposed to the "Apollonian"—the terms involved are the same as those we have already seen. What Staël adds in *Corinne* is the inspiration of her travels and eighteenth-century belletristic anthropology. The terms we have already dealt with are now distributed according to a geographical differentiation: if the masculine sublime is northern, then the feminine beautiful is southern.[99] The south, and in particular Italy, is always identified in terms of the beautiful, as a land of sensuous, pleasurable distraction. For this reason, Oswald, the man of the north, is initially "quite biased against Italians; he thought them passionate but flighty, unable to feel deep and enduring attachments" (*C*, 33). But Oswald comes to appreciate Italian passion in another form when he succumbs to the allure of Corinne, who, as the title suggests, is in fact the essence of Italy.

Oswald immediately has strong feelings for Corinne, and those feelings unsettle him not just because they go against his national character but also because his encounters with the beautiful and gracious Corinne remind him painfully of an earlier and fateful lapse from the imperatives of national identity (*C*, 39, 47). Eventually Oswald explains to Corinne the background to his current melancholy and illness, and with this we find out that the opposition of north and south, of the sublime and beautiful, involves more than England and Italy.

In 1791 Oswald made what was supposed to be a six-month trip to France. In these early years of the Revolution he encountered what seemed like a happy fusion of old-regime sociability and Revolutionary ardor. "It seemed," he says, describing those days to Corinne, "that conversation had inherited the deepest ideas, and that the whole world was in a state of revolution only to make social life in Paris more attractive. I met well-educated, highly talented men, inspired even more by the desire to please than by the need to be useful, seeking a salon's approval after winning acclaim at the speaker's rostrum, living in the society of women to be applauded rather than loved" (*C*, 209). Oswald's first encounter with Revolutionary France is the ideal realization and reconciliation of Staël's contradictory ideas; the best elements of aristocratic civility—the salon, its conversation, and its governance by intellectual women—fuse with the ideas and events of the early Revolution; this wishful phantasmatic reconciliation is shown to be such not just because its ideal harmony soon deteriorated with the radicalization of the Revolution, but also because Oswald found that there was more to refined French civility and beauty than his first impressions of it. Civility was accompanied by its usual problems. Oswald's feelings about French civility moved from charmed acceptance to disillusionment, as the pleasing appearances of civility, in the figure of a woman, showed themselves to be dissemblance, seduction, and moral corruption. Oswald met the beautiful and charming Madame d'Arbigny, whom he describes as the embodiment of "perfect grace." Flattered by her attentions, he grew close to her, until, as Oswald later recognizes, "she ruled over me tyrannically" (*C*, 212–213).

Oswald was charmed by d'Arbigny, but even in this state he found something out of proportion; her self-presentation seemed to him less natural expression than theatrical performance: "I sometimes thought," he says, "that her language was a bit artful, that she spoke too well and in too soft a voice, that her sentences were too studied" (*C,* 212). Staying in France much longer than initially planned, Oswald was called back to Britain by his father; Madame d'Arbigny contrived to keep him in France. She preyed on his sense of honor, calling on his protection as she pointed to the danger that as an aristocrat she feared from the Jacobin Revolution.

D'Arbigny deceived Oswald, and when he discovered the deception he returned to Scotland, where he found that his father had long been ill and had died in his absence. Oswald was overwhelmed with guilt at having sacrificed duty and obedience to the seductions of a dissembling French beauty. His actions constituted in effect the opposite of those of *The Oath of the Horatii:* he forgot his duty and disobeyed his father in order to pursue a pleasurable life of civility with a sociable woman who was precisely the opposite of David's deferential and domestic women. Staël here dramatizes the Rousseauian antithesis of simple natural morality (i.e., obeying one's father) and dissembling and corrupting civility, an opposition that is stylized as an opposition between English men and French women. What is significant is how Staël after representing that simple binary then seeks to go beyond it.

The characterization of D'Arbigny and the ultimately deceptive, seductive nature of French civility are meant both to resemble and to differ from what Oswald finds in Italy. As the novel makes clear in Oswald's associations of Corinne with d'Arbigny (*C,* 39, 47) and in descriptions of Corinne, she is similar to d'Arbigny in her presentation of an alluring beauty that immediately seduces Oswald. But unlike D'Arbigny, whose bad character lies beneath the dazzling surface, Corinne's beauty gives signification to moral substance. Her feminine and Italian charm is always characterized in ways that emphasize its difference from a dissembling French civility. Her beauty, we are told, is unadorned and unaffected (*C,* 22). She expresses her feelings directly and is genuinely sensitive to the feelings of others. She plays no social games. Thus, although she is all "grace and gaiety," those qualities in Corinne have "no trace of mockery" and are "owed only to a lively mind and radiant imagination" (*C,* 23).

We also learn that Corinne's defining achievement—her talent for improvisation—is in fact a form of French civility's ideal mode of sociability, but purified of pretense and narcissism and made into genuinely spontaneous and empathetic communication. Corinne describes her art: "I shall say that for me improvisation is like a lively conversation. I . . . go along with the impression my listeners' interest makes on me, and it is to my friends that I owe the most of my talent. . . . The conversation inspires my passionate interest. At times the interest lifts me beyond my own powers, brings me to discover . . . bold truths and language full of life that solitary thought would not have brought into being" (*C,* 44). Corinne's improvisation stands in for and stabilizes the uncertain conversation and sociability of French civility. She produces performances that operate like the purest, most sentimental conversation, as direct circuits of communication and intense feeling.[100]

The relations among Oswald, d'Arbigny, and Corinne can be represented in a modified structuralist schema. Oswald, England, and the masculine sublime constitute the opposite of d'Arbigny, France, and beautiful feminine civility. Corinne's attributes are not the opposite of d'Arbigny's but different inflections of them, inflections that give them a positive moral valence. The relationship of the characters looks like this:

morally defective (−)

Oswald/England/depth/   d'Arbigny/France/performance/
gravitas   dissemblance

north/masculine/sublime   south/feminine/beautiful

_____   Corinne/Italy/improvisation/
transparency

morally affirmative (+)

Oswald's attraction to Corinne, from a structuralist perspective, is the second attempt of the narrative to find a successful solution to the problem of linking opposing terms. The second attempt also fails, not because Corinne is a faulty alternative to d'Arbigny but because Oswald turns out to be on the wrong horizontal axis: he is on the side of the flawed d'Arbigny and therefore is flawed himself. In the novel, Oswald's structural problem is registered in different ways. The narrator repeatedly and explicitly points out that Oswald's character is weak and vacillating (*C,* 201, 215, 288, 336, 372, 406). Oswald's structural problem also defines the plot: his failure to act on his and Corinne's mutual professions of love culminates in his ultimate marriage to Lucile, the embodiment of silent, retiring English domesticity. Corinne, abandoned, chooses to waste away and dies.

Oswald's decision not to marry Corinne is precipitated by the command of his father, who in a letter left for Oswald tells him to marry Lucile. The father's letter has for Oswald the force of a self-renunciating oath, an inescapable duty that Oswald follows not only because doing so is in keeping with his northern masculine character but also because he is weak. Unlike the lesson of *The Oath of the Horatii,* male submission to paternal authority in *Corinne* is not an exaltation of male strength and autonomy but a sign of infirmity of character, one that necessarily results in affliction for both the unhappy Oswald and Corinne.

The novel thus enacts the terms of cultural conflict—between feminine civility and its masculinist critique—as an ostensible triangle, one that redeems aristocratic civility by splitting it, conferring its conventional problems onto France and d'Arbigny, and its benefits, including the ideals of sociability, conversation, and the elite public woman, onto Italy and Corinne. The novel also responds to the new ideals of masculine emergence—here thought of as "Romantic" but still classicist in character and function. This masculinity, predicated on an affirmation of an elevating duty that renounces the love of independent women, is here exposed by Staël as submission to an overbearing patriarchal authority. And this submission implies the lesson of Goethe's *Hermann and Dorothea:* that while giving men the appearance of freedom and power, submission to authority—to a sense of civic male duty—actually marks their tutelage; and what precipitates their autonomy is the influence of the public woman, as Hermann is able to enter adult autonomy in his own right only after Dorothea has changed him. The corollary of ongoing masculine tutelage to authority is the relegation of women to a passive domestic sphere, a condition that means a tragic loss for both the son and the public woman. Oswald's marriage to Lucile leads to the suicide of Corinne, and it soon shows itself to be a stagnant, unhappy union.

The novel is mapped out as an ostensible triangle formed by France, Italy, and England, but what underwrites this triangular relationship, what ensures that it ends in tragedy, is an absent but implied fourth term. This absent but still crucial structuring term must be related to Oswald in the same manner that Corinne is related to d'Arbigny. It must complement Oswald's and England's defects and, in that sense, offer a suitable partner for Corinne. The absent fourth term would offer a masculine and northern figure of the sublime that would without vacillation appreciate a virtuous feminine beauty.

That crucial missing term is the subject of *On Germany*.[101] There Staël presents a northern nation where men such as Kant, Goethe, and Schiller unite masculine moral rigor with an appreciation of art and poetry. Like English men, German men are profound and melancholy, but, unlike the English, they are more sensitive to emotion and beauty; they are sentimentalists in possession of *Innerlichkeit*.[102] In other words, German men are a positively charged version of English masculinity. But though positively charged, the character of German men is still incomplete. As we have already noted, Staël observes that for different reasons, including the seriousness and the abstract metaphysical character of German thought (and language), Germans have a less developed public life and a poorer sociability than those found in France: Germans, Staël says time and again, are highly deficient in the art of lively conversation. This is particularly the case of German women, who, Staël suggests, promote rather than mitigate this weakness in German men.

The lack of a refined sociability and lively public women in Germany finds its problematical opposite in France, where those institutions and figures are present but in a negative manner. German men find their tenable complement and completion in the variant form of feminine French civility—in Italy and Corinne. With *On Germany*, we might then complete the structuralist rectangle that governs *Corinne:*

morally defective (–)

England/empty depth/	France/false appearance/
bad masculinity	bad femininity
north/masculine/the sublime	south/feminine/beautiful
Germany/sincere depth/	Italy/moral appearance/
good masculinity	good femininity

morally affirmative (+)

The proper complement to Italy is Germany. These are strongly attracting cultural types, whose attractions are not cancelled out but strengthened by their differences. German men need a Corinne to provide their depth with a pleasing sociability and a gracious appearance in a manner that does not carry the French taint of dissemblance and corruption. And Corinne needs German men to fulfill her own sentimental desires—which, given her suicide at the end of the novel, means that she needs German men to live. We might say, in other words, that in this structuralist shuffling of terms and types, the ideal phantasmatic match is between Corinne and Goethe. Motivating the antitheses of *Corinne* and *On Germany*, as a solution to the cultural traumas of the period, is a dream of complementarity—between Germany and Italy, men and women, cultural depth and sensuous appearance, the classicist sublime and the beautiful of the old regime.

This structuralist reasoning, shuffling, and ultimate rearrangement of terms also imply a development in the sense and gender of classicism. In Staël's antitheses of north/south, masculine/feminine, and sublime/beautiful, classicism—identified as "southern"—is now displaced onto the entirely feminine and beautiful (even as Staël continues a covert link along a horizontal structural axis to classicism's sublime/masculine aspect, now deposited in the "north"), as Corinne is strongly associated with her location in Rome and its ruins. Her fluent improvised speech is meant to suggest a remnant of some ancient female art. The gender shift is thus complete: from David's masculinist classicism to Goethe's rehabilitated feminine classicist agent to Staël's new classicist woman, emerging as the play of type and antitype on the classical authority of Rome.

Staël's *Corinne* and *On Germany* seek to give sense to the cultural and political conflicts of the period, and together they imagine a solution that, while ingenious, remained phantasmatic. Staël's dream of complementarity was at work only in its absence. There was no actual enduring linkage—in fiction or in life—between the spirit of the best of Germany and of the best of France displaced onto Italy. Corinne dies, and Staël after *On Germany* remained in restless exile, awaiting the time when she could return to Paris. Staël's divided loyalties—on the one hand recognizing the need for some liberal reform, but on the other hand still attached to the way of life of aristocratic French civility—shaped an intricate maneuvering of terms of identity among different putative national characters. In the European and German reception of Staël that intricacy and its principle of complementarity were lost, and Staël's views of Germany were instead made into fodder for a conservative reaction in Germany, one strongly hostile to liberal reform and to any alignment with France, even in some displaced form. That skewing of Staël's *On Germany* was the result of another conflict in stylizations of Germany and France, one that concerned the question of whether Germany belonged to a "modernity" defined by the French Revolution.

CHAPTER FIVE

The French Revolution and the Problem of Time

Hegel to Marx

Each phantasy of identity that we have considered in this book entails a stylization of time. The liberal Enlightenment imagines that time flows in a linear, progressive, and universalizing fashion. Such is the temporal structure of sound empirical knowledge and benevolent commerce spreading, sometimes slowly and fitfully but also inexorably, across Europe to the rest of the world.[1] The progressivism and universalism of Enlightenment time were moreover reinforced by its assimilation of the discourse of civility, according to which European society had slowly evolved from barbarism to a present and future refinement and civilization. Against the teleological temporal schemas of Enlightenment time and the French discourse of civility, Herder, in the persona of a German cultural nationalist and historicist, asserted the incommensurability of different cultures and their temporalities. For Herder, there was not one, universal development for all countries, passing through the same set stages, but many developments, corresponding to the fundamental differences between cultures. Each nation followed its own historical rhythms and trajectories.[2]

Historicist disavowals of the Enlightenment's linear, teleological progressivism sometimes issued in simple Rousseauian inversions that imagined historical time as a fall from an original, archaic authenticity and moral certainty into modern artifice and moral corruption. Or, as Herder put it, "the eighteenth century's triumphant talk of the 'light of our century'" was actually an admission of "its frivolity and exuberance, its warmth in theory and its coldness in practice, its apparent strength and freedom and its real moral weakness and exhaustion under the weight of unbelief, despotism, and luxury." The direct converse of this depraved current culture was an older, feudal German society that, notwithstanding its roughness and coercive practices, was a place of clear moral purpose and social harmony: "In the patriarch's hut, the humble homestead, or the local community, people knew and clearly perceived what they talked about, since the way they looked at things, and acted, was through the human heart." In this German historicist phantasy, an idealized past served as a privileged origin, the fountainhead of the basic good character of Germans, which then disseminated itself through Germany's subsequent history, regardless of attempts to assimilate that character into a current Enlightenment and Francophile temporality.[3]

Winckelmann's classicism offered a conception of time that differed from both the linear progressivism of the Enlightenment and the idealization of the distant past in historicism. For Winckelmann and those influenced by him, the ideal temporal condition was at once a return and a transcendence—a return to a vision of *Ur*-rational forms, of eternal verities, that then allowed the viewer to step outside of contingent historical change. As Schiller tells us in *On the Aesthetic Education of Man in a Series of Letters,* in the contemplation of perfect aesthetic form "we are no longer in time"; "time itself, the eternally moving, stands still."[4] Other eighteenth-century classicists, such as Rousseau and David in France, looked to classicist atemporality (or supratemporality) with a more political purpose. They imagined that classical republicanism offered a timeless model of political and moral virtue and masculine plenitude that could be reestablished against what they identified as the corruption and decadence of French society.

In the eighteenth century, as with identities in general, the temporalities available to writers or intellectuals were multiple and sometimes conflicting. But, as with identities, the multiple, contradictory nature of temporalities did not prevent a writer, artist, or intellectual from subscribing to them. In *Also a Philosophy of History,* Herder issued a crucial founding statement of historicist notions of time, one meant to affirm a distinct German past. But in its stylization of the archaic past as a condition of moral and communal transparency, it also bears strong similarities to Rousseau's classicist idealization of the ancient republic. And although Herder's essay showed him to be a determined relativist in matters of time, he sometimes alternated between that rigorous historicism and an Enlightenment belief in universal progress and reform. Hegel's philosophy of history showed both a progressive and a universal character—and in this sense resembled Enlightenment histories—but it was also classicist in its much-discussed notion of an "end of history" in the present, when the major conflicts of history would have culminated in a system of rational completion that was now available for recognition and contemplation.[5]

What made it more difficult to subscribe to multiple temporalities or what led intellectuals to opt for one decisively against others was the French Revolution. The Revolution did not introduce new notions of temporality, but it did unsettle them, intensifying, separating, and reifying each against the other. To many Europeans, the Revolution signaled a quickening of historical change, conveying a sense that historical events had suddenly accelerated, so that Europe now seemed in the throes of a breakthrough into an entirely new stage of history.[6] Many German intellectuals initially welcomed the Revolution, regarding it as the long-awaited realization of the Enlightenment's calls for political reform. Friedrich Gentz expressed a typical sentiment: the Revolution "is the first practical triumph of philosophy, the first example of a form of government, which is based on principles and on a far-reaching, interconnected system." Kant reiterated this sentiment when he wrote that the Revolution had transformed the abstract principle of rational autonomy into a political reality.[7] Hegel expressed the same view in his lectures on the philosophy of history of the 1820s, asserting that the Revolution had cleared away an anarchic mass of antiquated social and political institutions and had allowed the most advanced moral and political tendencies in Europe to assume concrete form. In France, he said, it had abolished aristocratic privilege and arbitrary royal authority, replacing them with social equality and constitutional, representative government. Carried by Napoleon's armies into central Europe, the Revolution had led to the removal of a moribund empire and remnants of feudal privilege and servitude and had helped to establish rational legal codes, freedom of property and person, and equal access to government service.[8]

Because the Revolution had eliminated traditional obstacles to social equality and constitutional government, German intellectuals such as Kant and Hegel, who believed in the Enlightenment idea of universal reason and reform, could view it as a crucial fulfillment of the Enlightenment's promise of progress. For them, the Revolution marked the arrival of a new time, when unfettered reason had at last achieved some substantial reality. Or, as Hegel said, invoking the significance of the Revolution in his lectures on the philosophy of history, "Never since the sun had stood in the firmament and the planets revolved around him had it been perceived that man's existence centers in his head, i.e., in thought, inspired by which he builds up the world of reality" (*PH*, 447). In characterizing the Revolution as a new era when rational social and political forms attained institutional reality, these Germans (and many commentators today) identified it as the decisive arrival of "modernity."[9]

These Germans who initially welcomed the Revolution, seeing in it the definitive sign of a new, Enlightenment era, also subsumed Germany into that temporal condition. Perceived as the achievement of universal reason, the Revolution offered a model of social and political principles that rational people everywhere were obligated to follow.[10] A surprisingly large cross-section of German intellectuals—from Friedrich Gentz, Justus Möser, and Friedrich Schlegel to Herder and the young Hegel, Friedrich Hölderlin, and Friedrich Schelling in Tübingen—looked on the initial events of the Revolution as signaling the arrival of much-needed social and political reform in Germany. The Revolution's passage into intensified violence, international war, regicide, and Terror altered the initial euphoric support of many German intellectuals. Significant figures who had welcomed the Revolution, such as Gentz, Schlegel, and Schelling, turned into intellectual and political conservatives. Some historicists, including Möser, who had acknowledged the importance of social and political reform, even if within a historicist framework, now repudiated those ideas and emphasized the historicist idealization of a particular German past against Enlightenment and Revolutionary universalism.[11] The French Revolution honored Goethe and Schiller on the basis of their *Sturm und Drang* writings as allies in the realization of the Enlightenment's mission of human emancipation; the National Convention granted Schiller honorary French citizenship. But both writers became extremely critical of the Revolution as it unfolded. We have seen this in the case of Goethe's classicist writings, which offer a running indictment of the Revolution's particular classicism, its conception of masculinist revolutionary transformation.[12] Schiller's response to the Terror was to write *On the Aesthetic Education of Man* (1795), where he reiterated principles of classicist temporality, of a timeless eternity of perfect classicist form. Schiller self-consciously turned to classicist time as a succor from the appalling shifts of a tumultuous and overbearing political time. "Here alone," he writes, in the contemplation of eternal form, "do we feel reft out of time, and our human nature expresses itself with a purity and integrity as though it had as yet suffered no impairment through the intervention of external forces."[13]

Unlike Schiller, with his escape into a classicist fullness of time, republican classicists—David and the Jacobins—looked on the Revolution as the opportunity to return France to an earlier period, to the ancient republic and its putative powerful masculine order of transparent virtue and heroic self-sacrifice. This desire to start over from that propitious beginning, to erase the intervening corrupt time of decadent and feminine aristocratic civility, manifested itself in the creation of a calendar that marked the Revolution as Year I, the beginning of a new scale of historical time.

The Revolution thus both problematized and intensified the temporal choices of French and German intellectuals, reifying certain choices to the exclusion of other possibilities. The existence of multiple and conflicting temporalities was increasingly felt to be problematic as events now pressed writers and artists to follow a particular temporality, and identity, with rigorous and sometimes oppressive consistency. This process of entrenchment and problematization was evident not just for some Germans in the shift from a mild reformism to dogmatic reaction and in the taking refuge in a sealed classicist eternity, or, for some French, in the monomaniacal commitment to a classicist return to republicanism. It was also—and perhaps most problematically—evident in those who continued to subscribe to the Enlightenment's conception of linear, progressive, and universal time and who continued to identify the fulfillment of that time with the Revolution. These proponents of Enlightenment asserted and reasserted their belief in that conception of time even as they felt its tenability challenged by the Revolution's turn to extreme violence. One well-known case of this predicament in the Revolution was the situation of the liberal heir of the liberal French Enlightenment, the Marquis de Condorcet, who composed his great treatise on inevitable progress and the perfectibility of humanity while he was in hiding from the Terror. More than other reform-minded historicists, Herder—likely showing his Enlightenment loyalties—was enamored of the view that the Revolution had announced the arrival of a new age of liberty; and unlike other historicists, he held this view even after the Terror began. Living in Weimar at the court of Goethe's duke, Herder continued to express his enthusiasm for the Revolution after it went to war with Germany; this enthusiasm scandalized Goethe and the court, who then pressured Herder into silence.[14] Even after its darkest period of violence and the Terror, when most other onetime German supporters of the Revolution had repudiated it, Immanuel Kant continued to affirm in his writings that the occurrence of the Revolution offered proof of the progress of the human race.[15] And as we have already noted, Hegel also showed a similar affirmation of the Revolution in his lectures on the philosophy of history. These believers continued to use the Enlightenment trope of the Revolution as the breakthrough of abstract freedom into actuality.

The French who continued to think in terms of progressive Enlightenment time had to contend with the apparent abuses and setbacks of the Terror. Germans, who embraced some notion of Enlightenment time and who looked on the Revolution as the sign of a new "modern" era, faced additional problems that were both political and cultural. Identified by German sympathizers as the breakthrough of a universal reason into "modernity," the Revolution issued a clarion call to other rational peoples who also wished to don the mantle of modernity. But for Germans, that summons was a daunting challenge; it was not at all clear that Germany could meet the standard of reason and modernity set by the Revolution. There was no comparable social and political change in Germany.[16] The

Napoleonic conquest precipitated social and political reform, notably in Prussia; but that reform ultimately proved ambiguous in its results and was followed by varying degrees of political reaction.[17]

It was also unclear what the Revolution as a measure of social and political progress implied for German culture. Eighteenth-century German intellectuals had only recently freed themselves from what they had perceived to be their tutelage to French culture. As early as Herder, but with increasing conviction as German cultural accomplishments accumulated, German intellectuals had gained not just a sense of cultural autonomy but also a feeling that they had reconstituted Germany into a privileged realm of spirit and intellect. "It is a national characteristic only among the Germans," Schlegel wrote in 1799, "to honor art and learning as divinities just for the sake of art and learning themselves."[18] This image of Germany as a nation of the *Dichter und Denker* (poet and thinker) was authoritatively disseminated throughout Europe by Germaine de Staël's immensely popular *On Germany*.

Those German intellectuals who believed in the Revolution's reason and modernity were part of this efflorescence of intellectual activity, and they shared in its new sense of cultural autonomy and accomplishment. Yet in the cultural politics of turn-of-the-century Germany their faith in the Revolution's modernity and Enlightenment threatened to invalidate their claim to membership in Germany's new cultural identity. Writers and thinkers opposed to the Revolution sought in the 1790s to lodge German cultural identity in temporalities that they construed as radically opposed to the linear, progressive reformist time of the Enlightenment and to the sense of accelerated change marked by the Revolution. Classicists such as Schiller wanted to insulate German culture from the unruly political world by enveloping it in classicist eternity. Historicists (with the exception of the multifarious Herder) argued that Germany's unique past defined its culture, and hence distinguished it from France in particular and social and political modernity in general.[19] In *On Germany*, Staël made use of this historicist impulse when she identified Germany—in contradistinction to Revolutionary France—as distinctively "Romantic," a condition, she argued, that was indicated by the ongoing vitality of its medieval culture and the backwardness of its dormant politics. German intellectuals who subscribed to Enlightenment time and wanted a stake in Germany's new cultural identity therefore needed to accomplish several different objectives. They needed to show that German political developments could be subsumed into the putative rational modernity of the Revolution; they had to demonstrate that that modernity did not necessarily issue in violence and terror, as conservatives claimed; and they had to show that Germany's cultural achievement belonged to the temporality defined by the French Revolution, to a new modern age of rapid social and political change.

This project, difficult from its beginning, became ever more problematic during the first half of the nineteenth century. From Hegel to Marx, there emerged a growing disquiet with Germany's ability to meet the new standard of modernity and a growing skepticism about the accomplishments of German culture. By midcentury, the project of aligning Germany's cultural identity with the putative modernity of the French Revolution had collapsed. And in its collapse, it paradoxically yielded the conclusion it was initially designed to prevent: that Germany was deeply and intractably resistant to modernity.

HEGEL: ALIGNING FRANCE AND GERMANY

When Hegel delivered his lectures on the philosophy of history at the University of Berlin in the 1820s, he had become one of Germany's most important philosophers, whose presence and power in academic institutions had grown under the aegis of important officials in the Prussian educational bureaucracy. His theory of the state in this period offered an intricate compromise of traditional and modern institutions that, he asserted, were appropriate to the modern period and could be regarded to constitute a system of rational completion. In crucial respects this political system was meant to support (without directly corresponding to) the reform of Prussian institutions that had been started after the defeat of Prussia by Napoleon but had become stagnant in the 1820s.[20] But the issue of political reform, for Hegel, also involved issues of cultural identity and of measuring Germany against the French Revolution's standard of modernity. Hegel's concern was not just to endorse political reform in Germany, but also to link that reform to the achievements of cultural identity and to the arrival of the Revolution as a standard of modernity.

In his lectures on the philosophy of history, Hegel asserts that the French Revolution marks the appearance of a new principle in the concrete world of social and political institutions. What underlies and empowers the Revolution's achievements of social equality and representative constitutional government is the principle of the "absolute will." The absolute will is purely formal; it acts without regard for particular individual or social concerns. Unrestrained by prior desires, interests, morality, religion, history, or politics, the will strives for a complete autonomy. And in seeking to free itself from all given constraints, the will aspires to an abstract universality. It wills that unconstrained willing be made a general principle (*PH*, 442–443).

The arrival of the abstract and universal absolute will as a standard of political life has both positive and negative consequences. On the one hand the principle of the absolute will is radically incompatible with traditional notions of social hierarchy and political domination, and it supersedes those historically, producing in their place modern social equality and constitutional government. On the other hand, the will's unmooring from convention and traditional authority also means that it recognizes no necessary limits to its restructuring of political life; hence it also produces the most extreme measures in order to realize itself: terror, dictatorship, and continuing political instability (*PH*, 450–453).

The French Revolution thus establishes for Hegel a new reality and standard of political modernity, but it does so with some unsettling results. The principle of the abstract will has delegitimated traditional institutions but not yet offered a stable political principle in their place. The arrival and influence of the principle of the abstract will in the spectacular form of the French Revolution are not, moreover, confined to France. That will is not exclusive to a particular nation, but defines a broader condition, a generalized present—"*the last stage in history,*" Hegel writes, "*our world, our time*" (*PH*, 442). In keeping with the Enlightenment, Hegel recognizes that the absolute will is a universal principle, and hence establishes a new generalized age. What this means in particular for Hegel is that the absolute will must also have realized itself in contemporaneous German developments.

Hegel's philosophy of history thus translates the linear, progressivist, and universalist time of the Enlightenment into his particular philosophical idiom, and it does so in a way that acknowledges that the Revolution offers not just a solution to the blockages of traditional politics but also a new set of problems. One of those problems is the Revolution's apparently unstable dynamic, which, while the embodiment of modern reason, also seems to develop beyond rational control. Another problem for Hegel is whether Germany can now meet the imperatives of the universality of the French Revolution, of the new standard of modernity it sets for all states.

Hegel plainly recognizes that Germany has not experienced a political transformation similar to what has occurred in France (*PH*, 443). To bring Germany under the purview of the modernity of the French Revolution while doing away with the latter's unsettling consequences is the challenge Hegel faces as he turns to consider the significance of Germany's recent cultural achievements. He proceeds to argue that the principle of the absolute will has manifested itself in German cultural developments that he considers equivalent to the political developments of the French Revolution. His strategy is to create a parallelism or homology between diverse forms of phenomena, a procedure that assumes that homologous or parallel forms express the same principle or essence.

The homology that he constructs invests a parallelism observed by earlier Germans with momentous philosophical significance. German commentators had noted well before Hegel's lectures that as events in France issued in the Revolution, German philosophy and culture had produced its own upheaval. In 1781 Immanuel Kant's groundbreaking *Critique of Pure Reason* had raised challenging questions in epistemology. But in an even more influential work in 1788, the *Critique of Practical Reason,* Kant asserted the radical autonomy of human beings. Possessed of a rational, ethical will, human beings, according to Kant, could and should promulgate universal ethical principles that they would then be obligated to follow. German writers compared Kantian ethics, with its affirmation of radical and universal autonomy, to the French Revolution; and Hegel converted that analogy into a full-blown philosophical homology, according to which the same absolute will showed itself in the parallel forms of the politics of the Revolution and the philosophy of Kant.[21]

In France, Hegel observes, the abstract and universalizing will assumed a "practical effect" in the form of the Revolution, but in Germany the absolute will appeared in a different shape, in "no other form than that of tranquil theory." More specifically, the absolute will "obtained speculative recognition" in "Kantian philosophy" (*PH,* 443); Kant achieved for Germany what the Revolution accomplished in France.[22]

By asserting a homology between the disparate forms of philosophy and politics, Hegel aligns Germany with the French Revolution: the Germans, he tells us, have accomplished in "theoretical abstraction" what the French have accomplished in practice (*PH,* 444). Drawing this parallelism between German theory and French politics, he is implicitly making a claim for Germany's participation in modernity. Germans are no less advanced in their thinking than the French are in their politics. Hegel thus subsumes Germany into the universal and progressive time of the French Revolution; he establishes a measure of German modernity. But as he himself recognizes, this attempt to align Germany with the French Revolution in a unified vision of the present immediately is bound up with a further, pressing question: "why did the French alone and not the Germans set about realizing [the principle of the absolute will]?" (*PH,* 443).

Why France, not Germany, for the will's practical realization? Hegel seems to be faulting Germany's particular intellectual version of modernity vis-à-vis France's practical realization. But as we have seen, Hegel did not consider Germany's putative character—its profound *Innerlichkeit*—to be a disadvantage, but on the contrary superior to what he found in French culture. Hegel subscribes to that same favorable view of German interiority in his lectures on the philosophy of history, and in fact he appeals to interiority to solve the other pressing issue of how to continue to affirm the Revolution as a progressive historical development in the face of the Terror and war.

Like many other German commentators, Hegel locates the source of German interiority in the Reformation. Following a conventional formula, he states that Luther detached German consciousness from external authority and forced it to rely on itself. Since Luther, German thought has been characterized by an increasingly introspective and soulful inner life, by a constant deepening of *Innerlichkeit*. This unique German characteristic of enhanced interiority conditions Germany's acceptance of modernity. Because of the Reformation, Germany developed a broad and secure spirituality, an interior life that could absorb the exertions of the absolute will (*PH*, 444, 449). Thus the first expressions of the absolute will in the German Enlightenment were entirely compatible with religion, indeed, were "conducted in the interest of theology" (*PH*, 444). In France, however, the absence of a Reformation resulted in a weak and fragmented spirituality. Consequently, when the absolute will made its appearance in the Enlightenment, it entered into an intense and external conflict with the Catholic church. The French never established a general, harmonious spirituality; the will was instead channeled into an adversarial politics (*PH*, 444, 449). Unlike the situation in Germany, in France there was no soothing and all-encompassing *Innerlichkeit* to render the agitations of pure will against social institutions into agitations within thought.

Hegel's appeal to German *Innerlichkeit* to explain why Germany has a theoretical, rather than political, modernity vindicates the new German cultural identity and in a way that preserves the political significance of the French Revolution. At least since the Reformation, Hegel argues, Germans have become spiritual people par excellence. Their special spirituality has not precluded modernity but, on the contrary, has allowed them to attain it without succumbing to the excesses of the Revolution. Hegel not only claims for German culture a share in modernity; he also employs the German culture to banish the potential social and political problems of modernity. German culture offers a safe passage to modernity, a way of realizing the absolute will while avoiding the violence and war that accompanied the arrival of political modernity in France. Hegel goes on to say that no revolution can make lasting political gains without a preceding Reformation, since no revolution can establish free institutions without first cultivating inward spirituality (*PH*, 453). An enduring modernity can be founded only on an established *Innerlichkeit*.[23]

With his strategy of plotting parallelisms or creating homologies, Hegel redeems German culture for the modern age and, even more, identifies it as the preferred form of modernity. But even as he justifies Germany's cultural identity and protects its claim to modernity, he recognizes that German culture remains an incomplete embodiment of modernity. He cannot be content with *Innerlichkeit* alone. For if the freedom of the will is limited to the inner life of human beings, a disjunction could arise between internal states of mind and external states of objective social existence. The will cannot be fully free if its domain is confined to thinking. To avoid this potential dissonance between thought and reality, Hegel's answer to the question of why the will realizes itself in France, not in Germany, ultimately leads to a second assertion about the nature of German politics. Hegel returns from *Innerlichkeit* to political reality.

He proceeds by claiming that the Reformation brought some social and political reform, particularly in areas associated with the church and with the religious foundations of government (*PH,* 445). These developments are harbingers of further and deeper change: "Thus the principle of thought was already so far reconciled [in German religion]; also *the Protestant world had the consciousness that in the earlier developed reconciliation the principle was present for the further formation of right.*"[24] The Reformation and the creation of an intensive German spirituality promise future social and political reform. From the homology between the French Revolution and German *Innerlichkeit*, Hegel projects another harmonizing alignment of German politics. Indeed, without this promise the original parallelism is unstable; it threatens to collapse into fixed dichotomies of thought and being, *Innerlichkeit* and political reality, Germany and France. In this sense, both the original parallelism and Germany's claim to the modernity of the French Revolution are sustained by the promise of reform. That promise ultimately guarantees the coherence of Hegel's interpretation of the modernity of German culture.

HEINE: REINVENTING AND RECUPERATING GERMAN CULTURE

In the decade after Hegel's lectures, a strengthening conservatism dominated political life in Germany. Prussian reforms failed to establish a representative constitution; German liberal movements, particularly after the 1830 revolutions in France and elsewhere, were subject to intensified censorship and repression. The growing conservatism of German governments appeared to go hand in hand with that of many Germany intellectuals. Friedrich Gentz, Friedrich Schlegel, and Hegel's university friend Friedrich Schelling, for example, moved from an initial reformist receptiveness to the French Revolution to a strenuous rejection of the Revolution and any liberal reform. Because of such shifts and other developments, German Romanticism in particular was identified as a politically conservative cultural movement and often stylized as the movement that then generally summed up German culture. Ironically, the writing that served to lock into place the equation of German cultural life, German Romanticism, and political reaction was the liberal Germaine de Staël's *On Germany*. In that work, Staël identified Germany—erroneously, as we have noted—as "Romantic," and she attributed that character to the enduring influence of the Middle Ages and its Christian culture. The medieval Romanticism of Germany, according to Staël, had made Germans abstract-minded, spiritual, intensely inward, but also politically quiescent. By the 1830s a simplified version of this view of German culture—as Romantic, Christian, and politically undeveloped—had been disseminated across Western Europe, conveying to European liberals and reformers that Germany was in essence an archaic and retrograde culture. As Jules Michelet put it in 1831: "Germany is only naiveté, poetry, and metaphysics."[25] Thus, as German politics was becoming manifestly more conservative, that political character was increasingly identified as the correlate of German Romanticism, which in turn was taken to be the culture proper to Germans.[26]

After the revolutions of 1830, as the possibility of political reform dwindled and the threat of political persecution expanded, one of the most celebrated German poets of the period, the liberal Heinrich Heine, transplanted himself to Paris. As Heine made his way into Parisian cultural and publishing circles, he decided to write a study of German culture, to be published in serial form in French journals and republished in Germany as a book. The work was explicitly intended to correct the impression of Germany he believed was communicated in Staël's influential work; Heine's project, in fact, was to carry the same title: *On Germany*. The various parts, appearing from 1833 to 1835, were ultimately combined into two books, entitled *On the History of Religion and Philosophy in Germany* and *The Romantic School*. The latter offered a scathing critique of German Romanticism; the former, a positive alternative to the view of Germany as a Romantic and reactionary culture.[27]

Intending to correct what he believed was a mistaken, excessively conservative stylization of German culture, Heine was in fact carrying on Hegel's project of aligning Germany with France, of integrating the new German cultural identity into a unified view of modernity.[28] But the now-altered circumstances of the 1830s required Heine to offer a bolder interpretation linking German culture to French politics. He could no longer rely, as Hegel had, on the promise of imminent political reform to complete the alignment of Germany with political modernity. The unfolding of events had invalidated Hegel's simple "guarantee." Moreover, the increasing stylization of German *Innerlichkeit* as Romantic and apolitical required Heine to offer a strong rejoinder, claiming for forms of German *Innerlichkeit* an external, practical power that they seemed to lack by definition. Preserving a claim to modernity required that the German cultural identity be made to address the more clearly constrained political and cultural situation. To save German culture for modernity, Heine now found that he had to reconstruct it.

The new political situation marks the beginning of Heine's *On the History of Religion and Philosophy in Germany.* He begins by stating that Germany's present social and political situation is equivalent to France's before the Revolution. The German people are still dominated by an authoritarian Christianity and the institutions of the old regime. Germany, Heine admits, is thus socially and politically retrograde in relation to developments in contemporary France.[29] But like Hegel before him, Heine does not believe that this discrepancy between German and French politics signifies a total lack of modernity in Germany. Setting out an interpretive strategy similar to Hegel's, Heine points to a "remarkable parallelism" between German philosophy and the French Revolution (*RP,* 200).

Heine constructs a homology between German theory and French politics, and, like Hegel and other Germans, he sees this parallelism as initiated by Kantian philosophy. Kant's *Critique of Pure Reason,* Heine writes, "began in Germany an intellectual revolution which presents the most striking analogies to the material revolution in France and which must seem . . . just as important" (*RP,* 200). From this parallelism Heine then projects other homologies. He tells us that the German revolution in philosophy and the French revolution in politics passed through the "same stages." Where Robespierre and the Terror overthrew all past forms of political authority and abolished the monarchy, Kant criticized all previous epistemological authority and did away with deism. Napoleon, the conqueror of Europe, found a German alter ego in Fichte's world-creating *Ich.* Schelling's nature philosophy and his ultimate turn to Catholicism and absolutism mirrored restoration in France. The overthrow of the restoration and the resulting political situation in France found its equivalent in the defeat of conservative *Naturphilosophie* by Hegel and his followers. Hegel, Heine notes, "closed" the "great circle" of philosophical revolutions (*RP,* 199–240).

By asserting this homology between German thought and French politics, Heine seeks to accomplish the same aim as that of earlier German sympathizers of the Revolution who also had a stake in Germany's new cultural identity: to claim for German culture a share of modernity. But for Heine the political dissident in the more conservative 1830s, the conventional parallelism of German culture to France's political modernity has become problematic. In the end, Heine is still in exile, and his fellow Germans continue to live under unconstitutional rule and censorship. In his homology between German thought and French action, Heine reaches the same issue that Hegel was forced to confront, but one that is now made more pressing by the political circumstances of the 1830s. The problem for Heine, as it was earlier for Hegel, is how to demonstrate that German practice will now align with German theory. How, in other words, can Germany move from a parallelism or homology between its culture and French politics to a further synchronization of German politics with a modern German culture, and hence with the modernity of the French Revolution?

To deal with this problem, Heine reverses Hegel's procedure. Hegel argued that reason was increasingly present in history, assuming in Germany introverted forms that in turn created an inner disposition or *Innerlichkeit* that was suitable for rational political reform. Heine, however, as a more radical liberal reacting against the Romantic appropriation of *Innerlichkeit*, argues that dispositions of pure *Innerlichkeit* are inherently authoritarian. They distract one from the concrete concerns of politics and hence implicitly provide support for tyranny. What Heine seeks in German thought, to make it issue in political modernity, is no longer a principle of idealist interiority, but a principle taken from Saint-Simonian social theory, which was popular in France and Germany in the 1830s. Heine invokes the Saint-Simonian notion of "sensualism"—the centrality of material or sensuous satisfaction and drives in history.[30] The principle of sensualism, Heine tells us, is a radical agent in history, since its concerns with material satisfaction and desires necessarily lead to the real world of politics (*RP,* 146–147, 167, 177–181). To establish a similar possibility of political change in Germany, Heine must now locate a source of "sensualism" in German cultural institutions and traditions. In France, he argues, sensualism appeared in the uncompromising materialist philosophies of the Enlightenment (*RP,* 168–169); in Germany, it took on a more mystical form, rooted in that country's pagan past. Sensualism in Germany assumed the form of pantheism, the belief in the unity of the divine and the natural, of god and matter (*RP,* 137).

Heine's argument for the possibility of political change in Germany thus follows a different tack from Hegel's; and at first glance the two seem to proceed in different directions. To maintain the possibility of political change in Germany, Heine identifies in Germany's past a radical sensualism, thereby repudiating Hegel's belief in a characteristic German interiority. By extension, one might conclude that Heine will also be forced to repudiate Germany's new cultural identity. The idea that German culture is defined by a deep interiority must seem to him hopelessly reactionary.

But Heine does not repudiate that cultural identity. Against the conventional emphasis on German interiority, he identifies a different content in German culture, sensualism; but he places this new content into the same forms of German culture that Hegel determined as the defining manifestations of German spirituality. Heine, in other words, retains the progression of cultural forms that conventionally defined Germany's new cultural identity. He adheres to the conventional terms that add up to a special German culture, but he gives those terms a new substance and consequence.

With Hegel, Heine sees Luther's Reformation as a watershed in the development of Germany in particular and of humanity in general. It marks a qualitative advance in freedom. But in direct opposition to Hegel, Heine identifies the Reformation's progressive aspect in Luther's "sensualism," in his recognition of the legitimacy of ordinary, material life. Here Heine ignores the Luther of *Innerlichkeit*, identified with the doctrine of the justification by faith alone, and emphasizes instead Luther's humble origins, his well-known earthiness and crudity in manners, his blunt personality, his repudiation of celibacy for priests, and his abandonment of supernatural miracles (*RP*, 152–162). Luther's sensualism passes into the pantheistic philosophy of Spinoza and, through Spinoza, enters German philosophy, finding its highest manifestations in Schelling and Hegel. Pantheism thus entrenches itself in German religion and philosophy. And because Hegel has "closed" the "great circle" of philosophical revolutions, because pantheism has reached its highest point in theory, it will now, according to Heine, necessarily empty into reality. "Because of these doctrines, revolutionary forces have developed that are only waiting for the day when they can break out and fill the world with terror and with admiration" (*RP*, 242). Heine concludes with a prediction of imminent revolution in Germany, warning the French that, should they interfere, the coming bloodbath in Germany will engulf them as well (*RP*, 244).

Like Hegel, Heine establishes a parallelism between German culture and the French Revolution in order to preserve the former's historical legitimacy. Germany's new cultural identity can thus be shown to participate in modernity. But given the preceding decade of political reaction, Heine can no longer guarantee that relation by simply asserting the imminence of the synchronization of German politics with German theory. To argue that German culture presages further political improvement now requires a reworking of the meaning of German culture, a Hegelian *Aufhebung*, or elevation, that will at once transform that culture, render it more compatible with the radical requirements of the age, yet preserve its customary, defining forms. In Heine's rewriting of German cultural identity, Germany remains unique and praiseworthy for the increasing depth and sophistication of its religious and philosophical achievements; but those achievements are no longer to be seen as substantively ones of interiority. The conventional signifiers of Germany's cultural identity represent, behind their apparent interiority, a deeper, subversive sensualism.

Heine's attempted renovation of the project to align Germany with the French Revolution indicates that the project had become ever more problematical since Hegel's lectures in the 1820s. That Heine experienced considerable difficulty in carrying out this project of cultural legitimation is evident as well in another, striking way. In reconstructing a modern German cultural identity, he betrays an unsettling anxiety that such a project is ultimately untenable. In a burst of ironic self-criticism, he in fact defeats his own attempt to preserve the modernity of German culture.

As we have seen, Heine's argument has two steps. He first argues that Germany's philosophical development—from Kant to Hegel—mirrors France's political development; this establishes Germany's participation in modernity. To get from thinking to acting, Heine then argues that the revolution in German thought marks the culmination of the development of a pantheism that is inherently revolutionary. Now that the theoretical revolution is over, modern pantheism will pour into the real world. Heine never fully explains, however, this passage from theoretical pantheism to revolutionary action. He does not show how it will happen empirically or institutionally, but merely asserts the development as a kind of logical deduction that follows necessarily from the internal workings of pantheist consciousness.[31] But this assertion is difficult to accept. It is neither logically self-evident nor, as Heine shows, justified by how his pantheists actually behaved.

Few of his pantheists were revolutionaries. Heine tells us that some, such as the Romantics and Goethe, were politically conservative or at best politically indifferent. And he acknowledges that Schelling, one of the most accomplished pantheists of Germany's philosophical revolution, has become increasingly conservative in politics and religion, ultimately converting like other Romantic pantheists to Catholicism.[32] Heine notes that not just Schelling but also Kant and Fichte "can be accused of desertion"; in their later years, they became apostates of their own philosophies (*RP,* 239).

Heine's extended reflection on Schelling's actual political behavior thus spirals into a refutation of his argument about pantheism's revolutionary potential, and hence denies German culture's claim to modernity. He cannot stop himself from dismantling the elaborate system of interpretation he is simultaneously erecting. As he dwells on the real consequences of pantheism, his carefully demarcated system of oppositions (spiritualism versus sensualism, conservatism versus radicalism) and affinities (Germany and France, thought and action) begins to collapse into a confusion of categories: sensualism can lead to political conservatism, modern philosophy consorts with retrograde romanticism, thought repudiates action.

Heine thus works toward contradictory aims. He both argues for a position and undermines it. In *On the History of Religion and Philosophy in Germany,* this contradictory, self-negating procedure ends at a rhetorical impasse as Heine abruptly halts the flow of his exposition. Immediately after claiming that Germany's great pantheists have frequently turned "apostate," he interjects: "I don't know why this last sentence has such a depressingly paralyzing effect on my feelings that I am simply unable to communicate here the remaining bitter truths about Mr. Schelling as he is today" (*RP*, 239). Despondently facing the imminent failure of his argument, he then tries to make his way back to his argument about the essential radicalism and ultimate modernity of German pantheism. He arbitrarily suppresses his doubts and turns to happier thoughts: "Instead [of dwelling on the late Schelling] let us praise that earlier Schelling . . . for the earlier Schelling, like Kant and Fichte, represents one of the great phases of our philosophical revolution, which I have compared in these pages with the phases of the political revolution in France" (*RP*, 239). Forcibly fixing his attention on the more promising youth of pantheism, Heine continues his argument about the inherent political radicalism of German theory. His answer to his anxieties is to evade them.

But his evasions catch up with him. In the 1852 preface to the second edition of *On the History of Religion and Philosophy in Germany,* Heine in effect repudiates the central argument of his study. He admits that he was wrong to claim practical power for what he had identified as the most radical of German philosophies. Hegel's radical followers have proved incapable of changing reality.[33] Even in its most developed form, then, German pantheism does not automatically empty its energies into reality. With this striking confession in his preface, the entire argument of the subsequent text is fatally damaged, and, even more clearly than in Hegel's case, Germany's cultural identity again runs the risk of being cut adrift from the modernity of the French Revolution.

RUGE TO MARX: FROM HOMOLOGY TO INVERSION

In the decade following Heine's *On the History of Religion and Philosophy in Germany,* the fortunes of German liberals and radicals further deteriorated. The 1840 accession of Frederick William IV to the Prussian crown ultimately brought renewed political repression, which in 1843 closed the Prussian newspapers of some of those apostate Hegelians to whom Heine referred in his *History of Religion and Philosophy in Germany.* Two prominent radical followers of Hegel, Arnold Ruge and Karl Marx, made their way to Paris in 1843. For Ruge and Marx, the political persecution that they had faced in Prussia and Germany led them to repudiate both Hegelian theory and any notion that Prussia and other German states might institute liberal reforms.[34] The two planned to publish, as joint editors, a new political-philosophical magazine, the *Deutsch-Französische Jahrbücher,* which they hoped would begin a new collaboration of French and German politically active intellectuals. The magazine turned out to be exclusively German in tone and substance, and its financing collapsed after the first issue.[35] Ruge and Marx now parted ways, a separation caused not just by events but also by very different views of the relationship between France and Germany.

Like Hegel and Heine before them, Ruge and Marx reconsidered the cultural and political situation in Germany, measuring it against the standard of modernity identified with the French Revolution and subsequent French politics. In his letters and writings Ruge expresses views that are initially more in keeping with the conventional strategy of homology, but they include a variation that suits his political and journalistic ambitions in France. Like Heine, Ruge argues that the most advanced theory of the period—the one that is most modern—is German philosophy in the form of radical, atheistic Hegelianism, or "Young Hegelianism," which repudiates what it now considers the conservatism of Hegel. And in keeping with the strategy of homology, Ruge acknowledges that the practical equivalent to radical Hegelian theory is to be found in contemporary France's activist political press and popular political movements. The modernity of German theory finds its complement in French political practice.[36] But unlike earlier strategies of constructing homologies, Ruge now calls into question not just the practical political situation in Germany, whose limitations are now all too apparent, but also the theoretical situation in France. He points out that although French politics are fully modern, French theory is not, embracing as it does, in various of its collectivist movements, including 1840s Saint-Simonianism, some continued, limiting form of religious belief.[37]

The intense conflicts of Germany's religious politics had made Ruge (and Marx) into atheists and prominent members of the Young Hegelian movement, and any continuing sign of Christian religiosity was for them the mark of what German philosophy had now historically superseded. Thus, according to Ruge, while the Germans are philosophically advanced but politically backward, the French are politically advanced but philosophically backward. This catachresis of French and German temporalities calls out, Ruge believes, for synchronization. Such a realignment of German politics and French theory according to the norms of modernity is for Ruge the historical mission of his and Marx's collaborative project. He believes that through the *Deutsch-Französische Jahrbücher* the French will teach Germans modern politics, while the Germans will bring the French politically up to date.[38] This program foundered, not just because of the failure of the magazine and its inability to attract French contributors, but also, as Ruge later emphasizes, because French radicals showed no interest in giving up Christianity. French theory continues to be stuck in the past.[39]

Ruge's responses to German political persecution and his experiences of Parisian politics lead him to adjust the Hegelian strategy of constructing a homology between German culture and French politics so that the homology addresses the further radicalization of Hegelian philosophy and what he feels are the more demanding political imperatives of the 1840s. While he continues to assert the modernity of radical German theory, he cannot find or hope to find in Germany the political correlate that earlier writers projected. Unlike Hegel and Heine before him, Ruge invests all his hopes in France to bring German politics into modernity. But that hope, initially made possible by the strategy of homology, ends up being undercut by it, as the notion of the modernity of radical, atheistic Young Hegelian thought makes accepting less-modern, still-religious French thought unpalatable. Ruge's attempt to manipulate the conventional homology of German culture and French politics results in a new, doubled impasse. Hegel and Heine are stymied in their desire for a uniform modernity because they cannot convincingly move from the modernity of German theory to that of German politics. Ruge's impasse undoes the strategy of homology in a twofold fashion: it asserts not only that a modern German theory continues to be misaligned with German politics, but also that the modernity of French politics is now in conflict with the archaism of its still-religious theory.[40] The dissemination of temporal dislocation—from Germany to France—indicates how badly that strategy of homology had fallen into disrepair, how it was now producing further problems rather than the promise of a solution.

Ruge's view of the homology of German culture and French politics shows that that form of analysis had reached a dead end. Marx's only published writing in Paris, his "Contribution to the Critique of Hegel's Philosophy of Law: Introduction," which was published in the *Deutsch-Französische Jahrbücher*, also uses the strategy of homology but in a way that transforms that strategy of interpretation. Marx constructs a homology in order to invert its conventional meaning. Unlike those of previous writers and his contemporary Ruge, Marx's parallelisms between German culture and French politics seek not to redeem German culture for the modern present but to abandon it to the archaic past.

Like Hegel and Heine before him, Marx measures contemporary Germany against the French Revolution and finds it politically wanting. Germany, Marx states bluntly, is "an anachronism, a flagrant contradiction of generally recognized axioms."[41] Indeed, German conditions are so retrograde that even abolishing them would not bring Germany up to date: "If I negate the German state of affairs in 1843, then, according to the French computation of time, I am hardly in the year 1789, and still less in the focus of the present" (*IN*, 176).

German politics, according to Marx, are stuck in the past, below the standard of political modernity established by the Revolution. But in a gesture characteristic of the German strategy of interpretation, Marx concedes that Germany is not altogether without modernity; he agrees that modernity has manifested itself in German thought: "We are the *philosophical* contemporaries of the present without being its *historical* contemporaries." Modern politics has appeared in Germany as modern philosophy: "In politics the Germans *thought* what other nations *did*" (*IN*, 180, 181).

To determine Germany's place in modern history, Marx begins with the same interpretive move of the intellectuals we have considered: he constructs a homology or parallelism between French politics and German thought. But he now deploys this tactic in the service of a quite different strategy. From Hegel to Ruge, writers draw their parallelism in order to align German culture with the putative modernity of the French Revolution. Germany can thus justifiably claim a share of modernity. To sustain this parallelism, these writers then argue that modern German ideas are harbingers of modern political reform. The modernity of German thought points to the imminence of a modern German politics.

Marx, however, sets the assertions of this interpretive strategy against themselves. He accepts the new German cultural identity—the idea that the German culture has a special, characteristic depth or profundity—and he grants that identity a modern character. But then departing from the earlier interpretive pattern, he refuses to take the next step; he refuses to predict or even hope for a subsequent harmonization of German politics with German theory. And in an ironic reversal of earlier conventional reasoning, he justifies this refusal by appealing to the modernity of German thought: in Marx's view, the modernity of German culture *precludes* the possibility of a modern German politics.

For Marx, the parallelism between German thought and French politics no longer portends a fulfilled German political modernity. On the contrary, this parallelism suggests that Germany is irredeemably anachronistic. Where other writers argued for the modernity of German theory despite the backwardness of German politics, Marx argues that the theory is advanced precisely because the politics are retrograde. "The abstraction and conceit of [Germany's] thought," he writes, "always kept in step with the one-sidedness and stumpiness of its reality. . . . The status quo of *German political theory* expresses the *imperfection of the modern state*, the defectiveness of the flesh itself" (*IN*, 181). German philosophy, in short, is the way Germans make up for a bad reality; it compensates in thought for an inadequate politics.

Marx sees German philosophy and politics locked in an inverse relationship: as politics becomes increasingly retrograde, theory compensates by becoming increasingly modern. And as theory continues to develop an advanced modernity, it allows politics to become more deeply and perversely anachronistic. German culture and politics are locked in an inverse relationship that amounts to a condition of extreme temporal contortion, the bizarre spectacle of at once rushing forward to the future and collapsing back into the past. The current state of German culture and politics, Marx writes, now begins "to combine the *civilized shortcomings of the modern world* . . . with the *barbaric deficiencies of the ancien régime*" (*IN*, 183). It shares "the restorations of modern nations" without sharing "their revolutions" (*IN*, 176). "Germany," Marx predicts, "will one day find itself on the level of European decadence before ever having been on the level of European emancipation" (*IN*, 183).

Contrary to Hegel, Heine, and Ruge, Marx does not believe that German philosophy foreshadows a modern German politics or works to realize it. On the contrary, the modernity of German philosophy depends entirely on its inverse, the backwardness of political reality. The existence of the former presupposes the latter. For Marx in 1843, the issue is not whether German reality can catch up to German theory and thereby match the political modernity of other nations. The perverse symbiosis between the modernity of German thought and its retrograde political practice precludes that possibility. Germany, in short, has no chance of ever reaching the present.

In Marx's view, Germany's new cultural identity merely shows that it is hopelessly anachronistic; bound to a retrograde politics, this identity ensures that German conditions remain "below the level of history" (*IN*, 177). Suffering from temporal contortion—its theory is fixed to the present, its politics to the past—Germany is stranded in time. In the last pages of the "Introduction," Marx in fact goes on to say that traditional Germany lacks the usual resources for concrete historical development; its petty states and enervated classes are inadequate agents of change.[42]

Germany's only hope for rejoining the historical mainstream is to repudiate the past and the present, and Marx insists it must do this without appealing to anything considered characteristically German—neither to German culture, nor to German politics and society. Marx looks within Germany for an agent of history that owes nothing to German culture and institutions. He paradoxically defines this new historical actor in terms of its exemption from the society and culture that generated it. It is a "class of civil society which is not a class of civil society; an estate which is the dissolution of all estates, a sphere . . . which can no longer invoke a *historical* but only a *human* title, which does not stand in any one-sided antithesis to the consequences but in an all-round antithesis to the premises of the German state" (*IN*, 186). With this obscure, paradoxical formulation, Marx for the first time calls on the proletariat to assume a decisive role in history. The proletariat in its first manifestation as an agent of history is to restore Germany to the progressive flow of time.[43]

THE END OF THE GERMAN DISCOURSE ON MODERNITY

The movement from Hegel through Heine to Ruge and Marx suggests the progressive erosion of a particular attempt to legitimate the new cultural ideal of German intellectuals, which was established in the late eighteenth century and projected through the nineteenth. From Hegel to Heine to Marx, the German cultural identity—the German as the supreme embodiment of cultural depth and profundity—became increasingly untenable when measured against the putative political modernity of the French Revolution. Hegel, Heine, and Ruge erect a parallelism between contemporary French politics and German thought in order to justify a German claim to modernity; by means of this homology, Germany can be counted as part of the avant-garde of history, of a new, compelling time defined by the French Revolution. They self-consciously erect this parallelism because of Germany's apparent lack of modernity. But while this interpretive strategy acknowledges that it derives from the absence of political modernity in Germany, it also denies that absence, asserting that the current homology between French politics and German theory must lead to further homologous developments in German politics. The modernity of German thought renders a modern German politics inevitable. The parallelism between French politics and German thought therefore seeks to rectify its own political preconditions—to overthrow the given of Germany's political "backwardness."

The apparent continued resistance of Germany to a political modernity ultimately undermined the optimistic belief that German politics would soon harmonize with German culture. As the prospect of political reform disappeared from the horizon, the attempts to ground it in a putative German cultural modernity became increasingly strained. In the mid-1840s Ruge intends his project for a German-French alliance to remedy this situation—to justify the modernity of German culture by attaching it to the new radical politics of France. Marx's solution is more radical yet. He no longer expects the inverse relation between German thought and German reality to correct itself in favor of the modernity of thought. In 1843 he turns the project of aligning German culture with the French Revolution against itself. For Marx, German thought is as advanced as French modernity, but that fact does not prefigure a modern German politics. On the contrary, Germany's culture has made great achievements in order to forget its retrograde politics; German cultural identity is constructed on a wishful suppression of its political preconditions. The inverse relation between German thought and German reality is necessary and inescapable. German thought is modern precisely because German reality is backward.

In turning the interpretive strategy of homology against itself, Marx provides an ironic commentary on his predecessors Hegel and Heine and his associate Ruge. On Marx's account, the attempts to justify the modernity of German culture are second-order manifestations of German perversity. They are faltering, self-deceived attempts at historical self-consciousness. They acknowledge Germany's anomalous place in history but then seek to escape it in wish-fulfillment, in the phantasy of an imminent and necessary political harmonization, in a false faith in a coming and uniform modernity. The self-consciousness of Hegel, Heine, and Ruge therefore ends up reproducing the condition it hoped to overcome; it issues in a powerless and isolated affirmation of the modernity of German culture. By turning upon the interpretive strategy that he himself deploys, Marx brings to a close in his "Introduction" a multigenerational discourse that strove to fit German culture into a general system or uniform temporality of modernity. His contribution to that discourse ironically condemns it: he accuses it of complicity in rendering Germany anachronistic.

The collapse of the attempt to link German cultural identity to the putative modernity represented by the French Revolution helped to clear the way for the disseminaton of the opposing view of German culture and its relation to modernity. This view of German culture, which has associated German profundity with the rejection of social and political modernity, became a truism of the German cultural elite of the late nineteenth and early twentieth centuries. It could be valorized in either a positive or negative fashion, depending on one's perspective on modernity. Thomas Mann's *Reflections of a Nonpolitical Man* (1918), for example, is one long diatribe against those who would link German culture to modernity, which he, in a new variant of one of the defining binary oppositions of German cultural identity, identifies strongly with French "superficiality."[44] The same notion of German culture's hostility to modernity, but now with a negative valence that put German culture into question, served as the basis for post–World War II liberal Anglo-American and German interpretations of the inherent authoritarianism of German culture and society. This pattern of interpretation persisted until the 1980s, when historians criticized models of synchronized historical development according to which social and economic modernity necessarily issued in certain political and cultural forms.[45]

From the point of view of macroconceptions of the relationship between modernization and culture, the early nineteenth-century failure to render German cultural identity suitable for modernity contributed strongly to another influential view of the general relationship between modernity and cultural identity. As we have seen, Marx's disgust with the political conditions of German cultural identity led him to offer his first formulation of a new historical agent, one owing nothing to the German past and its retrograde politics or to the German present and its strangely unmoored modern theory. In its first manifestation, Marx's proletariat is to clear away the impasse of German history, to abolish its contorted temporalities. A few years later, in *The Communist Manifesto* (1847), Marx thus imagines how the German proletariat will accelerate the transformation of German conditions.[46] Here Marx is drawing on his first formulation of historical materialism, which asserts the primacy of economic and technological change and the overwhelming power of industrialization. This construal of historical materialism had momentous consequences not just for how people thought of German cultural identity but for how they thought about cultural identity in general.

Even critics of Marx have noted his ambivalence about capitalist industrialization in *The Communist Manifesto*. While regarding it as exploitative and destructive, he also admires its dynamism and its ability to effect a massive transformation of society, which will destroy all the accumulated deceptions of tradition, religion, and cultural identity. In a famous passage in *The Manifesto*, Marx looks to the dynamism of capitalist industrialization to bring about a complete cultural effacement. It will place and maintain human beings in a new time of continuous change that will undercut all traditional and conventional cultural expectations. Modern capitalism implies a zero degree of cultural identity, and that outcome, for Marx, is a rebirth, an entry, at last, into reality. Under capitalism, Marx writes, "all fixed, fast-frozen relations, with their train of ancient and venerable prejudices and opinions, are swept away, all new-formed ones become antiquated before they can ossify. All that is solid melts into air, all that is holy is profaned, and man is at last compelled to face with sober senses, his real conditions of life."[47]

In predicting that capitalist industrialization will usher in a new, demystified condition of self-knowledge, Marx is subscribing to—indeed, helping to form—one of the primary assumptions and hopes of modernization and development theory. As we have seen in our age of advanced industrialization and globalizing capitalism, this projected emancipation from phantasies of cultural identity has turned out to be the most unlikely of all such phantasies.

Notes

Introduction

1. Voltaire sought to establish the dominance of French culture in *Essai sur les moeurs et l'esprit des nations* (1745–1750) and *Le Siècle de Louis XIV* (1751). Both are discussed in relation to German responses in Harold Mah, "German Historical Thought in the Age of Herder, Kant, and Hegel," in *A Companion to Western Historical Thought*, ed. Lloyd Kramer and Sara Maza (Oxford, 2002), 146–151; and see Friedrich Meinecke, *Historism: The Rise of a New Historical Outlook* (London, 1972), 56–57. For a general discussion of French influences on Germany, see James Sheehan, *German History, 1770–1866* (Oxford, 1989), 149–150; Rudolf Vierhaus, *Germany in the Age of Absolutism* (Cambridge, 1988), 6, 36–37, 67–68; and Harold James, *A German Identity, 1770–1990* (New York, 1989), 15–19.

2. In the late eighteenth century the desire to recognize Germany as a coherent and significant cultural unity animated a variety of writers, artists, and thinkers—including Herder and Hegel—but they had not yet conceived the idea that the many German states should be united into a single political and administrative unity, the German nation-state. The transformation of the idea of Germany as a cultural nation into the idea of Germany as a political nation-state took place in the nineteenth century. This is the theme of Meinecke's classic *Cosmopolitanism and the National State* (1963), trans. Robert B. Kimber (Princeton, 1970). Although the emergence of Germany as a political nation-state is not a theme of this study, while focusing on Germans who were concerned with Germany as a cultural entity I do sometimes touch on the link to German political nationalism.

3. Peter Gay, *The Enlightenment: An Interpretation*, 2 vols. (New York, 1966 and 1969), 1:ix, 3, xi. Gay's synthetic interpretation of the Enlightenment was well received both within and outside academic circles. Widely and favorably reviewed in the mainstream press, the first volume was awarded the National Book Award in 1967.

4. Carl Becker, *The Heavenly City of the Eighteenth-Century Philosophers* (New Haven, 1932); and Gay's strenuous critique, "Carl Becker's Heavenly City," *Political Science Quarterly* (1957), reprinted in idem, *The Party of Humanity: Essays on the French Enlightenment* (New York, 1964), 188–210. On the general uncertainties of liberal history in this period, see Peter Novick, *That Noble Dream: The "Objectivity Question" and the American Historical Profession* (Cambridge, 1988), 133–167, 347.

5. Gay, *The Enlightenment*, 2:3. Gay's interpretation of the Enlightenment and its popularity was tied to the politics of the 1960s, to the sense of a renewed liberalism associated

with the postwar emergence of U.S. power and prosperity. Gay makes a strong connection between the liberal Enlightenment and the United States in his "Finale" to the second volume, where he asserts that what the philosophers imagined and realized piecemeal in Europe was fully implemented only in the American Revolution and the establishment of the American republic (557–558). The United States above all other nations embodied the spirit and telos of the Enlightenment, a view that functioned as a liberal explanation and justification for the ascension of the United States to global power. In this respect Gay's book can also be understood as a liberal justification of America in the Cold War.

6. Gay's ringing reaffirmation of liberal values is mirrored, for example, in Daniel Bell's *End of Ideology: On the Exhaustion of Political Ideas in the Fifties* (New York, 1962). Whereas Gay's *Enlightenment* establishes a definitive past and origin for modern American liberalism, Bell's work establishes a definitive future, one in which liberal values will no longer be considered one ideology among others but the end of ideology per se. See also Novick, 320–360.

7. The most significant interpretations of European modern intellectual history in this era take as their point of departure the presumption of a normative liberal Enlightenment. These include Gay's own *Weimar Culture: The Outsider as Insider* (New York, 1968); H. Stuart Hughes, *Consciousness and Society: The Reorientation of European Social Thought* (New York, 1958); and see Novick, 324–325, on Hughes's endorsement of the "end of ideology." Important interpretations of an intellectual German *Sonderweg*, Germany's cultural divergence from liberal modernity, include Krieger; Fritz Stern, *The Politics of Cultural Despair: A Study of the Rise of the Germanic Ideology* (Berkeley, 1961); Carl Schorske's classic study *German Social Democracy* (Cambridge, Mass., 1955) and his essays of the 1960s and 1970s, collected in *Fin-de-Siècle Vienna: Politics and Culture* (New York, 1980); and Fritz Ringer, *The Decline of the German Mandarins: The German Academic Community, 1890–1933* (Cambridge, Mass., 1969).

8. See Robert Darnton's devastating review of Gay in "In Search of Enlightenment: Recent Attempts to Create a Social History of Ideas," *Journal of Modern History* 43 (1971), 113–133; and his argument about the co-optation of a liberal and reformist Enlightenment in "The High Enlightenment and the Low-Life of Literature in Pre-Revolutionary France," *Past and Present* 51 (1971), 80–115, reprinted in *The Literary Underground of the Old Regime* (Cambridge, Mass., 1982), 1–40.

9. Unlike the French Enlightenment, the German and Scottish Enlightenments enjoyed a generally friendly relationship with state religions, notwithstanding Kant's problems with religious censorship in the 1790s. The German Enlightenment was also more conservative than the French in its general acceptance of a traditional corporatism. See Richard Sher, *Church and University in the Scottish Enlightenment* (Edinburgh, 1985); Jonathan Knudsen, *Justus Möser and the German Enlightenment* (Cambridge, 1986).

10. J. G. A. Pocock, *The Machiavellian Moment: Florentine Political Thought and the Atlantic Republican Tradition* (Princeton, 1975). On civic republicanism in France, see Pocock, 462–505; Keith Michael Baker, *Inventing the French Revolution: Essays on French Political Culture in the Eighteenth Century* (Cambridge, 1990) and "Transformations of Classical Republicanism in Eighteenth-Century France," *Journal of Modern History* 73 (2001), 32–52; and Johnson Kent Wright, *A Classical Republican in Eighteenth-Century France: The Political Thought of Mably* (Stanford, Calif., 1997). On Germany, see Frederick C. Beiser, *Enlightenment, Revolution, and Romanticism: The Genesis of Modern German Political Thought, 1790–1800* (Cambridge, Mass., 1992); Knudsen; Laurence Dickey, *Hegel: Religion and the Politics of Spirit* (Cambridge, 1987); Paul Nolte, "Bürgerideal, Gemeinde und Republik: Klassische Republikanismus im frühen deutschen Liberalismus," *Historische Zeitschrift* 254 (1992), 609–656. Various commentators, including Pocock, have pointed out how this republicanism was used by American revolutionaries against the British monarchy; but see in particular Michael Warner, *Letters of the Republic: Publication and the Public Sphere in Eighteenth-Century America* (Cambridge, Mass.,

1992). A general overview of civic republicanism in late eighteenth- and early nineteenth-century America is Daniel T. Rodgers, "Republicanism: The Career of a Concept," *Journal of American History* 79 (1992–93), 11–38.

11. On the novelty of the Enlightenment view of progressive commerce see the classic work of Albert O. Hirschman, *The Passions and the Interest: Political Arguments for Capitalism before Its Triumph* (Princeton, 1977).

12. Pocock, *Machiavellian Moment*, especially 423–552; and idem, *Virtue, Commerce, and History* (Cambridge, 1985), 42–43. In *The Social Contract* (1762), the civic republican Rousseau notes that private property should be limited so that there will be neither too much nor too little—two negative conditions that would undercut the autonomous republican citizen; Jean-Jacques Rousseau, *The Social Contract and the Discourses*, trans. G. D. H. Cole (New York, 1973), 237.

13. See chapter 1 on Herder's ambivalence about trade and international contact. The same impulse lies behind Rousseau's argument against the introduction of French theater into Geneva; Jean-Jacques Rousseau, *Politics and the Arts: Letter to M. d'Alembert on the Theater* (1758), trans. Allan Bloom (Ithaca, 1960). And for isolationist thinking in the new American republic, which might again be attributed to civic republicanism, see Felix Gilbert's classic *To the Farewell Address: Ideas of Early American Foreign Policy* (Princeton, 1966), 37–43, 55.

14. Pocock's influential thesis has been opposed by those who wish to restore the centrality of liberalism to the American Revolution and political traditions. The result has been an attempt to argue that Enlightenment commercial liberalism was somehow compatible with civic republicanism. See Ralph Lerner, "Commerce and Character: The Anglo-American as New Model Man," *William and Mary Quarterly* 36 (1979), 13–26; Jeffrey Isaac, "Republicanism vs. Liberalism? A Reconsideration," *History of Political Thought* 9 (1984), 349–77. Pocock rejects this supposed synthesis of conflicting views; *Machiavellian Moment*, 493 ff.; and *Virtue*, 48. The importance of an Enlightenment liberal tradition in U.S. history has also been emphasized by Marxists, who prefer to criticize liberalism (and capitalism) rather than republicanism and identify the former as the center of American politics. See Isaac Kramnick, *Republicanism and Bourgeois Radicalism: Political Ideology in Late Eighteenth-Century England and America* (Ithaca, 1990), 1–42, 163–200, 260–289. Civic republicanism has been put in the service of both New Left and conservative critiques of liberal America.

15. While Darnton's populist critique of an elite Enlightenment seemed to be at one with the antielite countercultural concerns of the 1960s and the resulting reorientation of historical writing toward social history, Pocock's history of civic republicanism appeared to have no such motivation. But notwithstanding the apparent absence of direct influence of the events of the 1960s and 1970s, its opposition of ancient republican virtue to Enlightenment commerce was immediately adopted by those who sought to attack a liberal Enlightenment and a liberal modernity. In studies ranging from historians of Anglo-American labor unrest to "communitarian" philosophical opposition to the Enlightenment, ancient republican virtue serves as a source of critique and as an image of a social alternative to the apparent atomization of Enlightenment liberalism. See, for example, Sean Wilentz, *Chants Democratic: New York City and the Rise of the American Working Class, 1785–1850* (Oxford, 1982); and the work that inspired a left- and right-wing "communitarianism," Alasdair MacIntyre, *After Virtue* (South Bend, Ind., 1981).

16. The now-classic example of the use of Geertzian ethnography in history is Robert Darnton, *The Great Cat Massacre and Other Episodes in French Cultural History* (New York, 1984); and see Harold Mah, "Suppressing the Text: The Metaphysics of Ethnographic History in Darnton's Great Cat Massacre," *History Workshop* 31 (spring 1991), 1–20. A crucial work introducing semiotics and cultural analysis into historical analysis is the first half of Lynn Hunt, *Politics, Culture, and Class in the French Revolution* (Berkeley, 1984). Foucault's

most influential works on early modern institutions include *Madness and Civilization: A History of the Insane in the Age of Reason* (1961), trans. Richard Howard (New York, 1965); and *Discipline and Punish: The Birth of the Prison* (1975), trans. Alan Sheridan (New York, 1977). Foucault's influence on Enlightenment studies also has another trajectory issuing from his works on epistemology, notably *The Order of Things: An Archaeology of the Human Sciences* (1966) (New York, 1970).

17. Joan Landes, *Women and the Public Sphere in the Age of the French Revolution* (Ithaca, 1988); Sara Maza, *Private Lives and Public Affairs: The Causes Célèbres of Prerevolutionary France* (Berkeley, 1993).

18. See Landes, 152–159; George Mosse, *The Image of Man* (Oxford, 1995), 29–37.

19. Dena Goodman, *The Republic of Letters: A Cultural History of the French Enlightenment* (Ithaca, 1994), 90–135.

20. Jürgen Habermas, *The Structural Transformation of the Public Sphere: An Enquiry into a Category of Bourgeois Society* (1962), trans. Thomas Burger (Cambridge, Mass., 1992). On problems in Habermas's theory and in how historians have used it, see Harold Mah, "Phantasies of the Public Sphere: Rethinking the Habermas of Historians," *Journal of Modern History* 72 (March 2000), 153–182. Goodman's use of Habermas is indicated in Goodman, 12–15.

21. Though a Marxist of sorts when he wrote *Structural Transformation,* Habermas still accepts the "bourgeois" public sphere of the eighteenth century as a normative ideal, which, according to him, the further development of capitalism undercut to produce a degraded institution in the twentieth century. For some recent historians who have used Habermas, the French Revolution distorted the eighteenth-century public sphere (which they also take as an ideal) by basing it on a rigid gender differentiation and banishing women from its institutions. In this sense, the modernity of the Enlightenment seems more genuinely "liberal"—more consistent in its affirmation of personal autonomy for everyone—than the society that came after it. This is Landes's position in part; Goodman seems to subscribe to it as well; and see Daniel Gordon, *Citizens without Citizenship: Equality and Sociability in French Thought, 1670–1789* (Princeton, 1994), who also rehabilitates old-regime sociability in the liberal terms of Habermas's theory. Carla Hesse has recently argued for a different understanding of what happened in the public sphere, as she points out how notwithstanding a change in gender norms that seemingly banished women from public activity, the number of women's publications rose steadily in the period up to and through the Revolution; Hesse, *The Other Enlightenment: How French Women Became Modern* (Princeton, 2001), 31–55.

22. Besides the dispute over the compatibility of liberal Enlightenment commerce and civic republicanism, see Goodman's critique of previous criticisms of the salon and salonnière, including those of Robert Darnton, in Goodman, 52–89. Darnton issues his own counter-counterargument in "Two Paths through the Social History of Ideas," *Studies on Voltaire and the Eighteenth Century,* 359 (1998), 274–280.

23. A single text may not only give voice to conflicting identities but also make the presence and conflict of contradictory identities one of its explicit themes. Landes, 31–38, reads Montesquieu's *Persian Letters* as singlemindedly concerned with preserving austere virtue and attacking Parisian refinement. But although these views are evident in the character of the self-deluded Persian Usbek, a second Persian, Rica, is won over to Parisian sensibility, comes to celebrate the salonnière, and even assumes the voice of a Persian woman who engages in an uplifting phantasy of female rebellion. Montesquieu, *The Persian Letters* (1721), trans. C. J. Betts (London, 1973), letters 63, 141, pp. 129–130, 247–254. The pull of contradictory identities is also a theme in Diderot's *Rameau's Nephew* (1761). Here Diderot represents himself as the respectable philosophe committed to the progressive education of his daughter, but he also plainly enjoys consorting with the nephew, the grub-street oppor-

tunist who would teach her the direct opposite. Denis Diderot, *Rameau's Nephew,* trans. Leonard Tancock (London, 1966), 45, 56–57, 103.

24. Other historians have of course already considered some of the ways in which terms of eighteenth-century identity fell into conflict and how those conflicts influenced developments in the following century. Though often very perceptive, these studies have generally underestimated the multiplicity, instability, and ultimate strangeness of the conflicting terms of identity. Historians have in different ways sought to elide conflict and instability even as they register it. In addition to the discussion in the following chapters, see my discussion of the recent historiography of the French Revolution associated with François Furet, in Mah, "Phantasies," 168–172.

25. A recent, and more psychoanalytic, argument for the phantasmatic aspect of identity formation is the important article by Joan Scott, "Fantasy Echo: History and the Construction of Identity," *Critical Inquiry* 27 (winter 2001), 284–304. One implication of what I am asserting here is that there is considerable unrecognized "transference" in Enlightenment historiography (to borrow a term from psychoanalysis) whereby a historian, for whatever reason, uncritically takes over a phantasy of identity of the eighteenth century that reiterates the phantasy's own self-description as something unproblematic and fully corresponding to reality, even as evidence shows the opposite. On the idea of transference applied to historians, see Dominick LaCapra's *Representing the Holocaust: History, Theory, Trauma* (Ithaca, 1994), *History and Memory after Auschwitz* (Ithaca, 1998), and *Writing History, Writing Trauma* (Baltimore, 2001).

26. I sometimes refer to a *longue durée* of terms or discourses of identity. I do not use this expression lightly. In their remarkable persistence over centuries of historical change, durations of certain terms and discourses of cultural identity resemble the extended periods of social and economic phenomena identified by the *Annales* school of historians in the 1950s and 1960s. In one sense, in fact, cultural durations show even more longevity; whereas the *longues durées* of the *Annales* end with industrialization, those of culture persist well into the twentieth century.

Chapter 1. The Man with Too Many Qualities

1. Ernst Cassirer, for example, notes that Herder "parts company with his age" but then adds that this was possible only because he followed "trails blazed by the Enlightenment"; Cassirer, *The Philosophy of the Enlightenment* (Princeton, 1979), 233.

2. Friedrich Meinecke, *Historism: The Rise of a New Historical Outlook* (London, 1972), 296–297.

3. This was the precritical Kant of Wolffian rationalism; Hamann was a source of the ideas of the *Sturm und Drang.* Herder's father was a poor pietist cantor and schoolteacher in Möhringen in East Prussia. Herder was able to attend university first through the patronage of a surgeon in a Russian regiment that passed through his town and then by means of a stipend from the estate of the Möhringen Count Dohna. See Robert T. Clark Jr., *Herder: His Life and Thought* (Berkeley, 1955), 39–51.

4. Rudolf Haym, *Herder nach seinem Leben und seinen Werken,* vol. 1 (Berlin, 1880), 105–107; Frederick C. Beiser, *Enlightenment, Revolution, and Romanticism: The Genesis of Modern German Political Thought, 1790–1800* (Cambridge, Mass., 1992), 198. Beiser idealizes the "republican" nature of politics in Riga. As we see, however, serious tensions existed even at the level of conceptualization; and as we shall see, serious tensions existed in Herder's conception of Riga republicanism. Governed by Germans and Russians, native Livinians tended to be an economically submerged population in Riga.

5. Clark, 51.

6. Ibid.

7. Haym, 105–106.

8. These are, notably, the historical study of language, the opposition of a historical and contextualized aesthetics over a mechanical and formalistic one, the comparative study of national cultures, and the proper cultivation of a German literature and language.

9. Nicolai to Herder, 19 November 1766, *Johann Gottfried Herders Lebensbild*, 4 vols. (Erlangen, 1846), 1:204–207; Haym, 132.

10. Jürgen Habermas, *The Structural Transformation of the Public Sphere: An Enquiry into a Category of Bourgeois Society* (1962), trans. Thomas Burger (Cambridge, Mass., 1992).

11. Clark, 58–61; Haym, 84 ff.

12. Quoted in Albert O. Hirschman, *The Passions and the Interests* (Princeton, 1977), 60; and J. G. A. Pocock, *The Machiavellian Moment: Florentine Political Thought and the Atlantic Republican Tradition* (Princeton, 1975), 492 ff.; idem, *Virtue, Commerce, and History* (Cambridge, 1985), 49 ff.; Ralph Lerner, "Commerce and Character: The Anglo-American as New-Model Man," *William and Mary Quarterly* 36 (1979), 3–26; Jeffrey C. Isaac, "Republicanism vs. Liberalism? A Reconsideration," *History of Political Thought* 9 (1984), 349–377. See also the essays in David Wooton, ed., *Republicanism, Liberty, and Commercial Society, 1649–1776* (Stanford, 1994); and Istvan Hont and Michael Ignatieff, eds., *Wealth and Virtue* (Cambridge, 1983).

13. Pocock, *Virtue*, 48–50; idem, *Machiavellian Moment*, 470, 490–503; Lerner; and Hirschman.

14. Johann Gottfried Herder, "On Diligence in the Study of Several Languages" (1764), in *Selected Early Writings, 1764–1767*, ed. and trans. E. A. Menze and K. Menges (University Park, Pa., 1992), 32.

15. J. G. Herder, "Do We Still Have the Public and Fatherland of Yore? A Treatise Presented in Celebration of the Opening of the New Courthouse," ibid., 61, 59.

16. Quoted in Haym, 107–108; Beiser, 198–199. Herder's good relations with the city's Russian rulers do not appear to have been feigned. His public praise of Catherine II in 1765 as a benevolent ruler is a sentiment echoed later in his private journal of his trip to France. There he outlines a plan for educational reform, which he believes will be endorsed and, he hopes, implemented by Catherine. Johann Gottfried Herder, "Journals of My Travels in the Year 1769," trans. John Francis Harrison (Ph.D. diss., Columbia University, 1952), 250; German edition: *Journal meiner Reise*, in *Werke*, ed. Wolfgang Pross, vol. 1 (Munich, 1984), 381; hereafter cited as *J*, with page numbers from the English translation and the German, respectively. Excerpts from the English translation are reprinted in F. M. Barnard, ed., *J. G. Herder on Social and Political Culture* (Oxford, 1963), 63–117.

17. See the list of his major German biographer, Rudolf Haym, who wrote that Herder was "a stimulating and jovial member of society; an incomparable teacher and pastor; a Masonic lodge leader, a poet and writer"; Haym, 108.

18. Herder to Karoline Flachsland, 22 September 1776, *Lebensbild*, 3:145. In the same letter (145–146) he goes on to describe his situation: "loved by state and community, worshipped by my friends and a number of young people, who thought of me as Christ! The favorite of the government and of the nobility." See also Haym, 107–111.

19. Clark, 51.

20. See Clark; Haym; Beiser; Anthony LaVopa, "Herder's *Publikum*: Language, Print, and Sociability in Eighteenth-Century Germany," *Eighteenth-Century Studies* 29 (1995), 5–24; Benjamin W. Redekop, *Enlightenment and Community: Lessing, Abbt, Herder, and the Quest for a German Public* (Montreal, 2000), 168–220.

21. Notwithstanding attempts to blend a commercial and a republican ethos, the two could always be turned against each other. Even the most commercial-minded apologists

for republicanism acknowledged the potentially destabilizing effects of unconstrained commerce on the polity. This same recognition is also evident in Herder's early writings. Given the ultimate, inescapable antithesis between the values of commerce and those of republicanism, the two are not what Pocock calls "two sides of a dialectic," since they have proven resistant to reconciliation; they in fact operate as a radical antinomy. Pocock is very good at showing how this antinomy ultimately asserts itself, notwithstanding attempts to deny it. See Pocock, *Machiavellian Moment,* 492–503, on how Montesquieu, Hume, and others, notwithstanding their endorsements of *doux commerce,* ended up concluding that commerce must ultimately undercut civic virtue. On the opposition between republican virtue and self-interested egoism in early German liberalism, see Paul Nolte, "Bürgerideal, Gemeinde und Republik: 'Klassischer Republikanismus' im frühen deutschen Liberalismus," *Historische Zeitschrift* 254 (1992), 609–656. Nolte makes the very interesting observation that in this period the term *Bürger* evolved from a republican to commercial bourgeois meaning. In the case of Riga and Herder, the term carries both senses.

22. Rousseau quoted in Lerner, 21.

23. Herder, "On Diligence," 30–31.

24. Ibid.; Herder's "gallantries and ambiguous courtesies" is a reference to French manners and civility. His own position on these, as we shall see, is very ambivalent indeed.

25. Herder, "On Diligence," 30.

26. Ibid. His first polemic on history, *Also a Philosophy of History* of 1774, is written expressly against universalist Enlightenment histories. See Harold Mah, "German Historical Thought in the Age of Herder, Kant, and Hegel," in *A Companion to Western Historical Thought,* ed. Lloyd Kramer and Sarah Maza (Oxford, 2002), 145–151.

27. Herder, "On Diligence," 30.

28. Not altogether convincing because he plainly sees some things, such as the German language, as continuous with its original natural condition. From what Herder says a little later in the article, it would seem that his point is more sophistry than genuine belief.

29. Herder, "On Diligence," 30.

30. Habermas, 1–110. For commentaries on the current historiographical use of the idea of the public sphere, see Craig Calhoun, ed., *Habermas and the Public Sphere* (Cambridge, Mass., 1992); and, more critically, Harold Mah, "Phantasies of the Public Sphere: Rethinking the Habermas of Historians," *Journal of Modern History* 72 (March 2000), 153–182.

31. Hamann to Herder, 21 November and 1 December 1766, *Lebensbild,* 1:208–210; Herder to Hamann, December 1766, ibid., 210–213; Nicolai to Herder, 26 November 1768, ibid., 377; Nicolai to Herder, 24 December 1768, ibid., 391; Herder to Nicolai, 10 January 1769, ibid., 413.

32. LaVopa, 10; Redekop, 196 ff.

33. Haym, 304.

34. Ibid., 217–219.

35. *Über Thomas Abbts Schriften: Der Torso zu einem Denkmaal, an seinem Grabe errichtet* (1768).

36. Haym, 218–220, 304.

37. Ibid., 304–307.

38. Mah, "Phantasies," 166 ff.

39. Herder, "Do We Still Have the Public and Fatherland?" 58.

40. Mona Ozouf, "'Public Opinion' at the End of the Old Regime," *Journal of Modern History* 60, suppl. (September 1988), S21; and see Mah, "Phantasies," 165 ff.

41. Herder to Nicolai, 10 January 1769, *Lebensbild,* 1:413.

42. The republican desire for a community of moral transparency and mutual recognition is of course also central in Rousseau's republican politics, and, like Rousseau, Herder will later lament the loss of it. In *Also a Philosophy of History* (1774), he displaces this idea of

transparency in a republican community to his highly idealized view of an original German tribal society: "In the patriarch's hut, the humble homestead, or the local community, people knew and clearly perceived what they talked about, since the way they looked at things, and acted, was through the human heart"; Herder in Barnard, 204.

43. For these reasons, modern media manipulation has been inevitable; its accomplishment has been to manage the circulation of opinion in the public sphere even while making it seem unregulated, sincere, and critical. See Mah, "Phantasies."

44. Michael Warner, "The Mass Public and the Mass Subject," in Calhoun, 377–402; and Warner, *Letters of the Republic: Publication and the Public Sphere in Eighteenth-Century America* (Cambridge, Mass., 1990); LaVopa. The most compelling critical conceptual analysis of the distinction between writing and speaking remains Jacques Derrida, *Of Grammatology* (1967), trans. Gayatri Chakravorty Spivak (Baltimore, 1976).

45. The *Journal* was written from July to November 1769.

46. Herder to Hamann, from Nantes probably at the end of August 1769, *Lebensbild,* 2:60. Here Herder also emphasizes how his dream marked a break with his past.

47. See, for example, LaVopa and Beiser.

48. Following some earlier commentators, Herder's English biographer Clark suggests that another reason for his departure from Riga was his unrequited love for an older married woman. Clark admits that this connection involves considerable speculation. But whatever the nature and status of Herder's romantic problems, some kind of sexual longing figures in the train of associations in Herder's *Journal* and its dream of France. See *J,* 212/360.

49. Roger Chartier, "Civilité," in *Handbuch politisch-sozialer Grundbegriffe in Frankreich, 1680–1820,* ed. Rolf Reichardt and Eberhard Schmitt, 20 Hefte (Munich, 1985–2000), 4:1–50; Annette Höfer and Rolf Reichardt, "Honnête homme, honnêteté, honnête gens," ibid., 7:7–74; Daniel Gordon, *Citizens without Sovereignty: Equality and Sociability in French Thought, 1670–1789* (Princeton, 1994); Lawrence Klein, *Shaftesbury and the Culture of Politeness* (Cambridge, 1994); Carolyn Lougee, *"Le Paradis des Femmes": Women, Salons, and Social Stratification in Seventeenth-Century France* (Princeton, 1976), 52 ff.; Dena Goodman, *The Republic of Letters: A Cultural History of the Enlightenment* (Ithaca, 1994), 90–135.

50. See also Harrison, *J,* 110, on the views of Voltaire, and 61, n. 1, quoting Abbé Galiani to Mme d'Epinay, 12 May 1770.

51. Egon Cohn, *Gesellschaftsideale und Gesellschaftsroman des 17. Jahrhunderts* (Berlin, 1921), 9; Klein, 118–120.

52. Hans Ulrich Gumbrecht and Rolf Reichardt, "Philosophe, Philosophie," in Reichardt and Schmitt, 3:20, 45.

53. Ibid., 20; Robert Darnton, "Philosophers Trim the Tree of Knowledge: The Epistemological Strategy of the *Encyclopédie,*" in *The Great Cat Massacre and Other Episodes in French Cultural History* (New York, 1984), 199–205.

54. Gumbrecht and Reichardt, "Philosophe," 40–45; Robert Darnton, *The Literary Underground of the Old Regime* (Cambridge, Mass., 1982), 1–17.

55. Gumbrecht and Reichardt, "Philosophe," 51. The turn of educated opinion in their favor was evident in the theater public's hostile reception after 1760 of plays critical of the philosophes, as shown by the fate of Pallisot's *Les Philosophes,* which was staged at the Comédie Française in 1760. Greeted with angry criticism, attendance plummeted after the first few performances, and within two months it ignominiously closed. Ibid., 38–40; and Ira O. Wade, *The "Philosophe" in the French Drama of the Eighteenth Century* (Princeton, 1926).

56. Darnton, "Philosophers," 207 ff.

57. Gumbrech and Reichardt, "Philosophe," 34. See Klein on the same process in Britain.

58. Anon., "Philosophe," in *Encyclopédie; ou, Dictionnaire raisonné des sciences, des arts, et des métiers, par une société de gens de lettres,* 17 vols. (Paris, 1751–1772), 12:510.

59. Ibid. and 511. See also Herbert Dieckmann, *Le Philosophe* (St. Louis, 1948); and Voltaire, "Gens de lettres," in *Encyclopédie,* 7:599.

60. Denis Diderot, "Supplément au Voyage de Bougainville," in *Oeuvres philosophiques* (Paris, 1964), 457.

61. Herder thinks he will do this in a way characteristic of the most successful of French philosophes: he hopes to win over to his cause an enlightened monarch. In Nantes he asked a friend to help him approach Catherine II with his plan for reform. *J,* 236/373; Beiser, 200–201.

62. On the Prussian Aacademy see Adolf Harnack, *Geschichte der königlichen Preussischen Akademie der Wissenschaften zu Berlin,* vol. 1 (Berlin, 1900), 29 ff.; and Hans Aarsleff, *From Locke to Saussure* (Minneapolis, 1982), 142–210. Frederick would later write an essay against the German language and German literature and their revival.

63. One elegant statement of this view is Isaiah Berlin, *Vico and Herder* (New York, 1976), 180 ff.

64. *J,* 329/421. Herder goes on to say that French classicism achieved nothing on its own. Corneille's *Cid* was Spanish in origin; Mazarin and Lully were Italian, as were France's other main cultural figures and forms; *J,* 329–330/421.

65. Herder wrote the essays on Ossian and Shakespeare; Goethe's contribution "On German Architecture" is a meditation on the medieval Strasbourg cathedral.

66. Roy Pascal, *The German Sturm und Drang* (Manchester, 1953), 79–83; Clark, 271–283.

67. See Mah, "German Historical Thought," 145–151.

68. J. G. Herder, *Briefe zur Beförderung der Humanität: Neunte Sammlung,* in *Werke,* ed. H. D. Irmscher, vol. 7 (Berlin, 1964), 583–597.

69. Quoted in Pascal, 82; and see Clark, 256–257.

70. In *Also a Philosophy* Herder pointedly rejects the Enlightenment (and early modern) trope of the maturing of the human race, a metaphor that implies a single, teleological development for all cultures. See Herder in Barnard, 207. But his *Ideas* takes this trope as its organizing principle, dividing human societies according to their stage in humanity's evolution from infancy to full maturity. Beiser, 208, thinks that Herder's recourse to this trope of biological maturation saves Herder from Enlightenment universalism, not recognizing that it was an enabling principle of precisely that universalism. Gottfried Lessing bases his 1780 essay on universal history, "On the Education of the Human Race," on this same trope; and it is implied in Kant's famous opening line to his 1789 essay "An Answer to the Question 'What Is Enlightenment?'": "Enlightenment is man's emergence from his self-imposed tutelage"; Immanuel Kant, *Political Writings,* trans. H. B. Nisbet (Cambridge, 1991), 54.

71. On Herder's awkward support of the French Revolution while he served the Weimar court, see Beiser, 215–216.

72. This image of Herder was bound up with the conservative drive to reify Germany as a fundamentally Romantic culture. See Bernhard Becker, *Herder-Rezeption in Deutschland* (St. Ingbert, 1987).

Chapter 2. The Language of Cultural Identity

1. Denis Diderot, *Lettre sur les sourds et les muets à l'usage de ceux qui entendent et qui parlent,* in *Oeuvres complètes,* ed. Roger Lewinter, 15 vols. (Paris, 1969–1973), 2:546. On the seventeenth-century origins of this view, see Ulrich Ricken, *Grammaire et philosophie au siècle des lumières* (Lille, n.d.), 9, 18 ff.; idem, "Rationalismus und Sensualismus in der Diskussion über

die Wortstellung," in *Literaturgeschichte als geschichtlicher Auftrag,* ed. Werner Bahner (Berlin, 1961), 104–105.

2. See Daniel Mornet, *Histoire de la clarté française* (Paris, 1929), 316; Ricken, *Grammaire,* 126.

3. Ricken, "Rationalismus," 97–110; idem, *Grammaire,* 10–25. Ricken notes (24) that François Charpentier in his *De l'excellence de la langue françoise* (1683) argues that sentences of inversion require the listener or reader to perform two mental operations. One must reconstruct the natural order of an inverted sentence before reaching an understanding of it, and in this interval between the two operations there arise possible complications to understanding. Languages of inversion therefore impede the assimilation and dissemination of knowledge. The eighteenth-century grammarian César Chesneau Du Marsais relies on the same argument when he explains why the French have great difficulty in learning Latin; Du Marsais, *Oeuvres de Du Marsais,* 7 vols. (Paris, 1795–1797), 1:7. The creation of a language stylized in this manner was one of the reasons Cardinal Richelieu established the French Academy in 1634. Richelieu sought to "create a diplomatic instrument without equal, clear, precise, with the least distance from one's thought"; M. Le Duc de la Force, Les Quarante, "La Fondation de l'Académie Française," in *Trois siècles de l'Académie Française* (Paris, 1935), 4.

4. Voltaire, "François, ou Français," in *Encyclopédie; ou, Dictionnaire raisonné des sciences, des arts, et des métiers, par une société de gens de lettres,* 17 vols. (Paris, 1751–1772), 12:286–287. Also see anon., "Langue," ibid., 19:267; and Voltaire, *Dictionnaire de la pensée de Voltaire par lui-meme* (Paris, 1994), 762–764.

5. Nicolas Beauzée, "Inversion," in *Encyclopédie,* 8:853; idem, *Grammaire générale,* 2 vols. (1767; reprint, Stuttgart, 1974), 2:539; Ricken, *Grammaire,* 148. And see Foucault's discussion of early modern views of "general grammar" in *The Order of Things: An Archaeology of the Human Sciences* (1966) (New York, 1970). Foucault conflates seventeenth-century rationalist and eighteenth-century sensationalist views of language, assimilating both into a single "classical" frame of mind. The result is a considerable elision of significant differences and contradictions in the two views of language. But at the same time Foucault makes many brilliant observations about the logic of general grammar that withstand the empirical mistakes. Foucault, 82–124.

6. Gottfried Wilhelm Leibniz, "Ermahnung an die Teutsche ihrer Verstand und Sprache Besser zu üben" (1679), in *Politische Schriften,* vol. 3: *1677–1689* (Berlin, 1975–1980), 809.

7. Frederick II, *De la littérature allemande* (Berlin, 1780), 9, 18, 37.

8. Adolf Harnack, *Geschichte der königlichen Preussischen Akademie der Wissenschaften zu Berlin,* 3 vols. (Berlin, 1900), 1:312–314; Hans Aarsleff, *From Locke to Saussure* (Minneapolis, 1982), 178.

9. Antoine Rivarol, *Discours sur l'universalité de la langue française* (1784; reprint, Paris, 1966), 112–113; see also 97, 109, 115–116. The same point was made in the other winning essay, Johann Christoph Schwab's *Von den Ursachen der Allgemeinheit der französischen Sprache* (Tübingen, 1785), 8, 53, 76. Many point out that French sentences frequently use inversions, even if that is not the rule.

10. *J,* 320/418. As we shall see, when Herder performs the role of the German cultural nationalist, he will offer quite a different view.

11. Etienne Bonnot de Condillac, *An Essay on the Origin of Human Knowledge* (1746), trans. Robert Weyant (Gainesville, Fla., 1971), 226, 256, 172, 239 ff.

12. Diderot, 543–545.

13. Ibid., 587–588.

14. Rivarol, 113, 89 ff.; Voltaire, Beauzée, and Du Marsais continued to refer to the direct order of the French sentence as "natural."

15. Condillac, 271; translation modified.

16. From this breach between a primary language of direct sense impression and a secondary language of rational reordering, Condillac, Diderot, and others make a distinction between languages suited to sensuous poetry and those suited to abstract prose. Germans later take over this distinction. See Condillac, 295; Diderot, 546; Rivarol, 112–113; and Johann Gottfried Herder, *Über die neuere Literatur: Erste Sammlung von Fragmenten* (1766–67), in *Werke*, ed. Martin Bollacher et al., 10 vols. (Berlin, 1985), 1:221. The classic epistemological impasses of sensationalist epistemology, as they were manifested in the French Enlightenment, are closely analyzed in Keith Michael Baker, *Condorcet: From Natural Philosophy to Social Mathematics* (Chicago, 1975); and David Bates, "Idols and Insight: An Enlightenment Topography of Knowledge," *Representations* 73 (winter 2001), 1–23.

17. Diderot, 546.

18. See Peter French, *Rhetoric and Truth in France: Descartes to Diderot* (Oxford, 1972), 71–72.

19. Schwab, 11, 177; to make his point, he also tells the amusing story of how Cato the Elder, who hated the "decadent" Greeks, nonetheless sent his son to Athens to be educated; ibid., 10.

20. Sophia Rosenfeld, *A Revolution in Language: The Problem of Signs in Eighteenth-Century France* (Stanford, 2001), discusses a different debate of the 1750s between Condillac, Diderot, and Rousseau, concerning the creation of a lexicon that would directly correspond to sensation. Rosenfeld wants to argue that in the French Revolution, the Jacobins' anxieties about language should be traced back to this discrete debate, but what she in fact shows is that the Revolutionaries' linguistic concerns were manifold and conflicting, extending not just this particular debate of the 1750s but also concerns about the logical rigor of French syntax and the corrupting nature of civility. Also, contrary to her characterization of Diderot and Condillac as consistently sensationalist in their view of language, we have seen that they also continued to subscribe to a rationalist privileging of the French language. On language, as on other matters, they held multiple and contradictory views. See also Patrice L.-R. Higonnet, "The Politics of Linguistic Terrorism and Grammatical Hegemony during the French Revolution," *Social History* 5 (1980), 410–469, on the additional issue in the Revolution of creating a single national language over and against a host of regional dialects.

21. For example, Voltaire, "François," 286–287; Rivarol, 116.

22. Voltaire, "François," 287; Frederick II, 10–11.

23. Historians have emphasized how the civility of the court and the salon was employed to further politically different ends. Older historians argued that civility served as a mechanism for extending power over a resistant aristocracy, whereby a consolidating seventeenth-century absolutism imposed carefully articulated rules of courtesy both within and outside the court. All dealings between the nobility and the officers of the crown were to be governed by a code of politeness and deference. According to recent historians, the crown's political skewing of social interaction led to a reaction in the salon that generated a dissenting variant of courtly civility. In the Hôtel de Rambouillet and then other salons, nobles and nonnobles mixed with the aim of establishing a new sociability that, unlike the civility of the court, would be genuinely pleasing because it would be free of social deference and hierarchy. This more democratic sociability, as Gordon and Goodman have argued for France and Klein for England, served as an incubator of the Enlightenment and the modern public sphere. For the older view of the courtly hegemony of civility used to domesticate the aristocracy, see Orest Ranum, "Courtesy, Absolutism, and the Rise of the French State, 1630–1640," *Journal of Modern History* 52 (1980), 426–451; and of course Norbert Elias, *The History of Manners*, vol. 1 of *The Civilizing Process* (1939; reprint, New York,

1978). For more recent efforts to locate the origins of the Enlightenment and a modern public sphere in old-regime sociability, see Daniel Gordon, *Citizens without Sovereignty: Equality and Sociability in French Thought, 1670–1789* (Princeton, 1994); Dena Goodman, *The Republic of Letters: A Cultural History of the Enlightenment* (Ithaca, 1994); and Lawrence Klein, *Shaftesbury and the Culture of Politeness* (Cambridge, 1994).

My treatment of French civility only indirectly concerns this debate on the political functions of French sociability. Since I contend that civility had constitutive representation problems that could not be resolved by making it more democratic, my analysis implies that recent views of the effective and putatively democratic functioning of civility in the salon are necessarily overly sanguine. The criticisms of civility (in all forms) are inseparable, always available, in the elaboration or execution of its doctrine. These criticisms are in fact continuous throughout the longue durée of the discourse of civility and, as I point out in chapter 3, may in fact be seen as specialized reiterations of an even more general and older criticism of aesthetic representation, a criticism that goes back to the ancient Greeks.

My interpretation differs from the view of recent historians who, seeking to rehabilitate civility's putative modernity, argue that criticisms of it emerged later and were unjustified, the product of different resentments. See Gordon, 86 ff.; and Goodman, 53–89, who treats criticisms of civility as the result of misogyny. What I believe Goodman and others in fact show, and what I also argue in chapter 4, is that for different reasons the always-existing problems in the discourse of civility became of supreme cultural and political importance in certain periods—in this case, in the late eighteenth century.

There is also another way in which these recent arguments may be considered overstated—namely, in their sanguine view of a well-functioning progressive or democratic modern public sphere. I discuss problems in the idea of the public sphere in Harold Mah, "Phantasies of the Public Sphere: Rethinking the Habermas of Historians," *Journal of Modern History* 72 (March 2000), 153–182.

24. Erasmus, *La Civilité puerile* (Paris, 1877), 13–15; French trans. of *De civilitate morum puerilium* (1530); Maurice Magendie, *La Politesse mondaine et les théories de l'honnêteté, en France au XVIIe siècle, de 1600–1660* (Paris, n.d.), 351 ff., 413, 455, 457, 460, 823, 882, 886; Roger Chartier, "Civilité," in *Handbuch politisch-sozialer Grundbegriffe in Frankreich, 1680–1820,* ed. Rolf Reichardt and Eberhard Schmitt, 20 Hefte (Munich, 1985–2000), 4:17; Annette Höfer and Rolf Reichardt, "Honnête homme, honnêteté, honnête gens," ibid., 7:9, 11.

25. Erasmus, 43.

26. Domna C. Stanton, *The Aristocrat as Art: A Study of the Honnête Homme and the Dandy in Seventeenth- and Nineteenth-Century French Literature* (New York, 1980), 122; Henning Scheffers, *Höfische Konvention und die Aufklärung* (Bonn, 1980), 102; and Gordon, 265 ff., for d'Holbach's similar view of manners.

27. Chevalier de Jaucourt, "Honnêteté," in *Encyclopédie,* 8:288.

28. Jean Starobinski, *Blessings in Disguise; or the Morality of Evil,* trans. Arthur Goldhammer (Cambridge, Mass., 1993), 37, referring to the seventeenth-century theorist of civility the Chevalier de Méré.

29. All signifiers are of course sensuous, but in the logic of civility that sensuousness is foregrounded. To indicate that emphasis I refer to civility's signifiers as "sensuous" rather than the more awkward "sensuously foregrounded."

30. As will be evident in the following discussion, my idea of the multiple meaning of sensuous signifiers is indebted to some recent literary theories. But the idea itself was also suggested, if not fully worked out, by earlier critics. Kenneth Burke, in *A Rhetoric of Motives* (1950; reprint, Berkeley, 1962), 87, wrote: "there is a difference between an abstract term naming the 'idea' of, say, security, and a concrete image designed to stand for this idea, and to 'place it before our very eyes.' For one thing, if the image employs the full resources of the imagination, it will not represent merely one idea, but will contain a whole bundle of

ones that would be mutually contradictory if reduced to their purely ideational equivalents." If security were represented by the image of a mother, Burke continues, that single image would inevitably invoke other ideas, such as "affection, tradition, 'naturalness,' communion." The aestheticization of civility has been broadly noted, and recent discussions of the tendency of such a process to generate surplus meaning can be found in Starobinski, *Blessings*, 36, 38; and especially Stanton, 113, who compares it to the function of poetic language: "The notion of the poetic and connotational and nondiscursive content illustrates how a relatively small number of signifiers in one language can produce a veritable battery of signs. From this perspective, the system of the aristocratic self, which represents a set of signifiers in a set of languages—physical, behavioral, and verbal—may be viewed as a vast, polysemic text for semiological analysis." In the analysis that follows, I emphasize the self-collapsing nature of civility's polysemic text.

31. Starobinski, *Blessings*, 7.

32. Ibid.; Stanton, 107.

33. Chartier, 21–22.

34. *The Misanthrope* is the best-known example of Molière's criticism of civility. Starobinski, *Blessings*, 56–57, nicely analyzes its paradoxes. Also see Molière's preface to the 1654 edition of *Tartuffe* in *The Misanthrope and Other Plays* (London, 1959), 99–109, concerning his petition to the king in which he attempts to preserve for the authorities the ideal of civility even while criticizing its dissembling ways.

35. Quoted in Stanton, 186.

36. Chartier, 25; Höfer and Reichardt, 29–37.

37. Montesquieu, *The Spirit of the Laws*, trans. Anne Cohler et al. (Cambridge, 1989), 317.

38. Quoted in Starobinski, *Blessings*, 10.

39. Quoted in ibid., 8–10; Chartier, 47, points out that the valorization of politeness continued into the nineteenth century. Fluctuations in the usage of terms of civility were also affected by the diffusion of the idea of civility. In the eighteenth century that ideal migrated from the elite sphere of the court and the salons to other social groups, becoming a more generalized social ethos. This development resulted in the "banalization" of some of the terms of civility. Some now abandoned traditional usages, notably the *honnête homme*, as derogated terms. Höfer and Reichardt, 55.

40. This procedure has been continued in recent studies of eighteenth-century civility that, seeking to rehabilitate refined sociability, make a distinction between honest politeness and deceiving civility. But this distinction shows the same problem of inconsistency. These studies assert that politeness is honest and that civility deceives, but then, without recognizing what they are doing, they reverse that distinction to say that politeness deceives, while civility shows forth honestly. Goodman, for example, 4–5, 14, distinguishes between good politeness and questionable civility, a distinction that she then reverses on 118 ff., where she quotes eighteenth-century figures who refer to politeness in negative ways. She also oscillates between positive and negative meanings of civility, 113–114.

41. Scheffers, 102; Klein, 221–222, 34–47, 102–107, 111–119, emphasizes that this was the case for Shaftesbury, who made explicit attempts to strengthen the connections between virtue and politeness by establishing the connection between politeness and philosophy.

42. Chevalier de Jaucourt, "Civilité, politesse, affabilité," in *Encyclopédie*, 3:497.

43. Quoted in Starobinski, *Blessings*, 7; and see Elias, 38.

44. Jean-Jacques Rousseau, *A Discourse on the Moral Effects of the Arts and Sciences*, in *The Social Contract and the Discourses*, trans. G. D. H. Cole (New York, 1993), 6–7; and see Jean Starobinski, *Jean-Jacques Rousseau: Transparency and Obstruction*, trans. Arthur Goldhammer (Chicago, 1988).

45. See Starobinski, *Jean-Jacques Rousseau*, on Rousseau's idiosyncratic psychology.

46. Abbé Galiani to Mme d'Epinay, 12 May 1770, quoted in John Francis Harrison, "Introduction," in his translation of J. G. H. Herder, "Journals of My Travels in the Year 1769" (Ph.D. diss., Columbia University, 1952), 61, n. 1. See also Mornet, 190; Goodman, 111–135; Gordon, 41–42, 116–118, 127–128; Klein, 43–45, 96–100.

47. Voltaire, *Dictionnaire,* 762–764, who also writes: "It is through civility that the French language has come to shed any trace of inherent savagery."

48. Rivarol, 98.

49. Ibid., 122.

50. Diderot, 547, 564.

51. Condillac, 297; translation modified. Seventeenth-century theorists of language also feared that metaphorical innovation would undercut the rationality of the language. The Port-Royal *Grammar* closes with an attempt to remove reformed French from that danger: "I add only that there is scarcely a language that uses fewer of those figures [of rhetoric] than French, because it is particularly fond of clarity and of expressing things, as much as it can, in the most natural and uncluttered order, although at the same time it is second to none in beauty and elegance"; Antoine Arnauld and Claude Lancelot, *Grammaire générale et raisonnée de Port-Royal* (1660; reprint, Geneva, 1968), 161–162. See also Ricken, *Grammaire,* 17.

To forestall the slide of the language into rhetorical excess, discussions of the language attempted a partitioning of categories of style equivalent to the partitioning of categories of civility—here the distinction between a "natural" (i.e., rational) and a "metaphorical" style. But as we have seen, writers kept noting that the border between the two styles was permeable and that slippage from one to the other was seemingly inevitable.

One other tactic to regulate the aporia of civility is worth pointing out because it, too, is implied in the works discussed. Some writers tried to contain the instability of civility by confining it to one particular period. For example, Schwab, 71, after saying that seventeenth-century French "politesse" is "the most beautiful flowering of the love of humanity and always presupposes a certain goodness of soul," adds that although this was true of the preceding period, politeness could be different in the future: "For I readily grant that, for a nation whose refinement degenerates into corruption, it finally issues in mere ceremony and formula and becomes even the varnish and vehicle of deception." Schwab never explains how or why such a change would happen, nor does he tell us that this criticism was already conventional in the era he praises. The trick is to turn a structural aporia into a diachronic progression.

52. The manner in which the uncertainties of civility destabilized the claims of the French language can also be put in the terms of Paul de Man. What is supposed to be a logic of civility—a closed circuit of signification—thus unfolds as a system of tropes and images that, originally designed to give the logic persuasive power, end up undercutting its foundational claim to representation. The logic of civility turns out to be a "rhetoric" as Paul de Man has defined the term: "rhetoric radically suspends logic and opens up vertiginous possibilities of referential aberration." Rather than enacting the moral signified, the rhetoric of civility supplants it. Paul de Man, *Allegories of Reading* (New Haven, 1989), 10.

53. Johann Wolfgang von Goethe, *Wilhelm Meisters Lehrjahre* (1796; reprint, Munich, 1976), 357–358. Goethe uses what is perhaps the most common trope of the instability of the signifying forms of French civility: they constitute an enabling language of sexual deception and transgression.

54. *J,* 349/430.

55. *J,* 355/434–435; translation modified.

56. The criticism of civility in France took the form of a general attack on manners and taste considered to be "overcivilized" and contributed to a classical republican revival in the late eighteenth century. Elsewhere it assumed forms defined by varying political and cul-

tural contingencies. Germans put it in the service of German cultural nationalism and of a classicism that was not republican. In the war of the American colonies against Britain, the conventional criticism of politeness as dissemblance was given a republican purpose as it was used to attack what was regarded as corrupt monarchy and aristocracy. See Michael Warner, *Letters of the Republic: Publication and the Public Sphere in Eighteenth-Century America* (Cambridge, Mass., 1990), 132–138.

57. Herder, *Über die neuere Literatur,* 215, 217.

58. Ibid., 219, 256.

59. Ibid., 21. This is suggested already in his earlier essay "On Diligence in the Study of Several Languages" (1764), in *Selected Early Writings, 1764–1767,* ed. and trans. E. A. Menze and K. Menges (University Park, Pa., 1992), 30. See Roy Pascal's discussion of the direct connection between experience and the German language in *The German Sturm und Drang* (Manchester, 1953), 246 ff. On Romantic views of language, which follow this reasoning to other conclusions, see Eva Fiesel, *Die Sprachphilosophie der deutschen Romantik* (1927; reprint, Tübingen, 1973).

60. Johann Gottlieb Fichte, *Addresses to the German Nation,* trans. R. F. Jones and G. H. Turnball (New York, 1968), 5–37. On Fichte in general, see Anthony LaVopa, *Fichte: The Self and the Calling of Philosophy* (Cambridge, 2001).

61. Fichte, 47. He says that ethnic non-Germans can acquire a German character.

62. Ibid.: "More important . . . and in my opinion the cause of a complete contrast between the Germans and the other people of Teutonic descent is . . . the change of language."

63. Ibid., 50: language is "the designation of objects directly perceived by the senses."

64. Ibid., 52.

65. Ibid., 55.

66. Ibid., 57.

67. Ibid., 58, 67, 71–72. Because French troops were still occupying Berlin, Fichte is careful to avoid calling the French by name but refers to them as "neo-Latins"—his term for those Teutons who crossed the Rhine and adopted the language of the Romans.

68. Ibid., 202.

69. Foucault, 78–124, 232–237, 294–307. Foucault sees a sharp historical break where there was in fact a continuity of earlier views of language existing beside and eventually interacting with a new philology.

70. Georg Wilhelm Friedrich Hegel, *System der Philosophie: Dritter Teil, die Philosophie des Geistes,* in *Sämtliche Werke,* ed. Hermann Glockner, 22 vols. (Stuttgart, 1958), 10:84–86.

71. Hegel's letter to J. H. Voss, quoted in H. S. Harris, *Hegel's Development: Night Thoughts (Jena 1801–1806)* (Oxford, 1986), 409; Martin Heidegger, interview, *Der Spiegel,* 31 May 1976, quoted in Victor Farias, *Heidegger and Nazism* (Philadelphia, 1989), 298. In the twentieth century, especially after World War II, the United States and American English are perceived as the major threats to the profundities of the German language; see Theodor Adorno, "On the Question: 'What Is German?'" *New German Critique* 36 (1985): 121–131. For subsequent involutions of the eighteenth-century view of French and German languages, see Jacques Derrida's fascinating *Monolingualism of the Other, or the Prosthesis of Origin,* trans. Patrick Mensah (Chicago, 1990) for its view of the complication, first, of being assimilated as an Algerian Jew into French culture and language and, second, of how German-Jewish intellectuals relate to the German language in the shadow of the Holocaust. The second topic is addressed as a short essay in Derrida, 78–93, n. 9.

72. See Richard Wagner, "German Art and German Policy: German and French Civilizations Contrasted" (1867), in his *On Music and Drama,* trans. H. Aston Ellis (Lincoln, Neb., 1992), 421–443.

73. Friedrich Nietzsche, *The Birth of Tragedy and the Case of Wagner,* trans. Walter Kaufmann (New York, 1967), 134–138.

74. Friedrich Nietzsche, "On Truth and Lying in an Extra-Moral Sense" (1873), in *Friedrich Nietzsche on Rhetoric and Language,* ed. and trans. Sander L. Gilman, Carole Blair, and David Parent (Oxford, 1989), 248–249.

75. Ibid., 246–247.

76. Not yet the poststructuralist or the postmodernist that we now expect but a late Romantic who believed in an ultimate, accessible truth and a higher reality, in this period Nietzsche expresses views that are susceptible, as I argue in chapter 3, to exactly the kind of deconstruction that he will later help inaugurate.

77. See Harold Mah, "German Historical Thought in the Age of Herder, Kant, and Hegel," in *A Companion to Western Historical Thought,* ed. Lloyd Kramer and Sara Maza (Oxford, 2002), 159–160.

78. Friedrich Nietzsche, *On the Advantage and Disadvantage of History for Life* (1874), trans. Peter Preuss (n.p., 1980), 27, 25.

79. Ibid., 27, 25.

80. Ibid., 26.

81. Ibid.

82. Ibid., 64. In 1878 he dedicated his *Human All-Too-Human* to Voltaire and made a point of sending the book to Wagner. Walter Kaufmann, "Introduction," ibid., 149. In 1886, three years after Wagner's death and in an obvious jab at Wagner, Wagnerites, and German cultural nationalists, Nietzsche manipulates his view of a Greek transcendence of the French-German antithesis to foreground its linkage to France: "Oh, those Greeks! They knew how to live. What is required for that is to stop courageously on the surface, the fold, the skin; to adore appearance in forms, tones, words, in the whole Olympus of appearance. Those Greeks were superficial—out of profundity"; F. Nietzsche, "Vorrede Vier," "Die Fröhliche Wissenschaft," in *Werke,* ed. Rolf Toman, vol. 3 (Köln, 1994), 14. Eric Blondel, "Life as Metaphor," in *The New Nietzsche,* ed. David B. Allison (New York, 1977), 156, points out that this emphasis on appearance is also gender-coded as "feminine," another connotation that would have infuriated the masculinism of Wagnerism and German nationalist culture. In these references, Nietzsche is not strongly identifying himself as French or female, but playing with the terms of identity, manipulating their meanings and instabilities to try on new personae. A useful guide to the multitudinous views of Nietzsche is Allan Megill, "Historicizing Nietzsche? Paradoxes and Lessons of a Hard Case," *Journal of Modern History* 68 (1996), 114–152.

Chapter 3. Strange Classicism

1. Notwithstanding his initial *Sturm und Drang* sympathies, Goethe came to warn Germans against religious-patriotic art and a return to early German art. See Hans Belting, *The Germans and Their Art: A Troublesome Relationship* (New Haven, 1998), 21 ff. And writers on the *völkisch* side reacted negatively to the classical models for a German identity. Herder wrote in 1767 that German writers who followed classical models of prose style abandoned their own national character: "one sacrificed everything that stood in the way of . . . becoming a classical imitator! Oh cursed word—classical! The word has buried many a genius . . . who stoops under the burden of a dead language. The fatherland has lost blooming fruit trees, since they now stand on alien soil"; quoted in Dieter Borchmeyer, *Weimarer Klassik* (Weinharn, 1994), 30. Herder gets right to the contradictions and problems of one of the oddest arguments for developing a distinctive Germanness: namely, to imitate another

culture, that of the ancient Greeks. Herder was also skeptical of the important Winckelmann; see Francis Haskell, *History and Its Images* (New Haven, 1993). Classical revival in this period in Germany is conventionally called German "classicism," while the contemporaneous classical revival in French art is often referred to as "neoclassicism." I continue to use both these conventional terms, but in order to subsume them into their common method and strategy of using classicism to construct identity, I also refer to both as "classic*ist.*"

2. Useful general studies of German classicism in literature and neoclassicism in art include Hugh Honour, *Neo-Classicism* (London, 1988); Robert Rosenblum, *Transformations in Late Eighteenth Century Art* (Princeton, 1967); Eliza Marian Butler, *The Tyranny of Greece over Germany* (1935; reprint, Boston, 1958); Francis Haskell and Nicholas Penny, *Taste and Antiquity* (New Haven, 1994); Heinz Otto Burger, ed., *Begriffsbestimmung der Klassik und des Klassischen* (Darmstadt, 1972); Walter Rehm, *Griechentum und Goethezeit* (Bern, n.d.); and Henry Hatfield, *Aesthetic Paganism in German Literature* (Cambridge, Mass., 1964). In his controversial study *The Rise of Eurocentrism: Anatomy of Interpretation* (Princeton, 1993), Vassilis Lambropoulos asserts that Hellenism was generally denigrated by Western, including German, intellectuals in the nineteenth century. In fact the opposite seems to have pertained in that period; Lambropoulos is on surer footing in speaking of the twentieth century.

3. Plato, *Republic,* in *Collected Dialogues of Plato,* ed. Edith Hamilton and Huntington Cairns (Princeton, 1989), 832. Arguably, the fear of images has an even older, theological correlate: whether God can or should be known in images. See W. J. T. Mitchell, *Iconology: Image, Text, Ideology* (Chicago, 1986); and idem, "Ekphrasis and the Other," in *Picture Theory* (Chicago, 1994), 151–182.

4. For general commentaries, see Matthew Craske, *Art in Europe, 1700–1830* (Oxford, 1997), 145–217; Marian Hobson, *The Object of Art: The Theory of Illusion in Eighteenth-Century France* (Cambridge, 1982).

5. In an early writing Kant significantly assigned the problematic reliance on pleasing sensuous forms to France and southern Europe. The designation of the truly moral—those who had learned to refuse the seduction of beautiful forms—Kant located in Germany and northern Europe; Immanuel Kant, *Observations on the Feeling of the Beautiful and Sublime* (1763), trans. John T. Goldthwait (Berkeley, 1960), especially 51–75; 97–116.

6. Adolf Schlegel, quoted in Alexander von Bormann, ed., *Vom Laienurteil zum Kunstgefühl* (Tübingen, 1974), 108; Wilhelm von Humboldt, *The Limits of State Action* (1791–92), trans. Joseph Coulthard (Indianapolis, 1993), 75, 79; Friedrich Schiller, *On the Aesthetic Education of Man in a Series of Letters* (1795), ed. and trans. E. M. Wilkinson and L. A. Willoughby (Oxford, 1989), 65; G. W. F. Hegel, *Introductory Lectures in Aesthetics,* trans. Bernard Bosanquet (London, 1993), 6. On Kant's concern about the potential immorality of beauty, see Kant, *Observations;* and Robert E. Norton, *The Beautiful Soul: Aesthetic Morality in the Eighteenth Century* (Ithaca, 1995), 216 ff.

7. Anon., "Rococo," in *Oxford Dictionary of Art,* ed. Ian Chilvers, Harold Osborne, and Dennis Farr (Oxford, 1994), 427. The principal painters of Rococo were Jean-Antoine Watteau (1684–1721), François Boucher (1703–1770), and Jean-Honoré Fragonard (1732–1806).

8. Norman Bryson, *Word and Image: French Painting of the Ancien Régime* (Cambridge, 1981), 91–104.

9. Lambropoulos, 56 ff.; Rosenblum, 27 ff., 51 ff.; Honour, *Neo-Classicism,* 13–41; Francis Coleman, *The Aesthetic Thought of the French Enlightenment* (Pittsburgh, 1971), 74, 84.

10. Plato, *Symposium,* in Hamilton and Cairns, 561–563; and see Erwin Panofsky, *Idea* (Columbia, S.C., 1968), on how this idea was transmitted, *mutatis mutandis,* through Neoplatonism and the Western tradition. Also see Norman Bryson, *Tradition and Desire* (Cambridge, 1984), 64.

11. Johann Joachim Winckelmann, *Thoughts on the Imitation of the Painting and Sculpture of the Greeks* (1755), in *German Aesthetic and Literary Criticism,* ed. H. B. Nisbet (Cambridge, 1992), 36; and see Michael Podro, *The Critical Historians of Art* (New Haven, 1982), xxi–15.

12. Johann Joachim Winckelmann, *History of Ancient Art* (1764), 4 vols. in 2, trans. G. Henry Lodge (New York, 1968), 1:132; and see 1:194, 200, 210; cited hereafter as *H.*

13. Honour, *Neo-Classicism,* 104. Butler, 169, quotes a letter of August 1788 from Schiller, who was studying Greek plays, to his friend C. G. Körner: "I hope to learn more simplicity in plan and style in this way. And further by a closer acquaintance with Greek plays I shall finally be enabled to abstract those elements which are true, beautiful, and effective, and by eliminating the imperfections, I shall form a certain ideal from them by means of which my present one will be corrected and perfected."

14. Wilhelm von Humboldt to Goethe, 24 August 1809, quoted in Nisbet, 244. Schiller makes the same point in *On Aesthetic Education,* 157: "the unfailing effect of beauty is freedom from passion." See also Schiller, 183.

15. Quoted in Mario Praz, *On Neoclassicism* (London, 1969), 148.

16. See also Schiller's description of the effects of aesthetic contemplation: "In his senses there results a momentary peace; time itself, the eternally moving, stands still; and, as the divergent rays of consciousness converge, there is reflected against a background of transience an image of the infinite, namely form"; Schiller, 183 and 80–83, 151. Renato Poggioli, *The Theory of the Avant-Garde* (Cambridge, Mass., 1968), 73, offers a particularly elegant statement of the ancient doctrine of the fullness of time: "In the consciousness of a classical epoch, it is not the present that brings the past to a culmination, but the past that culminates in the present, and the present is in turn understood as a triumph of ancient and eternal values, as a return to the principles of the true and the just, as a restoration or rebirth of these principles." On this idea in the Renaissance, see Hans Belting, "Vasari and His Legacy: The History of Art as Process," in *The End of the History of Art?* (Chicago, 1987), 7–8, 72–76, 94. This classicist principle of timelessness is plainly at odds with modern notions of linear and progressive temporality, even as the former is incorporated into the latter. On this paradox, see Harold Mah, "German Historical Thought in the Age of Herder, Kant, and Hegel," in *A Companion to Western Historical Thought,* ed. Lloyd Kramer and Sara Maza (Oxford, 2002), 160–161.

17. On the classicist unity of the aesthetic and the ethical, see Kenneth Clark, *The Nude* (Princeton, 1990), 42. A sophisticated psychoanalytic reading of the same ideal can be found in Alex Potts's superb book on Winckelmann, *Flesh and the Ideal* (New Haven, 1994), 145 ff.

18. Johann Joachim Winckelmann, "The Beautiful in Art" (1763), in *Winckelmann: Writings on Art,* ed. David Irwin (London, 1992), 95. This ideal of subjectivity as one of harmonious rational plenitude and self-transparency is the same as that articulated in the new German ideal of *Bildung*—of giving a *Bild,* or form, to one's self. Humboldt's classic formulation of *Bildung* carries all the distinctive marks of Winckelmann's classicism: "The true end of Man, or that which is prescribed by the eternal and immutable desire of reason, and not suggested by vague and transient desires, is the highest and most harmonious development of his powers to a complete and consistent whole"; Humboldt, 10. The ideal enters British liberalism by way of John Stuart Mill. Humboldt provides the epigram at the beginning of Mill's *On Liberty,* and Mill quotes Humboldt's passage above as the ideal development of liberal subjectivity; Mill, *On Liberty* (New York, 1986), 66.

19. See Butler, 44–48, 59–63, 81, 90, 132, 162, 179–180, 208, 251; and, for example, Goethe's essay "On the Laocoön Group" (1798), in Johann Wolfgang von Goethe, *Goethe: The Collected Works,* ed. Victor Lange, Eric Blackall, and Cyrus Hamlin, vol. 3 (Princeton, 1994), 15–22. Lessing's *Laocoön* reiterates Winckelmann's description of Greek sculpture

in general and of the *Laocoön* in particular; he differs from Winckelmann in his identification of poetry as the proper Greek medium of expressing emotion. Gottfried Ephraim Lessing, *Laocoön* (1765), trans. Ellen Frothingham (New York, 1969).

20. Winckelmann, *Thoughts on Imitation*, 44; translation modified. The original is "die Einfalt und stille Grosse"; J. J. Winckelmann, "Gedanken über die Nachahmung der griechischen Werke in der Malerei und Bildhauerkunst," in *Sämtliche Werke*, ed. Joseph Eiselein, 12 vols. (1825; reprint, Osnabrück, 1965), 1:34.

21. Schiller, 151, 157, 153.

22. George Mosse, *The Image of Man* (Oxford, 1995), 29–37.

23. Potts, 131 ff.

24. Mosse, 33, 37; Bryson, *Tradition and Desire*, 70 ff.; Joan Landes, *Women and the Public Sphere* (Ithaca, 1988), 252; Thomas Crow, *Painters and Public Life in Eighteenth-Century Paris* (New Haven, 1991), 252; Dorinda Outram, *The Body and the French Revolution* (New Haven, 1989).

25. Butler, 31; Rehm, *Griechentum und Goethezeit*, 176 ff.

26. Butler, 146 ff.; Rehm, *Griechentum und Goethezeit*, 176, 193; Thomas Mann, "Schwere Stunde," in *Der Tod in Venedig und andere Erzählungen* (Frankfurt am Main, 1990), 280–289.

27. Praz, 134; Potts, 145.

28. Praz, 59. Rosalind Krauss, *The Picasso Papers* (New York, 1998), 141 ff., uses this trope of the deadly classical line to criticize Picasso's classical period. See also Bryson, *Tradition and Desire*, 30, 72–73; Potts, 145 ff. The connotation of death that classicism sometimes invokes has underwritten speculative connections between Winckelmann's violent death at the hands of a robber and his classicist aesthetics. See, for example, Butler, 35 ff. Potts is careful not to jump to such conclusions.

29. Butler, 236.

30. J. W. Goethe, "Winckelmann and His Age" (1805), in Nisbet, 238–239. We shall see that Thomas Mann in *Death in Venice* reverses the terms of Goethe's maxim: in an indestructible health we can detect the darkest moment of self-sacrifice.

31. Flaubert quoted in Praz, 147.

32. Bryson, *Word and Image*, 217, 214.

33. Potts, 230; Honour, *Neo-Classicism*, 171. See Rosenblum, 3–10, for varied eighteenth-century responses to the newly discovered Roman painting of the selling of the god of love. Abigail Solomon-Godeau, *Male Trouble: A Crisis in Representation* (London, 1997), 24, 36, points out that during the Revolution David's pictures of male and female nudes were criticized for their sensuality.

34. Quoted from Heinrich Heine's *Confessions* in Butler, 251. On German classicist sadomasochism, see especially Potts, 173; and Simon Richter, *Laocoön's Body and the Aesthetic of Pain* (Detroit, 1992).

35. Praz, 46.

36. Charles Baudelaire, "The Pagan School" (1852), in *Baudelaire as Literary Critic*, ed. and trans. L. B. Hyslop and F. E. Hyslop Jr. (University Park, Pa., 1964), 72–73; and see Derrida's interpretation of Baudelaire's essay in Jacques Derrida, *The Gift of Death*, trans. David Willis (Chicago, 1995), 110. That this, too, is a recurring trope in the history of European classicism is suggested by Haskell and Penny's story (14) of how in 1527 the Italian humanist Andrea Falvio condemned as "maliciously inaccurate" the story that Pope Gregory the Great had ordered the most beautiful classical statues to be thrown into the Tiber so that men, fascinated by the statues' beauty, would not be led astray from the new religion of Christianity. At the end of the nineteenth century, Aby Warburg noted the by-then clearly opposing possibilities in classicism and recommended a very down-to-earth understanding—how one reads classicism depends on one's particular sensibilities: "We must not de-

mand of antiquity that it should answer the question at pistol point whether it is classically serene or demonically frenzied, as if these were the only alternatives. It really depends on the subjective make-up of the late born rather than on the objective character of the classical heritage whether we feel that it arouses us to passionate action or induces the calm of serene wisdom. Every age has the renaissance of antiquity it deserves"; Warburg quoted in Podro, 174. Though eminently sensible, Warburg underestimates, on the one hand, the extent to which historical conditions dictate the reading of classicism and, on the other, the way in which the strangeness of classicism chooses its appreciating subject rather than vice versa.

37. Goethe quoted in Lambropoulos, 57. See also Butler, 34, 56, 59; and Rehm, *Griechentum und Goethezeit*, 2–10. Winckelmann avoids going to Greece, even though in *H*, 3:155, he emphatically states how much he wanted to go.

38. Rehm, *Griechentum und Goethezeit*, 58; Craske (24) describes the *History* as "art history's first international bestseller." And see Max L. Baeumer, "Klassizität und republikanische Freiheit in der ausserdeutschen Winckelmanns Rezeption des 18. Jahrhunderts," in *Johann Joachim Winckelmann, 1717–1768*, ed. Thomas W. Gaehtgens (Hamburg, 1986), 195–221. In his "Salon of 1765," Diderot calls Winckelmann a "fanatic" and compares him in his zealous pursuit of an ideal to the eighteenth century's political classicist par excellence, Rousseau; Denis Diderot, *Diderot on Art*, ed. and trans. John Goodman (New Haven, 1995), 156–157.

39. Mosse, 30–37; Potts, 225 ff.; Carla Hesse, *Publishing and Cultural Politics in Revolutionary Paris, 1789–1810* (Berkeley, 1991), 141; Rehm, *Griechentum und Goethezeit*, 20; Thomas Crow, *Emulation: Making Artists for Revolutionary France* (New Haven, 1995), 26–27, 57, 72; Solomon-Godeau, 146, says that the Revolutionaries treated Winckelmann as if he were a prophet.

40. *H*, 1:183. Other Germans make the same association. See, for example, Ludwig Tieck, "An einem Brief an Wilhelm Wachenroder," in *Von deutschen Republik*, ed. Jost Hermand (Frankfurt am Main, 1975), 90–91: "With delight, I greet the genius of Greece, which I see soar over Gaul. France is now in my thoughts day and night."

41. J. J. Winckelmann to Hieronymus Dietrich Berends, early July 1756, in *Sämtliche Werke*, 10:167. In another letter he says that he avoids the French in Rome and advises his friend not to visit France; Winckelmann to Berends, 29 January 1757, ibid., 181. In *H*, 2:257, he ridicules the claim of seventeenth-century French classicism to having equaled the ancients. In his essay on Winckelmann, Goethe points out that Winckelmann always hated French "superficiality"; Goethe, "Winckelmann," 256.

42. See Suzanne Marchand, *Down from Olympus: Archaeology and Philhellenism in Greece, 1750–1970* (Princeton, 1996), 24. Marchand mistakenly calls Winckelmann a "romantic." Winckelmann's actual political loyalties and cultural identifications were ambivalent and complex. While showing a certain Protestant and German loyalty, his feelings about Germany were conflicted. To work in the Vatican, he reluctantly converted to Catholicism, a fact that he apparently always found embarrassing. He criticized not just German courts but also the court of Pope Clement XIII. See the sensitive analysis in Potts, 189–199, of Winckelmann in relation to patronage, sexual identity, and cultural identification. The odd, unlikely nature of German classicism as a nationalist project is manifestly evident in the famous call of Winckelmann to his countrymen, a call that is often represented as inaugurating the movement: "There is but one way for the moderns to become great, and perhaps unequalled; I mean by imitating the Greeks." Here the suppression of cultural distinctiveness—i.e., imitation of another culture—serves as the condition of possibility of acquiring distinctiveness, of becoming, in Winckelmann's words, "unequalled." What makes this embrace of the Greeks as a model for German identity even stranger was that all the Germans

who accepted that model knew that others, including the French, were also engaged in classical revival. Winckelmann, *Thoughts on Imitation*, 33.

43. Schlegel quoted in Rehm, *Griechentum und Goethezeit*, 16; Goethe quoted in Honour, *Neo-Classicism*, 58; on how Germans enshrined classicism, see Rehm, *Griechentum und Goethezeit*, who is more sympathetic to German classicism than Butler and Lambropoulos. And see, most recently, Jeffrey Morrison, *Winckelmann and the Notion of Aesthetic Education* (Oxford, 1996). Schlegel repudiated classicism after his conversion to Catholicism. After an early enthusiasm for classicism, Herder rejected it because of its claims to universal validity. Friedrich Gottlieb Klopstock always criticized German classicism, seeing it as too French, given the long history of French classicism in the seventeenth century. See Rehm, *Griechentum und Goethezeit*, 52, 96; Podro, 1.

44. *H*, 3:158. See also Rehm, *Griechentum und Goethezeit*, 47–51; and idem, "Der Begriff der Stille als Vorbereitung der klassischen Humanitätsidee," in Burger, 203–227. In this chapter, I follow classicist uses of the metaphor of the sea, which I believe shows the ambivalences of classicist subjectivity. The functions of the metaphor of the sea differ from the metaphorical use of the shipwreck in Western philosophy and literature. On the image of the shipwreck, see Hans Blumenberg's elegant *Shipwreck with Spectator: Paradigm of a Metaphor for Existence* (Cambridge, Mass., 1997).

45. Winckelmann explicitly asserts the youthful male body as his ideal, but demonstrates as well an appreciation of the more mature and muscular male figure, as seen in the *Laocoön*. Mosse, 29 ff., overemphasizes the significance of the mature male figure in saying that Winckelmann takes it as his ideal and that Winckelmann has no appreciation of androgyny.

46. Winckelmann's description of one's first impression of the sea and the compensatory stabilizing gaze enacts as well the classicist response to Edmund Burke's notion of the sublime. Perception of the sublime initially overawes the viewer and compels the reasoning mind to exert control over perception; recognizing a deeper rationality behind the first impression of the phenomenon, the viewer's mind attains a state of rest. See Angus Fletcher, *Allegory* (Ithaca, 1994), 242–253; and Immanuel Kant, *The Critique of Judgment* (1798), trans. Werner Pluhar (Indianapolis, 1987), 97 ff.

47. The representation of this liminal condition between youth and maturity accounts in part for the undulating lines of the figure, since in the springtime of life, Winckelmann says, the carving of "muscles and sinews" has not yet taken place; *H*, 2:222.

48. *H*, 2:220. Bacchus in fact is liminality incarnate: "The type of bacchus is a lovely boy who is treading the boundaries of the spring-time of life and adolescence, in whom emotions of voluptuousness, like the tender shoots of a plant, are budding," and "who, as if between sleeping and waking," is "half rapt in a dream of exquisite delight"; *H*, 2:219–220.

49. This analysis of the passage from Winckelmann's glance to the gaze does not correspond to the opposition that Bryson sets up between the physiological "glance" and the rational "gaze." Winckelmann suggests that both the glance and the gaze can be construed as Bryson's "gaze"—namely, as an attempt to see with a masterful rationality; but as I further argue, both the rational glance and gaze are unable to sustain themselves in this kind of looking and slide into what Bryson calls the "glance," the looking that "proposes desire, proposes the body, in the durée of its practical activity." Norman Bryson, *Vision and Painting* (New Haven, 1995), 122. For a different view of how classical vision was displaced by a mobile, physiological eye, see Jonathan Crary, *Techniques of the Observer* (Cambridge, Mass., 1992). Crary exaggerates the rapidity and completeness of that shift.

50. *H*, 2:206. The construction of ideal beauty out of ambiguous lines leads Winckelmann to a sacrilegious conclusion: that modern artists should represent the figure of Jesus in the same ambiguous form as that of Greek statues, because, Winckelmann points out, according to prophecy, he was "the most beautiful of the children of men"; *H*, 2:229–230.

51. On the return of the gaze—the introjection of an external looking—see Bryson, *Tradition and Desire,* 65 ff., 77; Maurice Merleau-Ponty, *The Visible and the Invisible* (1964), trans. Alphonso Lingis (Evanston, Ill., 1995); Jacques Lacan, *The Four Fundamental Concepts of Psycho-Analysis* (1973), trans. Alan Sheridan (New York, 1981), 67–122; Martin Jay, *Downcast Eyes* (Berkeley, 1993), 263–380; James Elkins, *The Object Stares Back* (New York, 1996), 70–74.

52. This notion of development, as Potts, 66–81, observes, is still a common trope in historical writing. It guides, for example, Carl Schorske's analysis of the Vienna Secession in *Fin-de-siècle Vienna* (New York, 1980), 270–278.

53. Potts, 99; Herbert von Einem, "Winckelmann und die Wissenschaft der Kunstgeschichte," in Gaehtgens, 319.

54. Potts has an ingenuous explanation for why only these sorts of female figures are found in the high style—a further oddity given that Winckelmann characterizes the youthful masculine male as exemplary of ideal beauty. The high style embodies, according to Potts, the "sublime" of eighteenth-century aesthetics; Potts, 113 ff. According to convention, the sublime is coded as masculine. But, as Potts argues in his analysis of Burke's essay, the sublime of Burke can not be represented in art; by definition massive and terrifying, it would never be able to assume stylized aesthetic form, which must in some way be pleasing to the senses. For this reason, Burke chooses examples only from nature. Winckelmann gets around this problem by representing the sublime as a female figure, Niobe, whose sexuality and expression have been nullified. This is a clever explanation, but it turns on a misconnection. Nothing in Winckelmann suggests that when he uses the word *sublime* he is referring to Burke's theory, as Potts assumes but does not demonstrate. Winckelmann's ideas of the sublime are not Burkean but are drawn from conventional classicist notions of the sublime. The sublime here signifies masculine power in the classical form of loftiness, gravitas, and self-mastery—in short, what Winckelmann calls "nobility" and "stillness," which he does not regard as incompatible with beauty. In other words, the paradox of female figures exemplifying the grand style remains.

55. On classicism and Prussian education reform, see Marchand; Friedrich Paulsen, *Geschichte des gelehrten Unterrichts auf den deutschen Schulen und Universitäten vom Ausgang des Mittelalters bis zur Gegenwart,* vol. 2 (Berlin, 1921); C. Varrentrapp, *Johannes Schulze und das höhere preussische Unterrichtswesen in seiner Zeit* (Leipzig, 1889). On the centrality of *Bildung* in the construction of middle-class German identity, see James Sheehan, *German Liberalism in the Nineteenth Century* (Chicago, 1978), 14 ff.

56. Friedrich Nietzsche, "Attempt at a Self-Criticism" (1886), in his *The Birth of Tragedy and the Case of Wagner,* ed. and trans. Walter Kaufmann (New York, 1967); cited hereafter as *BT.* Nietzsche's conflict with orthodox academic classicism is played out with particular clarity in the review of *The Birth of Tragedy* by the preeminent German classicist Ulrich von Wilamowitz-Moellendorf. The beginnings of an academic classicism sympathetic to Nietzsche's views are reflected in the response to Wilamowitz by Nietzsche's colleague and friend Erwin Rohde. See Marchand, 128–133; M. S. Silk and J. P. Stern, *Nietzsche on Tragedy* (Cambridge, 1981), 90–107; Hugh Lloyd-Jones, "Nietzsche and the Study of the Ancient World," in *Studies in Nietzsche and the Classical Tradition,* ed. James C. O'Flaherty, Timothy F. Sellner, and Robert M. Helm (Chapel Hill, 1976), 1–15.

57. On the relationship, see Carl Pletsch, *The Young Nietzsche: Becoming a Genius* (New York, 1991), 115 ff.

58. Rehm, *Griechentum und Goethezeit,* 53–79; and see Rosenblum, 15 ff., for visual examples. On the "orientalization" of Greece, see Rehm, *Griechentum und Goethezeit,* 295 ff.; and Lambropoulos, 61 ff. In Romanticism, an opposition appears between Christianity and classicism; Rehm, *Griechentum und Goethezeit,* 277 ff.; Hugh Honour, *Romanticism* (New York,

1979), 212–213; Belting, *The Germans and Their Art,* 9; Madame La Baronne (Germaine) de Staël, *De l'Allemagne,* 2 vols. in *Oeuvres complètes* (10–11), ed. A. Staël (Paris, 1820), 2:272–273.

59. On Nietzsche's influence on academics, see Marchand, 144, 140 ff.; Lloyd-Jones, 1. On the book's influence on German intellectuals in general, see Steven Aschheim, *The Nietzsche Legacy in Germany, 1890–1900* (Berkeley, 1992). E. R. Dodd's influential *The Greeks and the Irrational* (Berkeley, 1951), 236–239, was influenced by German classicists who in turn had been influenced by Nietzsche. Nietzsche repudiates his book in his "Attempt at a Self-Criticism."

60. *BT,* 52–56, 102–105. See Arthur Schopenhauer, *The World as Will and Representation* (1818), trans. E. F. J. Payne, vol. 1 (New York, 1969), 255–267. The primacy and privileging of voice and music in Romanticism go back at least to Jean-Jacques Rousseau's *Essay on the Origin of Language* (1749), trans. J. H. Maron and Alexander Gode (Chicago, 1966), 11–16, 51–71. See also Jacques Derrida's analysis of Rousseau in *Of Grammatology* (Baltimore, 1976), 192 ff.; and Jay, 106–109.

61. Paul de Man, *Allegories of Reading* (New Haven, 1979), 83 ff.

62. *BT,* 42. Nietzsche calls this "the wisdom of Silenus": "'What is best of all is . . . not to be born, not to be, to be *nothing.* But the second best . . . is to die soon'"; ibid.

63. De Man, 83 ff.

64. Ibid., 99.

65. See also Sarah Kofman, *Nietzsche and Metaphor* (Stanford, 1993), 6–13.

66. *BT,* 126–127; de Man, 97–98.

67. Nietzsche's attempt to tell us that the structure of the disturbed visuality has this content comes across as contrived, melodramatic, and unlikely. In another instance, and without realizing it, Nietzsche slips into his own alteration of classicist vision, his own Winckelmann-like hallucination. At the end of the book he tells us how he imagines a person wandering back "into ancient Greek existence" (*BT,* 144). In his phantasy, this person experiences a more subdued, orthodox classicism: "Walking under lofty Iambic colonnades, looking up toward a horizon that was cut off by pure and noble lines, finding reflections of his transfigured shape in the shining marble at his side, and all around him solemnly striding are delicately moving human beings, speaking with harmonious voices and in rhythmic language of gestures." Nietzsche's imagined person, in other words, sees himself seeing from the point of view of the Apollonian. The Dionysian is only hinted at as he encounters an old man who reminds him of the paradox of this vision: "'how much did the people suffer to be able to become so beautiful.'" And the old man then invites the visitor to witness a tragedy and to make a sacrifice with him "to both deities" (*BT,* 147). The strangeness of the reverie lies in how easily Nietzsche slips into it, as if he were experiencing it. The dreamlike dissociated repose of orthodox classicism is also aligned with a recognition that such serenity is linked to suffering, tragedy, and sacrifice. The reference to sacrifice reverses a conventional trope of orthodox classicism, one that is used, for example, in the various versions of the play *Iphigenia* to mark out the rational humanism of classicism, namely, its refusal of sacrifice.

68. Nietzsche's post-Wagnerian views of Greece are limited to a few suggestive references. We never find out in a more systematic sense what he might have been thinking.

69. Lacan, 23–24; Jay, 364–365; and Bryson, *Word and Image,* 138, who eloquently describes this distinction: "The unconscious is a field of distortion, not a repertoire of contents, because the point is that the unconscious is precisely that which cannot be spoken (or painted); it is outside language, beyond the limit of retrievability—we cannot just translate the unconscious into images. Its very existence is a matter of inference, from observed distortion in normal continuities."

70. Among the numerous works that deal with this topic, see Schorske; H. S. Hughes, *Consciousness and Society* (New York, 1959); William McGrath, *Dionysian Art and Populist Politics* (New Haven, 1974); Fritz Ringer, *The Decline of the German Mandarins* (Cambridge, Mass., 1969); Jackson Lears, *No Place of Grace* (New York, 1981); Martin Wiener, *English Culture and the Decline of the Industrial Spirit* (New York, 1981); Elaine Showalter, *Sexual Anarchy* (New York, 1990); Daniel Pick, *Faces of Degeneration* (Cambridge, 1989); Rita Felski, *The Gender of Modernity* (Cambridge, Mass., 1995).

71. Commentators have found the classicism in *Death in Venice* to be peculiarly contradictory to what one conventionally expects of classicism, and have tried to explain it in terms other than what Mann ostensibly writes, i.e., as intended "parody," as showing the influence of Wagner, and as an example of *fin-de-siècle* masochism. See, respectively, T. J. Reed, *Thomas Mann: The Uses of Tradition* (Oxford, 1974), 156 ff.; Anthony Heilbut, *Thomas Mann: Eros and Literature* (New York, 1966), 248–249; Gerald Izenberg, *Modernism and Masculinity: Mann, Wedekind, Kandinsky through World War I* (Chicago, 2000), 140–143. I believe that Mann's story was a serious, self-conscious attempt to recognize the long-standing strangeness of German classicism, making a different aspect of classicist affliction the solution to his problem of classicist latecoming, of being an epigone.

That Mann stages German classicism's collapse in Italy can be seen as an uncanny, ironic commentary on early German classicism. The first eighteenth- and early nineteenth-century admirers of ancient Greece did not and would not visit Greece itself. If their glorification of Greece had a geographical locus, that locus was Italy. And in the case of Winckelmann and Humboldt, the Italian city identified with ancient Greece was Rome. The shift from Rome to Venice is comprehensible in terms of the latter's nineteenth-century reputation as the city par excellence of decay, both biological and cultural. In Mann's novel, German classicism is still staged in Italy, but in a *fin-de-siècle* period of cultural disquiet, the proper Italian location is Venice. On the image of Venice in the nineteenth century, see Tony Tanner, *Venice Desired* (Oxford, 1992); and John Pemble, *Venice Rediscovered* (Oxford, 1995).

72. Harvey Goldman, *Max Weber and Thomas Mann* (Berkeley, 1988), 52–53.

73. Thomas Mann, *Death in Venice* (1912), trans. Kenneth Burke (New York, 1970), 16; hereafter cited as *DV*. Of the various translations of *Death in Venice*, I believe that Burke's remains the most felicitous, especially since its errors were corrected in the 1970 reissue.

74. Goldman, 203 ff. See also Bernhard Boschenstein, "Apollo und seine Schatten. Winckelmann in der deutschen Dichtung der beiden Jahrhundertwenden," in Gaehtgens, 339–340; Reed, *Thomas Mann*, 156 ff.; and idem, *Death in Venice: Making and Unmaking the Master* (New York, 1994), 81–82; J. R. McWilliams, "The Failure of Repression: Thomas Mann's *Tod in Venedig*," *German Life and Letters*, n.s. 20 (1967), 233–234.

75. On Mann's reading of Nietzsche, see Reed, *Death in Venice*, 76–78.

76. Radicalized because Mann suggests that all Apollonian form is self-defeating repression, while Nietzsche argues that some measure of Apollonian is necessary to mitigate the disintegrative effects of the Dionysian; the Apollonian becomes problematic for the young Nietzsche when it becomes excessive, that is, "Socratic."

77. Reed, *Thomas Mann*, 156 ff., also points out that Mann borrowed from Platonic dialogues, but he does not discuss this in terms of classicism's contradictions.

78. *DV*, 40. And see *DV*, 24: "The sea, empty, like an enormous disk, lay stretched under the curve of the sky. But in empty inarticulate space our senses lose also the dimensions of time, and we slip into the incommensurate."

79. In *Death in Venice*, as in *The Birth of Tragedy*, interpreters point out that, following Nietzsche, the medium of Aschenbach's transfiguration is music. As he lapses into his dream of the baccanale, Aschenbach hears noise, the Dionysian "*u*-sound" and "persistent flutes"; *DV*,

89; and Reed, *Death in Venice*, 66. But again this is Romantic misdirection, because the crucial element in Aschenbach's transformation is that he *sees* himself seeing the bacchanal. The music is here, as in *The Birth of Tragedy*, a catalyst or trigger, but it is not the substance of an experience of the Dionysian.

80. Goldman, 257, n. 64. Heilbut, 261, also points out that Goldman's interpretation of Aschenbach's relationship with Tadzio misses the seduction of the former by the latter. Izenberg, 142–143, interprets the relationship in terms of "feminine masochism," which was part of the *fin-de-siècle* discourse on women. Heilbut's and Izenberg's points, however, do not change the fact that Mann rehearses and explicitly identifies the strangeness of a German classicism in a way that goes back at least to Winckelmann. These recent interpretations miss the *longue durée* of larger cultural anxieties. Different figures have been identified as the "model" for Aschenbach—Goethe, Wagner, even Sergei Diaghilev—but Nicholas Boyle's choice of Winckelmann is unusually astute; Boyle, *Goethe: the Poet and His Age*, vol. 1 (Oxford, 1991), 29.

Chapter 4. Classicism and Gender Transformation

1. Hugh Honour, *Neo-Classicism* (London, 1977), 34–35; Dorothy Johnson, *Jacques-Louis David: Art in Metamorphosis* (Princeton, 1993), 11–14, who calls the painting "mesmeric"; Thomas Crow, *Painting and Public Life in Eighteenth-Century Paris* (New Haven, 1985), 215 ff.; Saul Friedlaender, *David to Delacroix* (Cambridge, Mass., 1980), 22–25. On the aesthetic reasoning that culminated in this kind of prescribed response, see Michael Fried, *French Painting and the Beholder in the Age of Diderot* (Berkeley, 1980), especially 71–173.

2. Honour, 35.

3. For example, Honour, 75: "In painting the *Oath of the Horatii* and the *Brutus*, David expressed the mood of those French intellectuals who, like himself, were to be swept along on the wave of the Revolution. He rendered in artistic terms their stern morality, their idealism, their faith in reason and the rights of man." See also Matthew Craske, *Art in Europe, 1700–1830* (Oxford, 1997), 247 ff.; Anita Brookner, *Jacques-Louis David* (Princeton, 1980), 97; D. Johnson, 31–34, 72–120; Ronald Paulson, *Representations of Revolution (1789–1820)* (New Haven, 1983), 28–29; Honour, 69–80.

4. Brookner, 97.

5. Tischbein quoted in Craske, 248.

6. Joan Landes, *Women and the Public Sphere in the Age of the French Revolution* (Ithaca, 1988), 9: "I take David's 1785 painting *The Oath of the Horatii* . . . as a prefiguration of the problematic of the nineteenth-century bourgeois public and its representation of women." See also 156, 170; and George Mosse, *The Image of Man* (Oxford, 1996), 37.

7. Thomas Mann, *Death in Venice* (1912), trans. Kenneth Burke (New York, 1970), 17; and see 96. This rhetorical question at the beginning of the story is repeated and answered at the conclusion, 95–96.

8. Sara Maza, *Private Lives and Public Affairs: The Causes Célèbres of Prerevolutionary France* (Berkeley, 1993), 51 ff., 112 ff., 213; Craske, 233 ff.; Landes, 65–66; Robert Darnton, *The Literary Underground of the Old Regime* (Cambridge, Mass., 1982), 1–40.

9. Craske, 145–187, 225–250; D. Johnson, 31–34; Thomas Crow, *Emulation: Making Artists for Revolutionary France* (New Haven, 1995), 26 ff.

10. Carolyn Lougee, *"Le Paradis des Femmes": Women, Salons, and Social Stratification in Seventeenth-Century France* (Princeton, 1976); Landes, 20 ff.

11. Dena Goodman, *The Republic of Letters: A Cultural History of the Enlightenment* (Ithaca, 1994), 90–135. As a woman, the salonnière, according to Goodman, was perceived to be

free of *amour-propre* and egoistic self-assertion and therefore naturally sympathetic to the sensibilities of others. This absence of the qualities that conventionally characterized men and her other-directedness made the salonnière the ideal mediator between combative men and, in the Enlightenment salon, allowed her to promote fluid and conciliatory discussion where it might otherwise have broken down into intractable disagreement. Goodman cultivates this idealized eighteenth-century image against what she rightly identifies as the disparagement of the salonnière in contemporary and historical literature. But she does not seem to recognize that her image of the salonnière is also an idealization, and her desire to rehabilitate leads her to dodge the strongest criticism of the salonnière: that her concern with "good taste" and always-pleasing conversation made her sometimes act as a censor rather than as a facilitator of discussion. Robert Darnton provides a nice example of this in showing that Madame Geoffrin refused to tolerate criticisms of the government; Darnton, "Two Paths through the Social History of Ideas," *Studies on Voltaire and the Eighteenth Century* 39 (1998), 359.

Goodman's criticism of Rousseau's skewed characterization of the salon does not mean that he was entirely mistaken about the uncertainties of refined civility. The problems of signification Rousseau pointed to were always part of the conflicted discourse of civility; Rousseau gave them a particularly strong gendered formulation, which proved to be extremely influential in a period of cultural crisis. On the all-male Enlightenment salons of the time, see Alan Kors, *D'Holbach's Coterie* (Princeton, 1976).

12. Landes, 22 ff., 66 ff.; Craske, 145 ff., 164–166, 225 ff.; Maza, 41 ff., 62–63, 110, 168–172, 180; Abigail Solomon-Godeau, *Male Trouble: A Crisis in Representation* (London, 1997), 51; Liselotte Steinbrügge, *The Moral Sex: Women's Nature in the French Enlightenment* (Oxford, 1995), 107; Dorinda Outram, *The Body and the French Revolution* (New Haven, 1989), 124 ff.

13. This dualism of views is striking in Montesquieu's *Persian Letters*. According to Landes (31–38), that work illustrates the Enlightenment's misogyny in its criticism of elite public women. Montesquieu reiterates the conventional criticism of civility condensed in the figure of the dissembling and corrupting public women who should be returned to domesticity. See also Baron de Montesquieu, *The Persian Letters*, trans. C. J. Betts (London, 1973), on the actress, 80. But Landes considers only one of the two conflicting views of public women in *The Persian Letters;* she ignores the dissenting voice of the other of the two Persians, Rica, who celebrates the salon and the salonnière, and who in the story of Zulema phantasizes about female freedom and power. It is a story of an antiseraglio. Montesquieu, 129–130, 247–253.

This work, like many others that touch on these themes, presents both the disabling problems of civility and its advantages. Only an extremist position—such as that of Rousseau, Laclos, or David—emphasizes the problems while disregarding the advantages, from which each of them benefited. Landes's and Goodman's views of the salon operate as the binary opposite of the Rousseauian view.

14. Jean-Jacques Rousseau, *Politics and the Arts: Letter to M. d'Alembert on the Theatre*, trans. Allan Bloom (Ithaca, 1960), 48–49. In Rousseau's chain of equivalences (and those of the discourse of civility), both women and the theater are tropes of civility gone wrong and are described in similar terms. Rousseau on the theater could be expressing his views of public women: "the continual emotion which is felt in the theatre excites us, enervates us, enfeebles us, and makes us less able to resist our passions. And the sterile interest taken in virtue serves only to satisfy our vanity without obliging us to practice it"; 57, 29.

15. Rousseau, *Letter to d'Alembert,* 101; Maza, 168; Craske, 166; Goodman, 35 ff.; Landes, 72 ff., 87 ff.; Helena Rosenblatt, "On the 'Misogyny' of Jean-Jacques Rousseau: The *Letter to d'Alembert* in Historical Context," *French Historical Studies* 25 (2002), 91–114, puts Rousseau's views in the context of Genevan politics at the time and argues that he was repeating and

commenting on those politics, which were conducted in the terms of civic republican virtue opposed to a decadent, feminine civility. While placing Rousseau in a more focused perspective, the article does not acknowledge that the terms are not peculiar to Geneva but reiterate the terms of a more general discourse on civility.

16. On Madame de Pompadour, see Crow, *Painters,* 110; on Du Barry and Marie Antoinette, ibid., 176 ff.; Maza, 178–182; and Lynn Hunt, *The Family Romance of the French Revolution* (Berkeley, 1996), 89–123. See also Choderlos de Laclos, *Les Liaisons dangereuses* (1782), trans. P. W. K. Stone (London, 1961). On Laclos, see Steinbrügge, 84–90; Darnton, *Literary Underground,* 14–16, 29–32, 200–202.

17. The urge for reform shows up in a variety of ways: in Diderot's appeal in *The Natural Son* for a new form of serious, didactic theater, the *drame bourgeoisie;* in Greuze's moralizing paintings of village life; in the establishment of imitations of the *fête de la rose,* a highly popular celebration around the selection of the most virtuous maiden in a village; and in new ideas—particularly Rousseauian ones—about political reform, institutions, and agency. See Denis Diderot, *Conversations on the Natural Son* (1757), in his *Selected Writings in Art and Literature,* trans. Geoffrey Bremner (London, 1994); Maza, 68–111; Crow, *Painters,* 140–153; Keith Michael Baker, *Inventing the French Revolution: Essays in French Political Culture in the Eighteenth Century* (Cambridge, 1990); Jürgen Habermas, *The Structural Transformation of the Public Sphere* (1962), trans. Thomas Burger (Cambridge, Mass., 1989); and Harold Mah, "Phantasies of the Public Sphere: Rethinking the Habermas of Historians," *Journal of Modern History* 72 (March 2000), 153–182.

18. Jean-Jacques Rousseau, *A Discourse on the Moral Effects of the Arts and Sciences* and *The Social Contract,* in *The Social Contract and the Discourses,* trans. G. D. H. Cole (New York, 1993), 1–30, 180–400; Craske, 219–275; Outram, 68–105; Paulson, 1–36; Honour, 69–80. The use of classical revival for moral reform affected the reception of Winckelmann in France; French critics and artists saw the German as seeking to revivify a noble aesthetic tradition against the debased aesthetics and morals of an eighteenth century dominated by French civility; Crow, *Emulation,* 26–27. Diderot called Winckelmann and Rousseau the two great fanatics of the century; *Diderot on Art,* ed. and trans. John Goodman (New Haven, 1995), 156–157.

Late eighteenth-century neoclassicism also rethought its seventeenth-century predecessors. According to Crow, *Emulation,* 28, biographies of Poussain that appeared in the 1780s minimized his connections to the French court and aristocracy and emphasized his ties to antiquity.

19. The views of Germans were much more ambivalent. In fact, notwithstanding their own masculinist posturings German classicists, when confronted by the hypermasculine assertions of the French and of the French revolutionaries, recuperated the feminine and putatively civilizing aspects of the old regime. Aggressive, Revolutionary French Jacobin classicism led German classicists to become, in cultural terms, counterrevolutionary. In *On the Aesthetic Education of Man in a Series of Letters,* written against the background of the Terror, Schiller begins by reiterating the conventional criticisms of dissembling civility and beautiful surfaces, but at the end he celebrates aristocratic civility and declares it indispensable to society; Friedrich Schiller, *On the Aesthetic Education of Man in a Series of Letters* (1795), ed. and trans. E. M. Wilkinson and L. A. Willoughby (Oxford, 1982), 27, 65–67.

20. Rousseau's assumptions and prescriptions meshed with the sensationalist psychology of the Enlightenment, which seemed to give a scientific basis to gender stereotypes, with the sentimentalism or *sensibilité* of the late eighteenth century, and with the gender stereotypes of what in the eighteenth century was sometimes called "anthropology"; Anne C. Vila, *Sensibility in the Literature and Medicine of Eighteenth-Century France* (Baltimore, 1998); Steinbrügge, 34–37, 56–57, 67, 83 ff.; Craske, 168. For an example of "anthropology," see the

young Immanuel Kant's *Observations on the Feelings of the Beautiful and Sublime,* particularly section 3, "Of the Distinction of the Beautiful and Sublime in the Interrelations of the Two Sexes," 76–96; and Kant's *Anthropologie,* in Kant, *Werke,* ed. Wilhelm Weischedel, vol. 7 (Frankfurt am Main, 1968), 140 ff., 230 ff., 303 ff.

21. Quoted in Steinbrügge, 31. Sophie in Rousseau's *Emile,* as Steinbrügge, 55 ff., cogently shows, is the literary realization of Rousseau's ideal woman, whose own simple virtue instills virtue in the men around her.

22. Darnton, *Literary Underground,* 35–36; Landes, 158–168; Goodman, 281–300; Outram, 124–152; Joan Scott, *Only Paradoxes to Offer* (Cambridge, Mass., 1996), 19–56. "Gender," Landes, 170, concludes, "became a socially relevant category in post-revolutionary political and civil life in a way that it would not have mattered formerly." The dissemination of neoclassicism in France and Europe brought about, in Thomas Crow's words, "the masculinization of advanced arts," according to which artists not only were asked to paint scenes of "military and civic virtue in traditional masculine terms" but also were "compelled to imagine the entire spectrum of desirable human qualities, from battlefield heroics to eroticized corporeal beauty, as male"; Crow, *Emulation,* 2. Hunt raises the important issues of not reading a change in norms for a change in reality and of using the Jacobin view of women to characterize the Revolution as a whole; Lynn Hunt, "Male Virtue and Republican Motherhood," in *The French Revolution and the Creation of Modern Political Culture,* ed. K. M. Baker, vol. 4: *The Terror* (Oxford, 1994), 195–208. Carla Hesse has shown that in one respect women writers actually benefited from the Revolution: the abolition of privileged, protected publishing allowed more women to enter the literary market, so that female writing proliferated even when Jacobin ideology and repression were paramount; Hesse, *The Other Enlightenment: How French Women Became Modern* (Princeton, 2001), 31–55.

23. D. Johnson, 73 ff.

24. Norman Bryson, *Tradition and Desire: From David to Delacroix* (Cambridge, 1984), 76; and see 73–75 on David's "paranoid vision"; D. Johnson, 172 ff.; Crow, *Emulation,* 183–185; Brookner, 97 ff. Lynn Hunt, *Politics, Culture, and Class in the French Revolution* (Berkeley, 1984), 92–112, is interesting on David's role in the choice of Hercules as a Jacobin symbol. And see D. Johnson, 179–221, on David's continued republicanism under Napoleon.

25. D. Johnson, 66. On 64 she notes that their sculpted forms correspond to Buffon's contemporaneous description of the ideal male body. See also Craske, 169, 248.

26. This classicist conception of the sublime is non-Burkean, although it bears some similarities that allow the two to be conflated by writers such as Germaine de Staël. The classicist notion of the sublime is evident in other works, such as Kant's *Observations on the Feelings of the Beautiful and Sublime,* where he writes, 64 ff., of the tender—that is, beautiful—sentiment of women: "Nothing of duty. Nothing of compulsion. Nothing of obligation." Women, according to classicists like Kant and David, lack the ability to think their way to what is morally necessary, and should they somehow come to see that necessity, they would still lack the will to act on it. In David's painting their rootedness in quotidian life has made for them the swearing of an oath an unbearable, unwatchable scene. Their sensitive and sentimental nature renders them unable to put aside their feelings for home, family, and loved ones, even in the service of what David regards as a transparently higher duty. They cannot make the disavowal of ordinary human emotion that defines heroic masculinity. See Outram, 68–89, for another source of this classicist notion of the moral sublime in the revived stoicism of Justus Hermann Lipsius.

27. Crow, *Emulation,* 34 ff.

28. Pierre Corneille, *Horace* (1639) (Paris, 1966), 56.

29. This is of course what any reader of the *Ur*-text of classical heroism would expect. Is the ultimate meaning of Achilles in the *Iliad* that he kills Hector or the sense of affliction

that closes the poem when he weeps with Hector's father over their ruined families—a devastation that Achilles identifies throughout the poem as the result of his pursuit of glory?

30. Quoted in Crow, *Emulation*, 34; and see D. Johnson, 59.

31. Paulson, 30–31; Landes, 152, writes: "Their drooping, soft, sensual bodies evoke an atmosphere of deep sorrow."

32. Landes has a sense of something odd about this scene, as she notes, 152, that the women "are present but strangely passive."

33. See Corneille, 58, 94; Bryson, *Tradition and Desire*, 73; Landes, 157; Crow, *Emulation*, 43; D. Johnson, 59 ff. The young Horace not only unapologetically looks forward to killing his wife's brothers and sister's fiancé; he also proclaims that his disavowal of family ties offers him the prospect of a "fame" to which few men dare "to aspire"; Corneille, 56.

34. See, for example, Bryson, *Tradition and Desire*, 70: "The *Oath* is an exact image of visuality for the subject under patriarchy"; and Landes, 153.

35. Note the uncertain status of the boy, standing with women. He is a liminal figure. Like the women, he is outside the action; but he will one day also be the subject of male transformation, and hence, like the men, he watches intently. His looking appears equivocal, displaying awe but also fear, desire but also repulsion. Landes, in contrast, sees the boy as already gendered and resisting the mother (58).

36. See J. L. Austin, *How to Do Things with Words* (Cambridge, Mass., 1975), especially 155–156.

37. Nearly, because the fact that the women of the family are sleeping is in itself a deviation from the viewer's expectations, given Corneille's play, of how they would behave.

38. Iphigenia in the old regime also fits well into the tradition of female eloquence described by Hesse, 3–31. See also Sophia Rosenfeld, *A Revolution in Language: The Problem of Signs in Late Eighteenth-Century France* (Stanford, 2001), 165–167, on how Jacobins came to fear oratory. In works that bracket the *Oath*, in *Andromache Mourning Hector* (1783) and in *The Lictors Returning to Brutus the Bodies of His Sons* (1789), the year of the Revolution, David contemplates in a demystified way how male transformations have destroyed families. In these paintings, heroic transformation is plainly an affliction, and, as in Corneille's *Horace*, women provide the active voices, faces, and gestures of loss. The more intense of these works, the *Lictors*, directly reverses the narrative trajectory and semiotics of the *Oath*. The lifeless bodies of the sons are carried into the chamber as their father, Lucius Junius Brutus, sitting in the shadows, grimly stares away from them into the foreground. Brutus ordered the execution of his sons because they had conspired to overthrow the republic and establish a monarchy. To the right of Brutus, occupying the center and other side of the painting and increasingly in the light, are the grieving, gesturing women of the family. Unlike the expressive patriotism of the Horatii, Brutus's duty to Rome has left him emotionally empty or stymied; the call of the state has paralyzed his natural affections, and the result is the grim-faced stare, the slight clenching of the fist, and the tense twisting of feet. Brutus is a study in tortured emotional repression in the service of the state. And in further contrast to the mute, drooping women of the *Oath*, the women in the *Lictors* openly, extravagantly show their grief. In a nice reversal of the dominant signifying line in the *Oath*, David gives to a woman in the *Lictors* the gesture of the outstretched arm, which here points to affliction, the dead bodies of the sons, rather than to transcendence. The painting also contains a visual reference to the classical story of Iphigenia. See Crow, *Emulation*, 109. *Andromache* and the *Lictors* were produced during what commentators consider David's period of deepest commitment to the new militant masculinity of Revolutionary classicist republicanism. In the midst of his masculinist extremism, he strangely bears witness to the ambivalent character of male emergence and restores the idealized position of the elite woman of the old regime as a critical dissident voice.

Another powerful commentary on the affliction of masculine transformation, *The Intervention of the Sabine Women*, is less enigmatic in that it can be directly related to unfolding events. Conceived and begun while David was in prison in 1794 (but not finished and shown until 1799), it can be seen as a response to the extremism of his Jacobin period. As Crow writes, the painting was "a bid for future rehabilitation, a plea that the irresolvable conflicts of the past be set aside"; Crow, *Emulation*, 185; D. Johnson, 124–126. The Sabine women, abducted and raped by Romans, intervene in the resulting conflict between Sabine and Roman warriors. Here women act in the spirit of Camilla and offer a genuine antithesis to the Horatii. Militant males glare at each other across the picture plane, poised for combat but frozen in place by the central interposition of female figures, one stretching her arms across the picture (the gesture of the Horatii again inverted in significance and given to a woman), others pleading and displaying their children, all with awake, alert faces and exhorting the men to stop. Injured women emerge as active moral agents to halt another masculine transformation.

Crow also argues that the problems of holding to Jacobin ideals of assertive, heroic masculinity showed themselves in the recourse of David and his students to phantasies of male utopia, to images of beautiful ephebic males, evident, for example, in David's *Marat* (1793) and *Bara* (1794). The more coercive the Revolution became, Crow argues, the more "abstractly beautific" became the images of men; Crow, *Emulation*, 175 ff., 166. The problem with this argument is that the evidence does not fit the historical timetable. For example, the most powerful of these kinds of images, *Endymion* (1791), by David's student Anne-Louis Girodet-Trioson (Crow, 134), comes before the Terror. Crow, as others have done, is right to point out that these images unsettle the orthodox classicist male image explicitly asserted by David and his students; but that drift away from orthodoxy is not tied to events, as Crow argues, but to a resistance built into classicism, which we have seen in the cases from Winckelmann to Thomas Mann. David's slippage from assertive masculinity to a gentler homoeroticism is found throughout the history of classicist art, both before and after periods of intense political agitation. This tendency is well documented for the French case, if not fully explained, in Solomon-Godot's *Male Trouble*. Ewa Lajer-Burcharth's recent *Necklines: The Art of Jacques-Louis David after the Terror* (New Haven, 1997) offers a new psychoanalytic explanation of David's post-Terror representations of injured masculinity.

39. Nicholas Boyle, *Goethe: The Poet and the Age*, 2 vols. (Oxford, 1992, 2000), 1:677.

40. Ibid.

41. Ibid. See especially the scene in which Werther's faux pas in an aristocratic setting leads to his ejection and flight from society. J. W. von Goethe, *The Sufferings of Young Werther* (1774), trans. Harry Steinhauer (New York, 1970), 45–52.

42. Boyle, 1:194, 590.

43. Ibid., 380; on how the Diamond Necklace Affair delegitimated the French monarchy, see Maza, 167–211.

44. Euripides' two plays are *Iphigenia at Aulis* and *Iphigenia in Tauris;* Racine's is *Iphigénie en Tauride*. On the family of the Atreides in French literature, see Henriette Bonnéric, *La Famille des Atrides dans la littérature française* (Paris, 1980), especially Diderot's view on Iphigénie in a letter to Sophie Volland of 6 November 1760, 170 ff. Carl Van Loo's *Sacrifice d'Iphigénie* (1757) was a well-known painting on the subject. See also Kenneth D. Weisinger, *The Classical Facade: A Nonclassical Reading of Goethe's Classicism* (University Park, Pa., 1988), 133.

45. Harold Rosenthal and John Warrack, "Iphigenia," in their *Concise Oxford Dictionary of Opera* (Oxford, 1964), 189.

46. James Johnson, *Listening in Paris: A Cultural History* (Berkeley, 1995), 60 ff.; on 65 Johnson argues that Gluck's *Iphigénie* offered a musical equivalent of neoclassicism. Entirely

serious in action and reaching a level of intensity and directness not known in the conventional *tragédie lyrique,* Gluck's work, Johnson says, can be likened to the work of David. This striking observation should be qualified. Although these stylistic similarities apply, Gluck's choice of a classical theme opposed to the masculinist republicanism of David, as well as his reliance on Racine's play and his service to the court and to aristocratic institutions, ultimately place him in a company opposed to David's neoclassicism. Gluck marks a transition from the French classicism of the seventeenth century, still being performed in the eighteenth century, to an alternative new classicism that is opposed to the neoclassicism of David's *Oath of the Horatii.* The connection of Gluck's new subjectivity to the art of the late eighteenth century is better explained by reference to Michael Fried, especially 35 ff., on the importance of a subject's absorption as a turn against Rococo.

47. J. Johnson, 110.

48. Ibid., 110–158. That the story of Iphigenia operates as an antithesis to the story of David's Horatii is further suggested by the *Lictors,* in which he rethinks heroic emergence, and in which critics have noted an allusion to the story of Iphigenia. At the far right of the painting, the old nurse of the sons, the only figure whose face would be fully in the light, has in her intense grief covered her face. This shrouded figure, as Thomas Crow notes, is a visual allusion to the story of Iphigenia at Aulis. The dramatic shrouding of one's grief is conventionally considered to have been done by Agamemnon, but here the sign is displaced from the male figure and conferred on the lowliest of the women, a servant of the family. Brutus, the Agamemnon equivalent, is shown emptied of all feelings. All human sympathies—even the vestigial humanity signified by the allusion to Agamemnon's shroud—is invested in the women, and to emphasize that it is "womanness" and not class sensibility which is the source of sympathy, the shroud is given to a female servant. Crown, *Emulation,* 109.

49. J. W. von Goethe, *Iphigenia in Tauris,* in *Goethe: The Collected Works,* ed. Victor Lange, Eric Blackall, and Cyrus Hamlin, 12 vols. (Princeton, 1994–1995), 8:12, has Thoas say to Iphigenia: "Do your heart's bidding, / Ignore the voice of reason and good counsel, / Be nothing but a woman and surrender / To such ungoverned impulses as may seize you."

50. Ibid., 41, 51.

51. See also Jean-Pierre Vernant, *Myth and Tragedy* (New York, 1990), 242, concerning ancient Greek tragedy: "From the point of view of [fifth-century] tragedy, human beings and human actions are seen, not as realities to be pinned down and defined in their essential qualities, in the manner of the philosophers of the preceding century, but as problems that defy resolution, riddles with double meanings that are never fully decoded." As I argue, this same point applies to various manifestations of German and French classicism.

52. See, for example, Dieter Borchmeyer, *Weimarer Klassik* (Weinharn, 1994), 148–159. In Euripides, Athena intervenes at the end of *Iphigenia in Tauris;* in Gluck's *Iphigénie en Aulide* and *Iphigénie en Tauride* Diana intervenes to prevent further bloodshed and restores Iphigenia to her homeland. In Racine's *Iphigénie en Aulide* Iphigenia is saved by another standard classical device—a mistaken identity provided by the enigmatic prophecy of an oracle. In Gluck's *Iphigénie en Tauride* bellicose militancy seems a reflex on the part of all men, Greeks as well as Scythians. As Orestes is about to be sacrificed, Greeks appear with Pylades, the friend of Orestes, and, enraged by what is about to befall Orestes, they charge the Scythians, crying out: "Let us exterminate this odious people / down to the last vestige, / and serve heaven's vengeance!" But before the two sides clash, Diana intervenes. She stops the fighting, does away with sacrifice on the island, restores Orestes to sanity and to the role of king of Mycenae, and sends Iphigenia home; Christoph Willibald Gluck, *Iphigénie en Tauride,* act 4, scenes 5 and 6.

53. Iphigenia contradicts Thoas, for example, with this: "The gods do not demand blood-offerings. / If men think so, it is their own illusion, / The fantasy of cruel human lusts";

Goethe, *Iphigenia*, 14. See also idem, *Conversations of the German Refugees*, in *Collected Works*, 10:21–22, where the Baroness ridicules the pretext for male extremism, the invocation of a higher overriding principle: "How easily men can deceive themselves," she says, how easily they call something, when it serves their purposes, "necessary, unavoidable, indispensable."

54. Different versions of the Iphigenia story emphasize that men's first impulse is always a bad one, that masculine emergence is always about to erupt and needs to be forestalled, not once but repeatedly. In Gluck's *Iphigénie en Tauride*, for example, the Greeks at the end of the opera rally to the aid of Orestes and the chorus of Greeks cries out, against the island's inhabitants who would sacrifice Orestes: "Let us exterminate this odious people" (act 4, scene 5). This is what triggers Diana's timely, final appearance: she must prevent the collision of the two groups of overbearing males. In Goethe's *Iphigenia*, after Iphigenia has lifted Orestes' curse, he immediately reverts to male assertion and wants to deceive and steal from Thoas. The high-minded Iphigenia, however, refuses; she tells everything to Thoas and will leave the island only if all are happily reconciled.

55. J. W. von Goethe, *Hermann and Dorothea*, in *Collected Works*, 8:268–269.

56. Goethe, *Iphigenia*, 5.

57. Goodman, 53–136; Daniel Gordon, *Citizens without Sovereignty: Equality and Sociability in French Thought, 1670–1789* (Princeton, 1994), 41–42, 116–118, 127–128; Lawrence Klein, *Shaftesbury and the Culture of Politeness* (Cambridge, 1994), 4–5, 96–100.

58. Goethe, *Conversations of the German Refugees*, 23–24; and see Borchmeyer, 248–249. My argument reverses that of Sigrid Lange, that for Goethe the emancipation of bourgeois men, or their civilization, requires the sacrifice of women; Lange, *Die Utopie der Weiblichen im Drama Goethes, Schillers, und Kleist* (New York, 1993), 29, 33. In fact the opposite seems to obtain for Goethe: that to revert to nature, which is identified as the most brutish and masculine condition, men require the sacrifice of women and that their return to civilization is accomplished by the elevation and mediation of women. Lange incorporates this point when she says (53 ff.), contradicting her initial argument, that women also appear as "saviours."

59. J. W. von Goethe, *Italian Journey* (1786–1788), trans. W. H. Auden and Elizabeth Mayer (San Francisco, 1982), 379; idem, *Campaign in France 1792: Siege of Mainz*, in *Collected Works*, 5:743; Boyle, 1:345 ff., 422–450; Borchmeyer, 159.

60. Peter Andre Bloch, *Schiller und die französische klassische Tragödie* (Dusseldorf, 1968), 223, 227.

61. Boyle, 1:304; Cyrus Hamlin and Frank Ryder, "Preface," in Goethe, *Collected Works*, 8: ix. And see Maza, 76–78, on how "private" theatrical performances involving aristocrats were part of the elite cultural practices in France as well.

62. Boyle, 1:275, 177, 248 ff., 380–381.

63. In his memoirs of the German military campaign against France in 1792–93, on which he accompanied the participating duke, Goethe at a dispirited moment recalls himself pronouncing these now much-quoted words: "From this time and place a new epoch is beginning, and you will be able to say that you were there"; Goethe, *Campaign in France*, 652.

64. That aristocracy and monarchy did not all of a sudden disappear is less relevant than the belief of many writers and intellectuals, including Goethe, for much of the nineteenth century that those institutions were now obsolete. The Revolution had such a dislocating effect on the social and political imaginary of the turn of the nineteenth century that it resulted in the strong belief that monarchy and aristocracy had been superseded in principle and "historically"—a view that, as some have suggested, issued in a whole new conceptualization of classes, namely, the "construction" of the bourgeoisie and its antithesis, the proletariat. These were invented and believed to be dominant social forms, even as monarchy and aristocracy persisted into the late nineteenth century in France and much of the rest

of Europe. See Gareth Stedman-Jones, *Languages of Class* (Cambridge, 1983), on the invention of class as a product of the misrecognition of the nature of the French Revolution; and Dror Wahrmann, *Imagining the Middle Class: The Political Representation of Class in Britain, c. 1780–1840* (Cambridge, 1995). Arno Mayer, *The Persistence of the Old Regime* (New York, 1981), rightly points out that the more accurate historical dating of the end of that regime is 1918 and the precipitating cause of the end is World War I.

65. J. W. von Goethe, *The Natural Daughter,* in *Collected Works,* 8:168, 171, 172.

66. Ibid., 140, 155, 174. The conspiracy against her is the work of the king's son, who does not want to share influence with her. Forced into the conspiracy is an abbé, who, when he describes how he was drawn in, blames a familiar problem, the misleading nature of refined appearance. Once content with his modest circumstances, he was seduced by "flattery and honeyed words, made a slave" of pleasures and luxuries, the desire for which now compels him to go against his once virtuous character; ibid., 173.

67. Ibid., 140, 155, 174, 213.

68. Ibid., 18, 214–215.

69. Cyrus Hamlin and Frank Ryder, "Postscript," in Goethe, *Collected Works,* 8:317; Borchmeyer, 276 ff.

70. Most famously, in *Wilhelm Meisters Lehrjahre,* when Wilhelm repudiates a prosaic life in business for the theater. See in particular his exchanges with Werner the businessman. Johann W. von Goethe, *Wilhelm Meisters Lehrjahre* (Munich, n.d.), 31, 38 ff. On 299–307, Wilhelm, rejecting life as a bourgeois, identifies the aristocracy as the only class that is by its social character open to *Bildung;* he then identifies the theater as a substitute for membership in the aristocracy.

71. Goethe, *Hermann and Dorothea,* 253, 264, 269–270, 273.

72. See Borchmeyer, 276. Boyle, 2:530–531, regards the poem not as "ironical" but as "humorous"—Boyle's explanation of the poem's "incongruities."

73. As she says to Hermann, showing how the father's performative speech fails to perform: "for in his [the father's] headstrong way, he says many things, but when it comes to /Action he changes his mind, and forbids things, but then allows them"; Goethe, *Hermann and Dorothea,* 272.

74. Ibid., 296.

75. Ibid., 306–307.

76. Goethe, *Natural Daughter,* 214–215. Eugenia's situation, as she has defined it at the end of the play, would literally mean the end of society; since the marriage would be sexless, there would be no children.

77. Goethe, *Hermann and Dorothea,* 292.

78. Ibid., 296.

79. Ibid., 305.

80. Madame La Baronne (Germaine) de Staël, *De l'Allemagne,* 2 vols. in *Oeuvres complètes* (10–11), ed. A. Staël (Paris, 1820), 2:502; and see 241, 487 ff.

81. Ibid., 1:61, 32, 50.

82. One might want to conclude that Rousseau's criticism of civility had alternating manic and depressive forms in hypermasculine classicism and sentimentalism, respectively; but in fact each form contains both aspects.

83. On the amazing reception of *La Nouvelle Héloïse,* see Robert Darnton, "Readers Respond to Rousseau: The Fabrication of Romantic Sensitivity," in his *The Great Cat Massacre and Other Episodes in French Cultural History* (New York, 1984), 215–256; and the discussion of *sensibilité* in Norman Bryson, *Word and Image: French Painting in the Ancien Régime* (Cambridge, 1981), 154–177. On other aspects of sentimentalism or sensibility in France, see Vila; and David Denby, *Sentimental Narratives and the Social Order in France* (Cambridge, 1994).

84. Germaine de Staël, *On Literature Considered in Its Relation to Social Institutions* (1800), in *Major Writings of Germaine de Staël,* ed. Vivian Folkenflik (New York, 1987), 189, 192.

85. Staël, *De l'Allemagne,* 2:196, 60.

86. Vivian Folkenflik, "Introduction," in Staël, *Major Writings,* 4; Madelyn Gutwirth, *Madame de Staël, Novelist: The Emergence of the Artist as Woman* (Urbana, Ill., 1978), 46.

87. Gutwirth, 85–86.

88. Madame de Staël, *Ten Years of Exile* (1821), trans. Doris Beik (New York, 1972), 63–95. On Staël's political beliefs, see Marcel Gauchet, "Constant, Staël et la Révolution française," in *The French Revolution and the Creation of Modern Political Culture,* vol. 3, ed. François Furet and Mona Ozouf (Oxford, 1987), 166–167.

89. Staël, *On Literature,* 191–192, 199, 203; Staël, *Considerations on the Main Events of the French Revolution* (1818), in *Major Writings,* 371.

90. Staël, *On Literature,* 197.

91. Staël, *De l'Allemagne,* 1:53; with, of course, the significant exception of Goethe.

92. Ibid., 1:103. In another similar moment of enthusiasm for the salon, Staël in *On Literature,* 198, draws a conclusion that to Rousseau would have proved her corruption. She tells us that French conversational play is superior to coarse truth-telling: "One can even forget about serious wrongdoing, about fears inspired (perhaps rightly) by someone's immorality, if his noble language creates an illusion as to the purity of his soul. But what is impossible to bear is the coarse education betrayed by every word, every move, the tone of voice, the position of the body, all the involuntary signs of the habits of life."

93. Staël, *De l'Allemagne,* 1:58, 51–54.

94. Ibid., 115, 119; and on 125 Staël refers to Goethe's Aurelie in *Wilhelm Meister,* who is the victim of deceiving refined appearance.

95. In this sense she continues an eighteenth-century belletristic tradition of "anthropology"—a stylization of nations and genders according to conventional stereotypes. See Kant's *On the Beautiful and Sublime* for another example of this kind of writing.

96. Germaine de Staël, *Corinne, or Italy* (1807), trans. Avril H. Goldberger (Newark, N.J., 1987); cited hereafter as *C.* Published in over forty editions between 1807 and 1872, *Corinne* was one of the nineteenth century's biggest bestsellers; Gutwirth, 285. Staël's father, to whom she was much closer than to her mother, died during her trip to Germany. One of the themes of *Corinne* is the failure to live up to the edicts of the father, although this is displaced onto a son; a direct descent from a mother is effaced; and Corinne dies without children—all concerns that point to the possibility of interpretation *en abîme.*

97. Staël insists on calling the Scotsman Oswald English.

98. The source of the Romantic concept of the sublime was Longinus's supposedly classical *On the Sublime.* Strictly speaking, the sublime of Burke is by definition nonhuman; calling human traits sublime is a classicist practice.

99. Although Staël identifies Corinne as Italy incarnate, we learn that she is actually of mixed parentage: her father was English and her mother Italian. After her mother's death, when Corinne was a young girl, the father returned to England, where he remarried, but Corinne stayed in Italy to finish her education, which also fixed her character as Italian (*C,* 201). After school, she is sent for to live in England with her father's new family, which now includes an English daughter, Lucile. Corinne finds life in England unbearable, in particular the passivity that is expected of English women, for whom, she is told, "household duties are a woman's only vocation." After her father's death she repudiates her family name and returns to Rome, where she adopts the name of Corinne, the poet and friend of Pindar (*C,* 269). She then meets Oswald, whose father she earlier met in England. Oswald's father had decided that his son should marry Corinne's half sister, who fits the model of

domestic English womanhood. The tragedy of Corinne is thus also implicitly a critique of fanatical Anglomania and of the fear of interethnic union.

100. Corinne's improvisation, often in song, is of course "conversation" in only a metaphorical and sentimental sense. She is in fact a better fit with the old-regime tradition of female eloquence as Hesse, 3–30, has described it. But although Corinne is directly derived from that more general position of female eloquence, Staël characterizes Corinne's utterance as "conversation" to make a pointed reference to the specific kind of eloquent speech of French civility.

101. Although she identifies elements in the connection between *Corinne* and *De l'Allemagne* that are different from those discussed here, Simone Balayé has a sense of the intimate connection between the two works. She points out that Staël in 1805 constructs for Italy what she has already prepared herself to do for Germany; Balayé, *Les Carnets de voyage de Madame de Staël* (Geneva, 1971), 115.

102. Staël, *De l'Allemagne*, 1:197.

Chapter 5. The French Revolution and the Problem of Time

1. Enlightenment writings that link the ineluctability of progress to the expansion of knowledge (and, for some, commerce) are Anne Robert Jacques Turgot's *Discours sur les progrès successifs de l'esprit humain* (1750) and a work by his follower, the Marquis de Condorcet's *Esquisse d'un tableau historique des progrès de l'esprit humain* (1793–94). The notion that the inevitability of progress is underwritten by the indestructibility of reliable knowledge passes from the Enlightenment into European liberalism. It figures, for example, as a premise of John Stuart Mill's arguments in *On Liberty* (1859), whose view that "we are the most progressive people who ever lived" is ultimately based on a notion that truth, once established, can never be definitively extinguished; Mill, *On Liberty* (New York, 1986), 81, 36. Rousseau opens his great criticism of the Enlightenment's assumption of the benevolent dissemination of knowledge and civility by attacking its concomitant view of progress and history. In this sense, he both inspired and reinforced the emergence of "historicism." See Jean-Jacques Rousseau, *A Discourse on the Moral Effects of the Arts and Sciences* (1750), in *The Social Contract and the Discourses,* trans. G. D. H. Cole (New York, 1993), 4.

2. Herder's *Also a Philosophy of History for the Cultivation of Humanity (Auch eine Philosophie der Geschichte zur Bildung der Menschheit)* (1774) is a foundational document of the so-called historicist reaction against an Enlightenment conception of universal and progressive time. Here Herder writes against every Enlightenment and French writer "who taking our regimented century for the *ne plus ultra* of mankind finds occasion to reproach whole centuries for barbarism, wretched constitutional law, superstition and stupidity, lack of manners and taste, and to mock their schools, county seats, temples, monasteries, town halls, guilds, cottages, and houses." This historicist Herder explicitly abjured common Enlightenment tropes of progressive temporality, such as referring to the present "maturity" of the human race, a metaphor that suggests a single scale of historical change for all societies. Johann Gottfried Herder, *J. G. Herder on Social and Political Culture,* ed. and trans. F. M. Barnard (Cambridge, 1969), 191, 207. The translator of the essay has given it the misleading title "Yet Another Philosophy of History, for the Enlightenment of Mankind." On historicism, see Harold Mah, "German Historical Thought in the Age of Herder, Kant, and Hegel," in *A Companion to Western Historical Thought,* ed. Lloyd Kramer and Sara Maza (London, 2002), 143–151.

3. Herder, 207; and see Mah, "German Historical Thought."

4. Friedrich Schiller, *On the Aesthetic Education of Man in a Series of Letters* (1795), ed. and trans. E. M. Wilkinson and L. A. Willoughby (Oxford, 1989), 83, 183.

5. This means not that it is a system without conflicts, but that the many social and political conflicts it identifies can be seen to serve a rational purpose. See Mah, "German Historical Thought," 154–163.

6. Ibid.; Reinhart Koselleck, *Futures Past: On the Semantics of Historical Time*, trans. Keith Tribe (Cambridge, Mass., 1985), 148–150, 251–253.

7. Gentz quoted in Rudolf Vierhaus, "'Sie und nicht Wir': Deutsche Urteile über den Ausbruch der Französischen Revolution," in *Deutschland und die französische Revolution*, ed. Jürgen Voss (Munich, 1983), 1–2; and see 8. Georg Forster, in a letter to his father in July 1789, uses the same trope: "It is beautiful to see what philosophy nurtures in the mind and then realizes in the state"; Forster quoted in James Sheehan, *German History* (Oxford, 1989), 212. Kant's views are in Immanuel Kant, *The Contest of the Faculties* (1798), trans. Mary J. Gregor (New York, 1979), 159–161. General works on German responses to the French Revolution are Jacques Droz, *L'Allemagne et la révolution française* (Paris, 1949); Maurice Boucher, *La Révolution de 1789 vue par les ecrivains allemands, ses contemporains* (Paris, 1954); G. P. Gooch, *Germany and the French Revolution* (London, 1965); Horst Günther, ed., *Die französische Revolution: Berichte und Deutungen deutscher Schriftsteller und Historiker* (Frankfurt, 1985); Alfred Stern, *Der Einfluss der französischen Revolution auf das deutsche Geistesleben* (Stuttgart, 1928).

8. G. W. F. Hegel, *The Philosophy of History*, trans. J. Sibree (New York, 1956), 446–447; cited hereafter as *PH*.

9. See, for example, M. Rainer Lepsius, "Soziologische Theoreme über die Sozialstruktur der 'Moderne' und 'Modernisierung,'" in *Studien zum Beginn der modernen Welt*, ed. Reinhart Koselleck (Stuttgart, 1977), 12. This view is indirectly criticized by Rolf Reichhardt, "Die französische Revolution als Masstab des deutschen 'Sonderwegs'?" in Voss, 322–324.

10. The rational principles of the Revolution could be and were separated from the means used to realize them; the former were considered essential and universal precepts that did not have any necessary connection to the particular, "contingent" or accidental conditions of their realization. See Vierhaus, 8; Droz, 55.

11. As a conservative, Gentz now translated into German Edmund Burke's influential *Reflections on the Revolution in France* (1790). On Friedrich Schlegel, see Frederick C. Beiser, *Enlightenment, Revolution, and Romanticism: The Genesis of Modern German Political Thought, 1790–1800* (Cambridge, Mass., 1992), 245, 263; on Friedrich Schelling's conservative transformation, see Warren Breckman, *Marx, the Young Hegelians, and the Origins of Radical Social Theory* (Cambridge, 1999), 54–56; on Justus Möser's increasing conservatism, see Jonathan Knudsen, *Justus Möser and the German Enlightenment* (Cambridge, 1986), 165–174.

12. Recall that in Goethe's *Hermann and Dorothea*, Dorothea's original German fiancé leaves her to serve the Revolution in Paris, where he dies. This incident may have been an allusion to the well-known geographer and writer Georg Forster, an acquaintance of Goethe's who became a Jacobin in Mainz, joined the revolutionaries in Paris, and died there.

13. Schiller, 151.

14. On Condorcet's attempt to balance his Enlightenment views of knowledge and progress with his anxieties about democratic politics, see Keith Michael Baker, *Condorcet: From Natural Philosophy to Social Mathematics* (Chicago, 1975); on Herder and the Revolution, see Beiser, 215–221.

15. Kant, 159–161.

16. Vierhaus, 12; and Jürgen Voss, "Vorwort," in Voss, viii–ix. Kant nicely illustrates the political problem. For him the only political constitution compatible with the rational au-

tonomy of human beings was a republic. But how could a republic be established in the midst of still-authoritarian governments and undereducated populations, particularly in Germany? To solve this problem, he fell back on a favored default solution of Enlightenment political theory: he counseled obedience to existing monarchs, and in a formulation that sums up this strain of wishful political thinking of the Enlightenment, he says that the duty of these monarchs is to govern *as if* they were republican. The phantasmatic nature of this proposal is particularly striking if we remember that Kant offered it in the mid-1790s, precisely when the Prussian government under the conservative Frederick William II had imposed a new regime of censorship that had suppressed Kant's own writings on religion. Compare Kant's idea of the self-denying "republican" monarch with Rousseau's mythical primary legislator in *The Social Contract*. The problem that bothered Kant is transposed by Rousseau to the putatively historical origin of a republic, but the phantasm of a solution remains the same.

17. Reinhart Koselleck, *Preussen zwischen Reform und Revolution* (Stuttgart, 1975); Walter Simon, *The Failure of the Prussian Reform Movement* (Ithaca, 1955).

18. Quoted in Friedrich Meinecke, *Cosmopolitanism and the National State* (Princeton, 1963), 62; and see 45, 55, 148; Droz, 183–185, 483–485, 487–488. On how this new cultural identity made it into the universities, see the articles of R. Steven Turner: "The Growth of Professional Research in Prussia, 1818 to 1848—Causes and Context," *Historical Studies in the Physical Sciences* 3 (1972), 137–182; "University Reformers and Professional Scholarship," in *The University in Society*, ed. Lawrence Stone, vol. 2 (Princeton, 1974), 495–531; "The *Bildungsbürgertum* and the Learned Professions in Prussia, 1770–1830: The Origins of a Class," *Histoire sociale/Social History* 8 (1980), 105–136.

19. Droz, 483–487; Vierhaus, 14.

20. On Hegel's relationship to the Prussian state, see Harold Mah, *The End of Philosophy, the Origin of "Ideology": Karl Marx and the Crisis of the Young Hegelians* (Berkeley, 1987), 20–42; John Toews, *Hegelianism: The Path toward Dialectical Humanism* (Cambridge, 1981).

21. See, for example, George A. Kelly, *Idealism, Politics, History: Sources of Hegelian Thought* (Cambridge, 1969), 84; Lorenz von Stein, *History of Social Movements in France, 1789–1850*, trans. K. Mengelberg (Totowa, N.J., 1964), 281.

22. For Hegel the idea of the absolute will is at the center of both Kantian epistemology in its notion of a transcendental ego and of Kantian ethics in its notion of an uncompromising good will. See *PH*, 343.

23. See also G. W. F. Hegel, *Phenomenology of Spirit* (1807), trans. A. V. Miller (Oxford, 1979), 328–364. Here Hegel gives a fuller account of the linkages among will, Enlightenment, religion, the Terror, and Kantian philosophy.

24. *PH*, 445; translation modified. The original reads: "So war das Prinzip des Denkens schon so weit versöhnt; auch hatte *die protestantische Welt in das Bewusstsein, dass in der früher explizierten Versöhnung das Prinzip zur weiteren Ausbildung der Rechts vorhanden sei*"; G. W. F. Hegel, *Philosophie der Geschichte* (Stuttgart, 1961), 591.

25. On the influence of Staël's *On Germany* in France, see Raymond Poidevin and Jacques Bariéty, *Les Relations franco-allemands* (Paris, 1977), 28–31. The Michelet quote is from ibid., 31. In 1845–46 the young Ernest Renan could still subscribe to this view of Germany, writing: "I have studied Germany and I believed I entered a temple"; ibid.

26. In 1843, for example, the French correspondent of the radical French newspaper *La Réforme*, reporting from southern Germany, identified the cultural project of German conservatism as medieval and romantic: "the different governments of Germany try hard to resuscitate the mystical philosophy of medieval Christianity in preaching filial respect as respect for paternal absolutism, in praising the chimerical liberty of corporations, and in advocating the imaginary equilibrium of castes." This, he says, is what in Germany is called

"Romanticism." Anon., "Correspondence particulière de la Réforme—Prusse Rhenane," *La Réforme,* 18 October 1847, 1.

27. See Heinrich Heine, "Die romantische Schule," in *Beiträge zur deutschen Ideologie,* ed. Hans Mayer (Frankfurt, 1971), 116–117; idem, "Les Aveux d'un poète," *Revue des deux Mondes,* 15 September 1854, 1173; Jeffrey L. Sammons, *Heinrich Heine: A Modern Biography* (Princeton, 1979), 188–197. On Paris as a haven for European political exiles in this period, see Lloyd S. Kramer, *Threshold of A New World: Intellectuals and Exile Experience in Paris, 1830–1848* (Ithaca, 1988); Jacques Grandjonc, "Les Emigrés allemands sous la Monarchie de Juillet—Documents de surveillance policière 1833–Février 1848," *Etudes Germaniques* 1 (1972), 115–249.

28. On Heine's relationship to Hegel, see Sammons, 76–78; and on Heine's relationship to Hegel's radical followers, see Lucien Calvé, "Heine und die Junghegelianer," in *Internationale Heine-Kongress Düsseldorf 1972,* ed. Manfred Windfuhr (Hamburg, 1973), 307–317; Breckman, 187–191.

29. Heinrich Heine, "Concerning the History of Religion and Philosophy in Germany," in *The Romantic School and Other Essays,* ed. Jost Hermand and Robert C. Holub (New York, 1985), 129; cited hereafter cited as *RP.* A convenient German edition is Mayer.

30. On the impact of Saint-Simonianism in Germany, see Breckman, 151–176; Charles Rihs, *L'Ecole des jeunes hegeliens et les penseurs socialistes français* (Paris, 1978); E. M. Butler, *The Saint-Simonian Religion in Germany* (Cambridge, 1926).

31. Heine writes: "In my opinion, a methodical people like us had to begin with the Reformation, only after that could it occupy itself with philosophy, and only after completion of the latter could it go on to political revolution. I find this sequence very rational"; *RP,* 242.

32. *RP,* 237–239. Breckman, 54–62, shows how Schelling moved to a Christian personalism characteristic of the German restoration.

33. *RP,* 5. See Heine, "Les Aveux," 1169–1206. In "On the History of Religion and Philosophy in Germany," Heine in fact contradicts himself in his assessment of Hegel. He characterizes Hegelian theory as radical and even potentially bloodthirsty, yet at another point refers to Hegel as a moderate spirit; *RP,* 237. And in another writing he compares Hegelian theory to Orleanist government, which is full of rival political groups. This would also suggest that Hegelian theory might have a character other than the revolutionary one he imputes to it. Heine, "Introduction," in *Kahldorf concerning the Nobility in Letters to Count M. Von Moltke,* in Hermand and Holub, 246.

34. See Mah, *End of Philosophy;* Toews; Breckman.

35. Though failing to obtain sufficient French or German support, the collaborative project was sympathetically reviewed by some French liberals and radicals. See anon., "Projet alliance intellectuelle entre l'Allemagne et la France," *La Réforme,* 13 November 1843, 1; P[ascal] D[upret], "L'Ecole de Hegel à Paris," *La Revue indépendante* 12 (February 25, 1844), 481–486; Charles L. Bernays, "Lettre au redacteur," *La Réforme,* 14 February 1845, who identifies the project as serving "the development and defense of the principles of the French Revolution." And in general see Beatrix Mesmer-Strupp, *Arnold Ruges Plan einer Alliance intellectuelle zwischen Deutschen und Franzosen* (Bonn, 1963); and Jacques Grandjonc, "Les Rapports des socialistes et néo-hegéliens allemand de l'émigration avec des socialistes français, 1840–1847," in *Aspects des relations franco-allemands, 1830–1848,* ed. Raymond Poidevin and Heinz-Otto Sieburg (Metz, 1978), 73–86.

36. German "philosophy," Ruge wrote in 1843, "will not become a power, until it steps forth into Paris and with the French spirit"; Arnold Ruge, "Studien und Erinnerungen aus den Jahren 1843 bis 1845," in his *Sämtliche Werke,* 2d ed., 10 vols. (Mannheim, 1847–48), 5:59.

37. Ibid., 136; Ruge to Ludwig Feuerbach, 15 May 1844, *Briefwechsel und Tagebücher aus den Jahren, 1825–1880,* ed. Paul Nerrlich, vol. 1 (Berlin, 1886), 347; Ruge to Karl Moritz Fleischer, 20 May 1844, ibid., 353; and Ruge, "Plan der Deutsch-Französischen Jahrbücher" (1843–44), in *Sämtliche Werke,* 9:155–156.

38. Ruge, "Studien," 61. Pascal Duprat reports Ruge's intentions concisely in *La Revue indépendante:* "Germany will preach to France the discipline of its philosophy . . . France, on its side, will preach to Germany its practical vision and its revolutionary instincts"; Duprat, "L'Ecole de Hegel à Paris," 485. Ruge opted for a strategy of complementarity, but in the search to relocate Germany in a modern present, other strategies were also available. Another radical German thinker, sometimes identified as a onetime Young Hegelian, Moses Hess urged a triangulation of revolutions in Germany, France, and England, according to which the principle of German spiritual freedom (from the Reformation) would join with the principle of political freedom (from the French Revolution), and both would unite with the English principle of material revolution (from England's Industrial Revolution). See Moses Hess, "Die europäische Triarchie" (1841), in *Ausgewählte Schriften,* ed. Horst Lademacher (Cologne, 1962), 131 ff.; Calvé, 312.

39. See Ruge, "Studien," 160, 22, 300; and Mah, *End of Philosophy,* 129–133.

40. This religiosity, he writes, shows that the French have made a great jump backward in history, abandoning the heritage of the Enlightenment for the "muddy emotion" of medievalist romanticism; Ruge, "Studien," 160, 222, 300.

41. Karl Marx, "Contribution to the Critique of Hegel's Philosophy of Law: Introduction," in Karl Marx and Frederick Engels, *Collected Works,* 48 vols. to date (New York, 1975–), 3:78; cited hereafter as *IN* (all references from volume 3).

42. *IN,* 184–185. See also Karl Marx and Friedrich Engels, *The German Ideology,* in *Collected Works,* 5:193–196.

43. Marx's description of the proletariat here is clearly at odds with his description of it in subsequent writings. In *The Communist Manifesto* and other works, he speaks of the proletariat as strictly a class, rather than as also an estate. He further drops the obscure notion that it is not part of society, making it instead one of the polarities in the defining conflict of modern society. In the "Introduction," Marx seems to identify the emergence of the proletariat as the unique answer to Germany's particular cultural and political situation, but it is unclear how it fits into the development of other, more consistently "developed" countries. In later writings, of course, he removes the proletariat from a unique German situation and integrates it into the "normal" evolution of all industrial societies. At the same time, Marx in particular and German socialism in general progressively ignore the peculiarities that Marx originally saw in Germany. In other words, as Marxism becomes increasingly systematized, both the proletariat and Germany are fitted into a general, uniform development of industrial capitalism.

44. Thomas Mann, *Reflections of a Nonpolitical Man* (1918), trans. Walter D. Morris (New York, 1987), especially 35–46, on the antithesis of German "culture" and French "civilization"; and 281–291 on how the character of German culture resists the modern democratic politics ushered in by the French Revolution.

45. The idea of the "unpolitical" or "illiberal" German, linked to the idea of the German *Sonderweg,* was at the center of some of the classic studies of German culture, from Leonard Krieger's *The German Idea of Freedom* (Chicago, 1957), Fritz Stern's *The Politics of Cultural Despair* (Berkeley, 1961) and Ralf Dahrendorf's *Society and Politics in Germany* (Garden City, N.Y., 1967) to Fritz Ringer's *The Decline of the German Mandarins: The German Academic Community, 1890–1935* (Cambridge, Mass., 1966). It even finds its way, as an unstated premise, to Carl Schorske's *Fin-de-Siècle Vienna* (New York, 1981), in which the failure of Austrian-German liberals led their children to flee politics into aestheticism and psychoanalysis. The idea

220   *Notes to Page 180*

is given a twist to produce its opposite in Jeffrey Herf's *Reactionary Modernism* (Cambridge, 1984), which argues that German intellectuals, assumed to have a Romantic antipathy to modernity, surprisingly embraced technology. The notion of the German *Sonderweg* and to a lesser extent of the unpolitical nature of German culture was dealt a mortal blow by the searching critique of David Blackbourn and Geoff Eley in *The Peculiarities of German History* (Oxford, 1984), a debate summed up in William Reddy, *Money and Liberty in Modern Europe* (Cambridge, 1987).

46. Karl Marx and Friedrich Engels, *Manifesto of the Communist Party*, in *The Marx-Engels Reader*, ed. Robert C. Tucker (New York, 1972), 362.

47. Ibid., 476.

Index

Page references in italics refer to figures.